CURRENCIES OF CRUELTY

PERFORMANCE AND AMERICAN CULTURES

General Editors: Stephanie Batiste, Robin Bernstein, and Brian Herrera

This book series harnesses American studies and performance studies and directs them toward each other, publishing books that use performance to think historically.

The Art of Confession: The Performance of Self from Robert Lowell to Reality TV
Christopher Grobe

Realist Ecstasy: Religion, Race, and Performance in American Literature
Lindsay V. Reckson

The Queer Nuyorican: Racialized Sexualities and Aesthetics in Loisaida
Karen Jaime

Black Patience: Performance, Civil Rights, and the Unfinished Project of Emancipation
Julius B. Fleming, Jr.

*F*ck The Army! How Soldiers and Civilians Staged the GI Movement to End the Vietnam War*
Lindsay Goss

Disability Works: Performance After Rehabilitation
Patrick McKelvey

Like Children: Black Prodigy and the Measure of the Human in America
Camille Owens

Redface: Race, Performance, and Indigeneity
Bethany Hughes

Currencies of Cruelty: Slavery, Freak Shows, and the Performance Archive
Danielle Bainbridge

Currencies of Cruelty

Slavery, Freak Shows, and the Performance Archive

Danielle Bainbridge

New York University Press
New York

NEW YORK UNIVERSITY PRESS
New York
www.nyupress.org

Please contact the Library of Congress for Cataloging-in-Publication data.
ISBN: 9781479829552 (hardback)
ISBN: 9781479829569 (paperback)
ISBN: 9781479829606 (library ebook)
ISBN: 9781479829583 (consumer ebook)

This book is printed on acid-free paper, and its binding materials are chosen for strength and durability. We strive to use environmentally responsible suppliers and materials to the greatest extent possible in publishing our books.

The manufacturer's authorized representative in the EU for product safety is Mare Nostrum Group B.V., Mauritskade 21D, 1091 GC Amsterdam, The Netherlands. Email: gpsr@mare-nostrum.co.uk.

Manufactured in the United States of America

10 9 8 7 6 5 4 3 2 1

Also available as an ebook

For Mama and Daddy, with love

CONTENTS

PROLOGUE

An Ethnography of the Archive

Entering the archive is often transactional, a curious blend of reciprocal exchange and an exercise in extraction. Whatever the cause of the trip, whether it is scholarly or personal, I've found that the expectations we bring to the archive as a site of knowledge collection and production inherently carry with them the desire for a certain kind of yield. Either we are looking for the piece of information that will complete our project, conclude our personal search, or sate our own lingering curiosities, or we are trying to uncover the essential fact that we need to satisfy some sort of external query (such as when we serve as a research assistant for another scholar, a foundation, or an archive's administration). When thinking about the terms of the exchange, the natural conclusion I draw is associated with the labor attached to that transactional exchange. More precisely, who is gaining and who is losing? Why are these terms (*gaining* and *losing*) associated with the idea of transaction? And how can we think through the terms of the transaction to disrupt the almost sanctified act of archival preservation within the world of academia and, more specifically in the case of this book, within the world of performance and theater scholarship, since theater itself is an exchange of labor, ideas, talents, and often money?

It is this final exchange that most interests me for the purposes of this book. What happens when the exchange of money for talents extends to the bartering of human life for cash, as represented in the archive? Or to put it more precisely, what happens when enslavement and performance meet? In this text, I will analyze the intersections of these two phenomena alongside the process of enfreakment (or being made freakish through a nexus of disability, racialization, and marginalization) for nineteenth-century disabled performers. But before we explore the world of the nineteenth-century freak show stage, we must first analyze the dynamics of racial power that continue to dictate the performance archives where the traces of these performances still live.

When I first began doing research in North Carolina, I was struck by the number of personal genealogies that were taking place within the archives, often simultaneously, alongside, or instead of traditional academic searches. On my first trip to Chapel Hill, I met a researcher who told me that he supplemented his summer income by tracing the genealogical roots through the Civil War and antebellum South of families willing and able to pay him. Apparently, research labor and a willingness to sift through endless amounts of microfilm can also be big business. Upon returning to Raleigh on my next research trip, I found that every person who entered the state archive was required to fill out a slip of paper that noted if the search was personal (family history and genealogy) or academic. It seems that in the genre of Southern US history, there is an interwoven aspect of personal and scholarly pursuits that is at once fascinating and unavoidable.[1] The archive takes on the role of a character in and of itself, stretching out to encompass a part that both memorializes historical figures in the past and ensnares present actors and subjects as those who are affected by history's legacies. This focus within US Southern historical repositories on genealogy and personal history was fascinating to me when I began my project. Not only because it wasn't something that ever interested me before, although I can't trace my own family's history beyond my great-grandparents, but also because it seemed a strangely regional and local approach to the archive. In my PhD program, we were encouraged to ask big and pressing questions about history so we could explore and excavate how we came to be in our present moment. Somehow, tracing personal history felt strange and less vital in comparison. However, over the years of researching and writing this book, I've come to discover the deeply personal and lived nature of the performance archives I study.

Archives themselves hold an inherent connection to the past that is neither negated nor lessened by their own essential desire for futurity. For it is through and for the act of preservation in perpetuity that an archive exists. Although we most often understand the archive as a site of the past, of remembering, and of memorialization, I'd like us also to assume that the act of historical preservation carries within it its own desire for futurity through conservation and continuation. It is what drives us to the archives to begin our searches, whether they be personal or professional in nature. When we look for the personal, we're hoping to create a lineage between past versions of ourselves (effigies in the form of dead relatives standing in as the answers to various questions and curiosities). We project backward and imagine that this relative gave us our eye color, while another may have contributed to our sense of humor or love of a particular type of food. When the searches are professional, we turn to history as a sort of urtext of our present moment and hopefully use it to predict future trends and outcomes. But in each case, we rely heavily on the imagined futures that we cannot see. Therefore, here I evoke the necessity of the imagination, that which looks to, projects, and envisions the future, as we look to the intersections of the archive, performance, and slavery.[2] Each of these three points of inquiry not only benefits from but requires the use of the future and the imagination to detail the important transactional nature of the archival connections between the performers I will discuss in this book.

It was futurity and imagination that made possible the calculated business maneuvers of both these performers and those who profited from their acts (enslavers, showmen, and the family members of the enslaved and of the enslavers). It was also the sense of a future projection and imagination that drew these performers' historical remains into the archive, ensuring that their traces would continue their narrative legacies long after the final curtain. In this book, I evaluate what I've termed the future perfect tense of archival research. I argue that the future perfect, a tense that effectively communicates the uncertainty of the past tense in the future (or "that which will have been"), encapsulates the desires of historical analysis in the past, present, and future. Because the moment that someone decides to place something in an archival repository, they are determining not only what will be memorialized but also the shape of stories that will be told in the future. They effectively determine the history of the future. The future perfect is why a historical account of an event (say the Civil War) will differ based on when it was written. So an account from 1875 will look vastly different from one written in 1975. I assert that the future perfect accounts for these shifts in both temporality and desire throughout history. The interstitial space of the future perfect is also combined with performance methodology because it takes into account the desires of not only the historical actor but also the historians who craft and curate stories of the past.

In considering my inquiries into the future perfect tense, I turn to an evaluation of my own labor and transactional relationship with the performance archive. My intervention into the politics of nineteenth-century performance labor remains influenced by my own contemporary desires as an archival audience of these enfreaked performers. What demands do I place on these onstage laborers? Am I calling on them, through their archives, to perform and therefore labor once more for the purposes of my project? I would answer a tentative yes to the latter question. I am calling on these figures to do work, and it is through their work and legacies (along with the findings of previous researchers) that my own academic labor as both a scholar and a descendant of the enslaved is made possible. I draw on this consciousness here not only to evaluate my own personal and scholarly relationship to the archival process but also to investigate the ways that the legacies of performance and slavery continue to influence not only my research but also my quotidian movements. The method and site of preservation are called into question here. How do we memorialize slavery and its attendant traumas within archival institutions? This memorialization is affected by slavery's intersections with public performance and labor.

The conflation of the past and the present in the following anecdote perhaps best illustrates not only the ways that I am calling on these performers to labor again under the terms of this project, labor that cannot be ignored or pushed aside in this book's attempts to unravel the terms of free and unfree nineteenth-century enfreaked performance, but also the ways that personal desire, longing, and haunting continue to shape how slavery is memorialized in the archival space, specifically in terms of the specter of the plantation. For it is the plantation, as a site of national mourning, historical preservation, architectural beauty, and unfree labor in its arguably most naked, brutal, and coercive state, that casts shadows on both the margins and the centers of these performers' biographies and onstage personae.

In the summer of 2013, I departed from New York on a flight bound for North Carolina's research triangle. Unfamiliar with the South, North Carolina, and archival research in general, I began what I didn't know at the time would become my first exploration in a project on nineteenth-century freak shows and slavery. Arriving early to the site on a free hotel shuttle through the triangle, I was regaled with stories from my white Southern driver about the specialness of this place. "The triangle isn't racist like most of this damn state," I was assured over and over and over again. I wondered why this needed to be stated, but I never bothered to ask. When we arrived at the University of North Carolina at Chapel Hill's palatial library, I took off from my ride in search of Millie Christine[3] McKoy, whose lives and performance legacies had captured my researcher's imagination from the first image I saw of them in Yale University's Beinecke Rare Book and Manuscript Library. I would return to the same archive in 2016, only this time in search of Chang and Eng Bunker (1811–1874), freak show predecessors of the McKoys, fellow nineteenth-century North Carolinians, and the original "Siamese Twins." On my first trip to the University of North Carolina at Chapel Hill's North Carolina Collection in 2013, I remember my feelings of frustration at the focus on the Bunkers in lieu of the McKoys in the archival space. The Bunkers' images were prominently and permanently featured in the archive's exhibit in the foyer, where playbills and photographs of their homes accompanied more unusual items such as a timeline of their lives and the silverware they used. Walking deeper into the exhibit, unguided and unencumbered by any presuppositions about its contents, I went searching for the McKoys, assuming falsely that they would be as prominently featured as the Bunkers since, in their lifetimes, they were so often marketed as the "Two-Headed Nightingale" and the "North Carolina Twins." As an inexperienced researcher and writer, I essentialized their interest, presuming that bodies so spectacular, performances so remarkable, and lives so exceptional could not have escaped archival capture. Indeed, the nature of their archive seemed to resist obscurity. It was also on this first trip that I discovered a re-creation of the Hayes Plantation Library.

Gazing inside this structure as the granddaughter of four grandparents with only an elementary school education (and in some cases no education), I was overwhelmed by the historical weight of the peculiar institution not for the first time in my life. Here, on the brink of where it was most dangerous for an enslaved body to go (the library), I stood in search of the McKoys and they were nowhere to be found. My immediate response was one of outrage: The words *silence*, *violence*, and *trauma* immediately rang inside my ears in the echoing emptiness of the room. Where were *my* McKoys? It didn't feel right to use the possessive term *my*, unconsciously mirroring the language of the men who alternately enslaved, exploited, and employed them throughout their careers. On my return to the archive in 2016, I found myself inexplicably drawn again to the beauty of the plantation library. I was surprised to find the permanent collection of objects associated with the Bunkers remained intact, while the adjacent temporary display had been changed from defunct Confederate currency to generational fashion trends on campus, a slightly lighter and less controversial subject.

I stepped close to the edge of the library and peered inside, staying perhaps longer than is entirely necessary considering its small size. I noticed for the first time that the room is shaped like an octagon and the ceiling bore a beautiful eggshell-blue mosaic that surrounds a hanging chandelier. I was so transfixed by my connection to this plantation library that I jumped in surprise when I heard a voice behind me say, "Let us know if there's anything we can do to help you." I turned around and saw a college-age white woman smiling at me. I thanked her quickly and turned back to the library, trying to take a perfect picture for my archives. As a young Black woman, I have always been profoundly uncomfortable when people in authority refer to themselves in the plural first person, since "Can we help you?" is usually the precursor to raised eyebrows and accusations of theft in stores. I learned long ago not to touch anything, lest I raise suspicion. I learned this lesson especially well in museums in New York from my own father. Look, display interest, do not touch, move on. This careful choreography is as second nature to me now as covering my mouth out of politeness before I sneeze; the dust in the archive is strangely reminiscent of the thick yellow pollen that coats all the horizontal surfaces on my springtime research trip to the South.

I turned my back to the young museum worker and continued to snap my photos, growing increasingly dissatisfied that I could not get the right light and that the barricade in front of the door prevented me from entering and capturing the right angle. I switched to panorama and slowly swept my lens over the room to no avail. Suddenly I heard a tentative voice again. "We can move that"—she pointed to the barrier in front of the door—"and let you go in if you'd like?" I was taken aback. This seems to transgress everything I've ever been told about the museum space, but I was too eager to turn down this chance. I nodded a silent yes and watched as she slid the barrier to one side of the doorway and stood back to let me in. I hesitated. Not so long that it is noticeable to anyone but me, but my step stalled as I approached the door, as if an invisible force were pressing lightly against my sternum, holding me back.

I did not want to enter the room. I did not want to be lured in by its beauty or its historical significance or its hauntings. I know that I study slavery and, in some ways, these passings are the metaphorical cost of the ticket. And yet my step stalled as I approached the door. Finally, I girded myself and walked in. Here I was, no longer on the brink but in

Figure P.1: Re-creation of the Hayes Plantation Library, University of North Carolina at Chapel Hill North Carolina Collection. Photo by Jay Magnum.

the belly of this dangerous place. The first time I stood on the edges of the exterior, I cried by myself. This time I felt unease that is a cocktail of nausea and excitement at my permitted transgression. I stepped inside with the museum guide watching me closely at my side and took one long panorama picture of the interior before thanking her and hurrying out. The picture was not perfect, but it is good enough for my purposes. I only realized later, when I uploaded the picture to my computer, that my hands were shaking terribly, rendering the photograph unusable.

In both 2013 and 2016 I noted that the library is unexpectedly beautiful. I was anxious to run my fingers over unbroken book spines, to touch my lips to gleaming wooden surfaces, to acquaint my tired bones with the supple leather seats. To relax here. I wondered again at the danger of relaxing in this space, of becoming too comfortable, of being caught at ease instead of furiously laboring. After all, I was not at the archive to linger, I was there to work. And it struck me how perverse my connection to the library and, by extension, the library's beauty is. This is not a beautiful place. It is not a place where Black bodies would have engaged in leisure. It is a site where Saidiya Hartman's aptly named "scenes of subjection" would have occurred, close to the domesticity and intimacy of the master's home.[4] Both Toni Morrison and Salamishah Tillet note this strange connection that the modern descendants of the enslaved maintain to their ancestors' trauma in "The Site of Memory" and *Sites of Slavery*, respectively.[5] Hilton Als examines his own desperate attempts to see himself and also beauty in the film version of *Gone with the Wind* as a young Black queer boy growing up in the United States.[6] Hartman also describes her journey through archives of the transatlantic slave trade in her monograph *Lose Your Mother*.[7] In this regard I am not much different from any of these diasporic Black subjects, longing for connection and understanding, laboring toward those ends. The currencies of cruelty I trace in this work are often encapsulated by moments like this one, where in spite of the appearance of luxury and the performance of manners, there are still the ever-present horrors of slavery in every act. Although these performance acts often relied on the veneer of gentility (indeed gentility was the performance), they were still conducted under the dark shadow of unfreedom.

Even my desire to write about this space, this plantation re-creation, bothers me. Surely a place like this is haunted, nestled uncomfortably somewhere between Western ideals of social comfort and propriety, the immeasurable cruelty of slavery that built those same comforts, and horror tourism. In my undergraduate and graduate education, I was keenly aware that privileges such as this (comfort, ease, abundance, access) were never intended for my ancestors and therefore never truly intended for me. And yet I lived and continue to live and operate in worlds (academia and history) where it is completely normal to be covetous of spaces such as this one. Spaces that worked to break and ultimately destroy the souls of Black folk.

To return to my theorization of the future perfect here, I must first stop and ask myself, Why now, and why this project? Why this text, these words, this book? This moment, when I stood on the precipice of fact-finding, serves as evidence of my desire for the future perfect. Perhaps it was because at that moment I was young and idealistic enough to believe in the infallibility of things like archives and history without questioning their intentions. As time has passed, my beliefs have shifted, prompting me to conclude that I am not working against the archive, not truly. Rather, I am telling one version of an ever-evolving story with the hope that "what will have been" in the future perfect of history will include the stories I have dedicated so much time to. That the future history will have evolved to include a fuller spectrum of what collectively ails us: namely, the history of US enslavement and ableism.

In my life adjacent to academia, I create educational videos about history for general audiences. In one video we focused on the history of nineteenth-century "ugly laws" that sprang into being in some states across thc United States after the Civil War. What struck me as particularly cruel about these laws, which limited disabled people's access to public space and life, is that they came at a moment when there was a higher number of disabled veterans returning home from war. It seems our societal desire to marginalize and forget our sins against each other remains a hallmark of historical retelling. Despite their wide-reaching impact in their day, today you would hard-pressed to find anyone who has heard about "ugly laws" or why they mattered. And yet they did matter deeply to those affected. I have chosen to attempt to tell these stories from the past in part because I simply want them to be known. But in a greater sense I wish to wrestle with our remembering, our forgetting, and our unknowing through the lens of performance history and archival research. To find answers to my unanswerable questions. And while this book is a finished product, my negotiation with the archive will remain ongoing.

So much of my thoughts and feelings about archives and archival memory is fragmented and contradictory. My own family's archives exist in just that way. Without consistent access to cameras or money for studio sessions, it seems as if most of my relatives and ancestors sprang into being in the mid-1970s and early 1980s when cheap home cameras entered their lives. I have seen one photo of my father as a baby, and never anything earlier than a grade school yearbook photo of my mother. My grandparents, in my limited imagination, were always fully grown adults, as if they were born at the age of forty or beyond.

In contrast, there is a surplus of photographs of me and my siblings. This is in part because our father did not want to replicate the dearth of photos from his own childhood with his children. There are photos of us during every holiday, birthday, and other special event. We sit (mostly) still in our starched Sunday clothes and frilly socks with Mary Jane shoes gleaming. But there are also an equal number of photos of the mundane minutia of our lives growing up. Me sitting between my mother's knees as she patiently parts the hair on my tender head. My sister caught mid-laugh while eating her breakfast cereal. My brother grinning a toothless infant smile into the camera's lens. This plethora of pictures was somewhat the bane of my childhood existence. So often my father's small film camera would flash unexpectedly in our faces at inopportune moments. As he advanced the film after each shot, he would smile and insist he was "just finishing the roll" before he took the film canisters to Costco or the photo development place that would go out of business by the time I left high school in the early 2000s. This was before digital cameras made film photography almost obsolete for the average shutterbug.

This split reality of photographs and family documentation has always made me strangely tender about photographs of Black folk. I love to see us when we are young and beautiful. But even more, I love to see us get old, evidence that we can live long lives even in the wake of terror and oppression. I felt similarly as I stood on the precipice of the library, trying to imagine the hands that built and tended to these books they were forbidden to read. What would a portrait of them capture? What would it necessarily leave out?

And so, the first time I stand there in the plantation library, in awe, I cried. I released saltwater tears down my cheeks, familiar with the feeling. I cried because . . . It was beautiful. Because I wanted it and was ashamed. Because it was and was not mine. Because I did and did not want to step inside. Because there was no rest here. Because it all seemed to radiate light through the high arched windows, like a haven, and I wondered how so much beauty could exist right in the middle of so many people's hell. But I was here to labor, to search for the traces of labor, to extract, to deduce, to conceive, and to conclude. So I slowly walked away, farther into the caverns of the archives.

Introduction

I conversed with this these person-s and found her quick and of pleasant manner. Both at times have identical dreams.
—Photograph of Millie Christine McKoy, dated 1885

The first time I saw a picture of Millie Christine McKoy, I recognized them. Their posture. Their style of dress. Their straight-faced affect. Their grace. I recognized some indescribable, ineffable thing that immediately piqued my imagination as I gazed at a small black-and-white carte de visite under the glaring fluorescent lights of the archive. The hold they had on me was as inexplicable as it was immediate. As a twenty-two-year-old first-year graduate student only recently out of undergrad, I naively didn't even know it was possible to study and theorize performance without a video recording. So the nineteenth-century performance archive was both terrifying and strangely thrilling to me. This inexplicable feeling of unearned familiarity with the McKoys was so strong that I continued to rack my brain for days afterward to see where I knew them from. Was it from a live performance? Well, that would be impossible considering their heyday was between their births in 1851 and their deaths in 1912. Was it from another archive? Improbable, if not impossible, since my work at the time as a very young and inexperienced researcher had focused on late twentieth-century Jamaican feminist theater and novels, and the McKoys were nineteenth-century North Carolinians.

As I continued to stare at the photograph of two poised Black women who were conjoined twins attached at the hip in the nineteenth century, I soon lost track of time in the viewing room of Yale University's Beinecke Rare Book and Manuscript Library. The purpose of that day's visit was for students in the first-year cohort of the African American Studies PhD program to view pieces from the James Weldon Johnson Collection (the collection dedicated to the study of the African diaspora). On the table were some of the most interesting and coveted archival materials from Black thought and culture: poems by Langston Hughes on the original typewritten sheets, a screenplay by Richard Wright, and papers from the archives of James Baldwin. I remember these precious bits of paper clearly, and yet it was the image of Millie Christine, their hair parted down the middle and severely plaited, wearing identical conjoined dresses, that eventually caught my eye. I took out my pencil, the only writing utensil allowed in the reading room, and immediately began to jot things down. Those thoroughly uninspired and hurriedly scribbled notes went something like this:

"Conjoined twins"
"19th century"
"Black women performers"
"*They grew old together . . .*"

They grew old together . . . That final observation was taken from the barely whispered words of the professor who had taken us to the archive that day. She said them as she looked over my shoulder to see what I was hunching forward to write about. I repeated the words to myself, at first in my head and then later out loud to myself in my empty apartment. I ruminated on this observation for many days, contemplating what it meant for disabled Black women to live a comparatively long life in the nineteenth century after being born into slavery. Long life was not the intended lot of the enslaved, and although some did reach old age, many were lost to the never-ending cruelties of slavery's machinations. Overwork and undernourishment. Long hours unsupported by sleep and rest. Backbreaking labor. These were more often than not the determining factors of premature death for enslaved subjects. So the fact that these women survived at the nexus of slavery, disability, and disregard for Black womanhood raised questions that I was unable to answer for myself in the scant hour we spent in the archive that fateful day.

My initial feeling of uncanny recognition has lessened over time, since there is no greater humbling force to a new researcher than years of archival research. And yet, it has never truly gone away in its entirety. Perhaps it is a researcher's superstition. Perhaps it is all in my head. Regardless of the reason behind it, that initial instinct has driven this book from its inception. I went searching for the McKoys anywhere I could find them. In popular performance of the nineteenth through twenty-first centuries. In the archives. In books. In poetry. I craved the answers to those initial scribbled notes with a ferocity that surprised me. On the one hand, I was obsessed with finding answers to my questions about these famed twins who have in some ways fallen out of popular memory. On the other, I continued to resist this book at every turn, even going so far as to call it my "side hustle" project when people asked me what I worked on. I wanted my fixation on the McKoys to remain at the side and not the center of my scholarly research, in part because of my own internalized ableism and cultural elitism. I thought a project entirely centered on freak shows was somehow less serious and therefore less "rigorous" than a project on Black feminist twentieth-century Jamaican theater sounded. I was worried that this hyperfocus was somehow a mistake and that I couldn't possibly write a book about these women's lives and performances.

But as I continued to dig and found other enfreaked performers like the McKoys with intimate connections to US slavery, and confirmed how little I initially knew about the lives and performance strategies of these virtuosic nineteenth-century stars, I uncovered a world of popular performance culture enmeshed with the horrors and lived realities of slavery. Those performers include piano prodigy Thomas "Blind Tom" Wiggins, conjoined twins (the original "Siamese Twins") Chang and Eng Bunker, and P. T. Barnum performer Joice Heth. The McKoys, Heth, and Wiggins all performed as enslaved laborers, whereas the Bunkers performed and lived in their later years as enslavers on two adjacent plantations. Each performer deployed complex strategies of enfreakment to engage audiences and capitalize on their unique combination of mental prowess, business savvy, and spectacularized physical bodies. The more I studied this period, the more I realized that the intersection of disability and enslavement was something that raised more questions than answers, mostly of myself. Why hadn't I imagined that there were enslaved people born with disabilities during slavery? It's not as if disability has not existed in every population and every period throughout history. Why would the nineteenth century be any different? These were stories that weren't taught to me in any history class I had ever taken, even ones that centered on Black studies and Black history. It was a glaring hole in not only the performance history of the nineteenth-century United States but nineteenth-century US history more broadly speaking. Although there is scholarship surrounding this very intersection of identities (enslavement and disability), it was largely if not entirely unknown to me before starting this book.[1] Because of my own ignorance, I set out to give myself an education in this area of study. This book is the result of that education.

Currencies of Cruelty: Slavery, Freak Shows, and the Performance Archive takes up the three keywords in the subtitle through the critical lens of the future perfect archival tense and autoethnography, or an "ethnography of the archive," in order to explicate the ways racialized and enfreaked performers in the nineteenth-century United States engaged with the lasting legacies of their memories through performance. The future perfect posits that "that which will have been" is as important to the practice of archival collection and discovery as the past tense or the simple future tense. The past and the future create a clean dichotomy through which we are asked to view history as something cleaved into two neat pieces. However, this simplicity does not allow for the complexity of the decision-making that goes into entering something into the archival record. When evidence is entered into the archives, we are supposed to assume that it is impartial and objective. And yet we know through canonical works such as Michel-Rolph Trouillot's *Silencing the Past* and Saidiya Hartman's *Scenes of Subjection* that the archive is actually subjective and highly unstable, especially as it relates to telling the stories of minoritized and Black subjects.[2] What the future perfect asserts is that each piece of archival material that is entered into the official record is entered because someone was deeply concerned about how history would be narrated in history's unresolved future. This is evidenced in the performance archive, where nineteenth-century Black enfreaked performers like Millie Christine McKoy exercised a self-conscious engagement with their archival memory and participation through fugitive performances both in life and postmortem. Similar patterns of lived and postmortem engagements with the archive are evidenced in the lives, performances, and legacies of Blind Tom Wiggins, Chang and Eng Bunker, and Joice Heth. Each set out to defy the standards of abjection that were dictated to them through performance acts that both centered and decentered their enfreaked bodies and humanity.

I take up the use of the first-person pronoun *I* throughout the text to create a critical analysis of the continued resonances of slavery's afterlives for Black subjects who are descendants of the enslaved. We are not divorced from this reality but rather living through and alongside it. The *I* allows me to apply a critical eye to my own participation as a scholar, artist, and historian with the archives of slavery. This critical move takes up the archive not as a pseudoscientific objective catalog that summarizes the past but rather as a living subject with human ambitions and intentions folded into the margins, often invisible to the naked eye. By narrativizing this process of invisibilization and subjectivity, I shine a light on how we engage with the archive as a living thing possessing desires that are often outside the control of those of us who do archival research. The archive is alive, and it is both my source and my respondent. It is participating in this process in some ways. Ethnography of the archive allows me to take up a performance studies approach (D. Soyini Madison, Richard Schechner, et al.) to ethnography coupled with archival analysis as my methods.[3] Each is dependent on the other. The future perfect tense builds on other speculative approaches and grammatical approaches to the archive (Tina Campt's *A Black Gaze*, Hartman, Lisa Lowe, Hortense Spillers).[4] It posits that the archive contains within it the desire for the future perfect, or "what will have been." By speculating about the past tense of the unknown future, those who enter things into the archival record are concerned not only with the preservation of the past but also with how the past will be dictated in the future. This makes the archive a space of active memory and willful forgetting as it relates to Black subjects who have historically been both erased and overwritten in the archival record. This space of memory and forgetting is why the future perfect extends not only to my analysis of the archive but also to my use of the first-person singular pronoun. By calling on the subjective nature of memory alongside the subjective nature of archival collection, I ask why it is important to personalize and therefore strip anonymity away from the archives of slavery.

My work here is in conversation with that of others who have written and studied the connections between slavery, performance, and disability. Works like Daphne Brooks's *Bodies in Dissent*, Uri McMillan's *Embodied Avatars*, Cynthia Wu's *Chang and Eng Reconnected*, Benjamin Reiss's *The Showman and the Slave*, and Joseph Roach's *Cities of the*

Figure I.1: Images of Thomas "Blind Tom" Wiggins (1849–1908), Chang and Eng Bunker (1811–1874), Joice Heth (1756–1836), and Millie Christine McKoy (1851–1912).

Dead continue to inform this book's preoccupations with the ways that performance offered avenues to access newfound legal freedoms while also reinforcing the lasting binds of slavery for Black, disabled, or otherwise racialized performers.[5] These texts are deeply concerned with the ways that these performers negotiated their social circumstances while

Figure 1.1: (*continued*)

THE GREATEST
Natural & National
CURIOSITY
IN THE WORLD.

Nurse to GEN. GEORGE WASHINGTON, (the Father of our Country,)
WILL BE SEEN AT

Barnum's Hotel, Bridgeport,

On FRIDAY, and SATURDAY, the 11th. & 12th days of December, DAY and EVENING. also Monda

JOICE HETH is unquestionably the most astonishing and interesting curiosity in the World! She was the slave of Augustine Washington, (the father of Gen. Washington,) and was the first person who put clothes on the unconscious infant, who, in after days, led our heroic fathers on to glory, to victory, and freedom. To use her own language when speaking of the illustrious Father of his Country, "she raised him." JOICE HETH was born in the year 1674, and has, consequently, now arrived at the astonishing

AGE OF 161 YEARS.

She Weighs but FORTY-SIX POUNDS, and yet is very cheerful and interesting. She retains her faculties in an unparalleled degree, converses freely, sings numerous hymns, relates many interesting anecdotes of *the boy* Washington. and often laughs heartily at her own remarks, or those of the spectators, Her health is perfectly good, and her appearance very neat. She is a baptist and takes great pleasure in conversing with ministers and religious persons. The appearance of this marvellous relic of antiquity strikes the beholder with amazement, and convinces him that his eyes are resting on the oldest specimen of mortality they ever before beheld. Original, authentic, and indisputable documents accompanying her prove, however astonishing the fact may appear, that JOICE HETH is in every respect the person she is represented.

The most eminent physicians and intelligent men in Cincinnatti. Philadelphia, New-York, Boston, and other places, have examined this *living skeleton* and the documents accompanying her, and all, *invariably*, pronounce her to be, as represented, 161 *years of age!*

A female is in continual attendance, and will give every attention to the ladies who visit this relic of by-gone ages.

She has been visited in Philadelphia, New-York, Boston, &c., by more than TWENTY THOUSAND Ladies and Gentlemen, within the last three months.

Hours of Exhibition, from 9 A. M. to 1 P. M. and from 3 to 5, and 6½ to 10 P. M.

ADMITTANCE 25 Cents, CHILDREN HALF-PRICE.

Printed by J. BOOTH & SON, 147, Fulton-st N. Y.

Remains Monday the 14th

Figure I.1: (*continued*)

Figure I.1: (*continued*)

simultaneously opening up new possibilities for themselves and their descendants through their earning potential. Although they may have been considered less valuable as traditional enslaved laborers, their value as performers proved to be a double-edged sword that dictated their lives and their time in the spotlight. But what interests me here is not only their perseverance through adversity but the ways they altered and manipulated their performances to mirror these complex social conditions onstage.

The nineteenth-century United States often functions as a great historical axis around which many of our current understandings of our collective past as a nation rest. It was a century that encompassed both the horrors of slavery and failed promises of emancipation, as well as Reconstruction. It also serves as a site of contestation over the very questions of liberty and humanity for Black subjects that the United States is still wrestling with to this very day. So even though modern US popular culture often exhibits a desire to relegate the racial wounding of that century to a firm past tense, it cannot help but continue to rear its head time and time again because it remains, in many tangible ways, unsettled. Every new debate about the salience of Confederate Civil War monuments, institutional memory, and how, why, and when we should begin to tell the story of enslavement in our current moment makes plain this uncomfortable truth. Because the slaveholding past and the Confederacy are not uncharted and unknowable memories. No matter the attempts at division and reconciliation, in many ways that wound does not heal because many are unwilling to recognize that it is both dead and not dead. It is not a foreign contagion, but an essential part of our national DNA. The Confederacy was not dissolved. It was reabsorbed.

Freak shows, in many ways, bear this same unsettled modern positioning. They largely fell out of favor by the mid-twentieth century, and the responses to the realities of these performance histories now often range from understandable outrage to curiosity, unease, and disgust. I admit that at points during my interrogation of this archive, I have experienced the entirety of this spectrum of emotions. But despite the relative unpopularity of the freak show today, it was in its time a widely popular form of entertainment.[6] And like the memories of enslavement and shame that exist in our collective understanding of modern US culture, freak shows are both dead and undead. They did not disappear; rather they were reabsorbed as an almost ghostly marginal memory, neatly folded into our understanding of Americana and entertainment.

So although I did not extensively know the McKoys when I first encountered their archives, I did recognize them. I understood something in their erect posture and direct gazes looking into the camera on the first visiting card I viewed at the Beinecke, dated 1885 and surrounded by the firm handwriting of either the photographer or the owner of the image. The writer notes that the twins were thirty-four when this image was taken, years after their performance careers began and decades after their births in 1851 in North Carolina, yet years still from their eventual deaths in 1912. I sat under the light in the archive and recognized in them the photographs of famed racist and Harvard professor Louis Agassiz. I recognized the erect posture and self-fashioning of Black respectability politics. And even if I didn't know it at the time, I recognized the enfreaked body on display. I recognized them, even though I was (at that point) unaware of their origins or even their names. I became fixated on the marginalia, a piece of which is reproduced in the epigraph of this introduction. This passage runs along the right-hand side of the image. It reads, "I conversed with this these person-s and found her quick and of pleasant manner. Both at times have identical dreams." My fixation on these marginalia was multifaceted. In part, I was interested in the use of the singular versus the plural when addressing the McKoys' extraordinary condition and bodies. Were they, in fact, "this" or "these" "person" or "persons"? Yet when it came time to use a pronoun, the unknown author deferred to the singular "her," noting that she was "quick and of pleasant manner." My only assumption is that the observation about identical dreams came from conversing with the McKoys themselves.

My fascination with the McKoys' unrecorded and reportedly identical dreams became an integral part of my larger explorations into the intersections of freak shows and slavery. Similar to that initial encounter in the performance archive, which was marked by an inexplicable feeling of recognition, the marginalia about their dreamscapes raised more questions than answers. Namely, how can and should we address the compromised agency of these performers and their archival remains, when their lives and performances were both free and unfree? Also, why does our current moment bear the evidence of such resurgent and sustained interest in the McKoys and performers like them?[7] When I went to the archives at the University of North Carolina at Chapel Hill to research the McKoys and their contemporaries, fellow freak show performers and North Carolina residents Chang and Eng Bunker, a librarian retrieving my boxes inquired whether there was a reason both sets of twins lived in North Carolina. Making a small quip, she said, "Do we just have more freaks down here than anywhere else?" But despite her humor, there was an underlying sense of a real question. How and why were these performers so popular? And what should we make of their legacies in a twenty-first-century US context that is working furiously to fade the memories of both its freak show past and its persistent connection to nineteenth-century slavery? Surely the moment in which historical work is written bears as much significance as the final project itself. A text written on World War II in the 1950s will often have a radically different project from one covering the same events published in 2001 or 2023. Archives, and archives surrounding historical recordings of once live performances, bear evidence of this same shift. As a result, my book looks not only at the nineteenth-century intersections of slavery and performance but also into our own modern fixation on returning to the archive, the nineteenth century, performance studies, freak shows, and slavery, time and time again. To illustrate this methodological and historical straddling, this book moves between archival findings, autoethnography, an ethnography of the archive, and twenty-first-century creative works that reimagine our relationship to the archives of freak shows and slavery.

For there are and have always been, for the Black bodies caught in the crosshairs of the transatlantic slave trade and its rhizomatic afterlives (most often labeled modernity), "refinements of cruelty." That which is deemed acceptable and impermissible. Visible, spectacular, or unseen. Desirable or repulsive. Appalling or celebratory. Redemptive or abject.[8] The phrase is taken directly from C. L. R. James's canonical text *The Black Jacobins*. The text, a historical retelling of the Haitian Revolution and Caribbean slavery, serves as a methodological predecessor to my own work on nineteenth-century US slavery and freak shows because it is structured around the process of undoing historical silence and misremembering through narrative. The phrase "the refinements of cruelty," used to describe the process through which white masters evaluated the physical and fiscal worth of the Black subjects they enslaved, could include an evaluation of the strength and color of a slave's teeth, the tasting of her sweat to determine the health of her blood, or the public dispensing of corporal punishment, such as by digging a hole in the dirt to accommodate the pregnant stomach of a mother receiving the lash of the whip or, in a process known as burning, blowing "a little powder in the arse of a nigger."[9] As intimately violent as these acts were, James maintains a cynical and jarringly satirical tone throughout his descriptions, writing, "There are and always will be some who, ashamed of the behaviour of their ancestors, try to prove that slavery was not so bad after all, that its evils and its cruelty were the exaggerations of propagandists and not the habitual lot of the slaves. Men will say (and accept) anything in order to foster national pride or soothe a troubled conscience. Undoubtedly there were kind masters who did not indulge in these refinements of cruelty and whose slaves merely suffered over-work, under-nourishment, and the whip."[10] What struck me in James's description here was not only his indictment of the behavior of enslavers and torturers but his condemnation of those who wish, through the memorialization of slavery, to codify and sanitize these narratives through the veneers of "refinement" and the pseudoscience of taste inherent to these claims. The structures of the freak show acts that I analyze in this book often relied on making invisible the destructive exploitations of sideshow owners and proprietors under the guise of "refined" performance. Parlor music that audiences could sing along to. "Receptions" held in public venues. Ticketed shows. Collectible ephemera such as visiting cards and playbills. Archives also do this work. And it was at just such a moment of nationalist imagination, state pride, and a false memory of enslavement as a place of comfort, rare books, and refinement that I encountered Millie Christine McKoy, Chang and Eng Bunker, and their contemporaries.

In *Currencies of Cruelty: Slavery, Freak Shows, and the Performance Archive*, I borrow from James's theorizations of cruelty but couple them with my own evaluations of alternative ledgers of enslaved labor. More specifically, I am concerned with the ways that enslaved performers in freak shows and sideshows were evaluated for their worth in a system that viewed them as at once valueless because of disabilities that prevented them from performing traditional forms of enslaved labor and simultaneously exponentially more valuable as objects of spectacle onstage. This reversal of valuations is inherently tied up not only in the cruelty that was an integral part of the project of chattel slavery but also in the cruelties and exploitations of the nineteenth-century freak show stage. Additionally, both slavery and freak shows are fixated on accounting in ways both big and small, evident and unseen. This careful accounting is present in the bark of the showman and the overseer. It is there in the advertisements of human sales and freak show entertainments, each of which promised unfettered access to vulnerable flesh. I argue that these currencies of cruelty are the basis for freak shows featuring enslaved subjects.

In this book, I excavate the archives of six nineteenth-century freak show performers with intimate connections to the system of American slavery from 1811 to 1912. Although the McKoys are undoubtedly the central and primary figures in this book, the stories and narratives of the four other performers are also vital to my understanding of the phenomena of enslaved and disabled nineteenth-century performance. Some performed as enslaved laborers, like musical prodigy and pianist Thomas "Blind Tom" Wiggins, conjoined twins Millie Christine McKoy (whose performances at first centered on their shared genitalia and then shifted after emancipation to encompass singing, dancing, and recitation in multiple languages), and P. T. Barnum's performer Joice Heth, whom Barnum toured under the false claim that she was the 161-year-old nursemaid of President George Washington. In contrast, Chang and Eng Bunker, rose to fame as freaks who displayed their conjoined and racialized bodies and later became enslavers. I track these performers from the Bunkers' birth in Siam in 1811 to the McKoys' death in 1912. But this time period also marks the years of active performance for the subjects in my ongoing research, rather than merely bookending their lifespans, most notably Joice Heth, who was born around 1756. It also encompasses the transition from legal slavery, through emancipation, Reconstruction, and the dawn of the twentieth century. I theorize the archival remains of their lives and performances (playbills, visiting cards, newspapers, autopsy reports, reviews, photographs) as alternative ledgers of enslaved labor in order to expand the methods of accounting for enslaved bodies and their performance labor beyond traditional archival routes (such as plantation account books or bills of sale). Building on Ellen Samuels's understanding of "enfreakment" as the process of being actively made a "freak," this book reveals, at the nexus of race, gender, disability, and performance, the relationship between the spectacularized otherness of sideshow performance and the dehumanizing project of American slavery.[11]

This book is invested in an examination of the evidence of accounting present in the places where disability, slavery, and performance touch in the archive. To that end, my argument is broken into three main parts. First, I establish how the archival practices of both freak shows and enslavement (and history more broadly speaking) are animated by an anticipatory practice of past-tense futurity I've called the future perfect. Borrowing from other grammatical approaches to writing archival histories, the future perfect (just like the tense it draws its name from) considers the past tense of the future. Put more simply, it examines the "what will have been" of history rather than relying entirely on the strictly historical past tense. It acknowledges that the present situations and impulses that drive us to write history are ever shifting but always deeply concerned with futurity. For why else would we enter items into the archive if we were not concerned with how history will have been told ten, fifteen, twenty, or one hundred–plus years into the future? Both the performers I study (especially the McKoys) and the enslavers who were the proprietors of their acts were concerned with how their stories would be preserved, told, and disseminated over time. This concern is mirrored in how their stories and archives are taken up today. Second, I analyze how unfree or newly freed enfreaked subjects accounted for themselves, their performance strategies, and their labor pre- and post-emancipation. I argue that these methods of "giving an account of oneself" (to paraphrase Judith Butler) are equally reflected in the archive's intense accounting for the bodies and labors captured under US enslavement and also in its accounting for the performance labor of enfreaked subjects.[12] This accounting is one of the currencies of cruelty that this book draws its name from, since it is reflective of an attempt to control and profit off the enslaved people whose performances proved so lucrative to their enslavers' estates.

And last, I examine how archival structures that recorded enslavement and enfreakment on the sideshow stage are deeply invested in accounting equally for performers' physical bodies and their performance labor. This creates a system whereby the unfree enfreaked body accrues high value as an object of spectatorship and performance even as the terms of bondage render that same body abjectly valueless as a traditional enslaved laborer. This occurs both onstage during life and also in the archive after death. I combine these three critical questions to assess not only the process through which these performers became enslaved but also the ways they were enfreaked, marking both slavery and freakdom as active practices of subjection. This is evidenced in accounts of things like Blind Tom playing Confederate fundraising concerts at the order of his enslaver or the McKoys' (auto)biographies, which hold accounts of benevolent slavery. In each case, the value was in the presumption that these performers, because of their disabilities, could not generate income for the estate when in fact they proved to be massively profitable high earners both before and after emancipation.

The accounting for the enslaved body in life and postmortem that I am invested in excavating in this work has been well documented within Black studies, history, and adjacent disciplines. It is evident in Stephanie Smallwood's *Saltwater Slavery* as she accounts for what was lost in the bartering of souls in the transatlantic slave trade. It is also present in Miranda Joseph's work on debt, Jennifer Morgan's *Reckoning with Slavery*, and Daina Berry's *The Price for Their Pound of Flesh*.[13] Each author negotiates the balance between Black personhood and Black commodification inherent to the project of slavery, whereby the Black subject was deemed highly valuable (from conception to life to death) as a commodity even as it was socially devalued through punishment, torture, and often fatal forced labor. Even in death, enslaved bodies retained high value as cadavers for medical schools and experiments.[14] But my considerations are particularly invested in the intersections of enslaved labor and performance labor evident in nineteenth-century sideshows and freak shows. This labor is the focal point of my inquiries precisely because it was often masked by the thin veneer of the white audience's pleasure, which mandated a sort of forced compliance from Black enslaved and enfreaked performers. But even within this mandated compliance, there were fissures created by the maneuvering and savvy of the enslaved. It is those fissures that I will trace here.

Chapter 1, "Alternative Ledgers of Enslaved Labor: The Future Perfect and the Nineteenth-Century Performance Archive," focuses on a 265-page account book maintained by Chang and Eng Bunker from 1832 to 1841, as well as letters written to the Freedmen's Bureau by the McKoys' parents. In this chapter, I argue that both the archive and enfreaked performance strategies contain within them a desire for the "future perfect." The future perfect asserts that rather than simply accounting for the uncertainty of the conditional past tense (or "what could have been"), the archive and performance labor are both deeply invested in the unknown and unsettled past tense of the future (or "what will have been"). This is because the improvised freak show, both onstage and in the archive, is concerned with anticipating a future's past that has not yet materialized. I argue that this anticipatory gesture, a gesture that is entirely intentional but made to look effortless and invisible, is often mirrored in the improvisational stylings of the freak show performers whose narratives are the central nodes of this book. This includes performance strategies like Millie Christine McKoy's famous duet harmonies with audience participation, synchronized dance steps, and signature act of speaking to two people on two topics at the same time, often in separate languages, to prove intellectual autonomy outside their embodied freakdom.[15]

The conditional uncertainty inherent to the archival practices of slavery and its afterlives has been widely theorized in Black studies and cultural studies. It is in Fred Moten's theorizations of the "anti- and ante-slave" and Omise'ke Natasha Tinsley's "anti- and ante-modern."[16] These temporal undoings hold together the tension of the present tense as it struggles with the restrictions of the past and casts outward into the future. It is also woven through the grammatical approaches to history of scholars theorizing the instability of slavery's and race's subjective past, such as Saidiya Hartman's "critical fabulation," Lisa Lowe's "past conditional," and the question of parentage and inheritance built into Hortense Spiller's "Mama's Baby, Papa's Maybe: An American Grammar Book," where she famously notes, from the perspective of the omnipresent Black woman, "My country needs me, and if I were not here, I would have to be invented."[17] However, I argue that these same theorizations of past-tense fragility in Black studies, archival critique, and nineteenth-century performance must be extended to fully encompass the future perfect because it is the future perfect tense in the study of slavery that is echoed in statements like Spillers's famous, "If I were not here, I would have to be invented."

Chapter 2, "Slave Autobiography and the Performance Archive," turns to biographical and autobiographical playbills from the six performers central to this project to mark the shift from being narrated by white freak show proprietors to engaging in limited forms of self-narration after US emancipation. This chapter tracks how performers gave an account of themselves as former property and, in some cases, as property owners operating their own shows after emancipation. I argue that the content and form of the McKoys' biographical narratives remained relatively unchanged even after emancipation, demonstrating that the legal shifts of the nineteenth and early twentieth centuries were as slow to materialize for enfreaked subjects as they were for newly freed Black subjects. As a result, disabled performers, especially newly freed Black subjects, often relied heavily on narratives of contented enslavement or a tranquil Southern pastoral even when archival evidence such as letters to the Freedmen's Bureau (in the case of the McKoys' parents) or ongoing custody battles and attempts at recuperating performance profits (in the case of Blind Tom's parents) belie this representation. Instead, it points to the contentious grounds under which newly freed and enfreaked performers continued to rely on the antebellum objectification that allowed them to rise to freak stardom, in order to maintain financial stability through performance acts.

Chapter 3, "Autopsy and Enfreakment on the Nineteenth-Century Stage," turns to the popularity of public autopsies of enfreaked performers, such as Joice Heth's public dissection in 1836, as well as the display of such performers' bodies upon their death, as when the Bunkers' torsos were cast in plaster for display in Philadelphia's Mütter Museum in 1874. I argue that there is a direct exchange between these enfreaked performers' live performances and the circulation and value of their physical bodies after death that allows for the continued performance of the enfreaked body as a subject of archival fascination today. In this chapter, I also reckon with questions of ethics and the potential impossibility of repatriation for these US-based performers' bodies, a question I'm called on to reckon with often as I negotiate the ways their bodily remains have become tourist attractions (in the case of the Bunkers on display at the Mütter Museum) or monuments to American national identity (in the case of the McKoys, who were reinterred in a ceremony by the Whiteville North Carolina Historical Society and their new grave marked as a historically significant site in 1969). Others were simply discarded, as Joice Heth was when it was revealed at her public autopsy that she was too young to, in fact, be President George Washington's nursemaid, as P. T. Barnum claimed in order to promote her act. The juxtaposition of the discarding of Heth and the treatment of her successors, the McKoys and the Bunkers, marks this sharp difference. While some of these enfreaked performers still remain a part of the central makeup of American popular culture and historicization, others are discarded when their bodies no longer hold up under the weight of violent interrogation, examination, historical imagination, and public scrutiny.

The fourth and final chapter, "Aural Fugitivity in *Zong!*, *Olio*, and *Curio*," explores my theorizations of *aural fugitivity* in the archives of enfreaked performance and its twenty-first-century successors. Evaluating poetry collections like M. NourbeSe Philip's *Zong!* and Tyehimba Jess's *Olio* alongside my own 2018 performance piece and 2025 film based on the life of the McKoy twins, both titled *Curio*, in this chapter I interrogate the aural performance strategies used by the enfreaked to escape complete archival capture (such as musical and speech improvisations). Building on my theory of aural fugitivity, or a process through which an enslaved or formerly enslaved performer was able to evade all-encompassing archival capture through hard-to-define and hard-to-record sound acts, in this chapter I argue that aural fugitivity provided a method of fugitive performance that hid in plain sight. This could include but was not limited to speech acts and speech improvisations, musical performances, unrecorded utterances, and other types of sonic and vocal discord that managed to evade the performance archive. Building on theorizations such as Daphne Brooks's "spectacular opacity" and Uri McMillan's "sonic of dissent," aural fugitivity asserts that sound acts provided an escape for enfreaked and enslaved performers from the exploitative physical displays that were favored before emancipation.[18] Additionally, in a twenty-first-century reimagining of the archive, aural fugitivity allows modern artists the ability to theorize and re-create the archives of the enfreaked and enslaved without using verbatim the language that was deployed during their lifetimes to exploit and subjugate them.

Throughout this book I will also be conducting an interwoven "ethnography of the archive." Combining the methods of autoethnography and ethnography, the chapters will include material that excavates the process through which extraordinary stories such as these are entered into the official record. An ethnography of the archive combines the skills learned from Saidiya Hartman's "critical fabulation" and my theorizations of the future perfect to imagine the politics and procedures that nineteenth-century archival actors and those who followed them used to determine the historical significance and importance of these enfreaked and enslaved stories. How does one determine that something will be historically significant in the future? In ten years? Fifty years? One hundred fifty years? And how is this reliant on the future perfect, or the historical past tense of the future moment? Connecting the theorizations of this book is an undergirding interrogation of what made and makes these performances both entertainment and history, inside the United States and internationally. Although by the mid-twentieth century freak shows were often considered unfashionable and distasteful in the United States, we are still struggling with ways to narrate and memorialize the performances and labor of these archival subjects, just as we are still struggling with how to reckon with and narrate the legacies of nineteenth-century slavery. At the center of these struggles and debates is the archive, performance or otherwise, because it is the repository we most often turn to when we look to animate the historical record.

I come to this work from a variety of valence points, voices, and experiences that are at once scholarly, creative, and deeply personal. I write this book not just as a scholar of theater, performance, Blackness, and disability but also as an artist and maker who is the descendant of New World enslaved laborers. My labor and theirs, while not comparable, nevertheless run parallel to each other in this book. They often work from contradictory impulses. My experience as a Black performer is also folded into the pages of this text. As a historian and expert, I have built a sizable portion of my career performing and in some ways commodifying Black intellectual prowess for networks like PBS, the History Channel, and YouTube Originals. These performances were carefully cultivated and scripted largely by me in order to disseminate work from within the humanities and humanistic social sciences to a broader audience outside academia. My performances were not solely built on the idea of being an "expert" but rather sprang from a genuine desire to see a shift in the way research was shared and made available to those outside academia. I wanted to see a change, and so in 2017 I began making web series with PBS that eventually spawned numerous other shows and web series with different media partners.

This is not to say that any parts of my performances of Black intellect through script writing, podcasting, web series, and films were inauthentic. In fact, a large part of the shows' popularity was the perception that I was just being myself while on camera, rather than disappearing behind a role or persona. Rather, I want to note these experiences as what they were: namely, performances of Black virtuosity. This shared commonality of performing intelligence as a metaphorical talking head for audiences that can be at once admiring and also hateful (as online audiences are notably volatile) makes me feel a certain personal closeness to Black performing folk like the McKoys, Blind Tom, and Joice Heth, even as I fight against any false equivalences. It is possible to see something of ourselves reflected in the performance archive without collapsing the self and the other. My hope here is to simply point out the complexity of these interwoven narratives and voices at play in the *Currencies of Cruelty*. In addition to the claims of the future perfect in both practice and theory, I hope to demonstrate in form as well as words the ways Black performances are aligned with multiple rationales and reasons for existing. There is not merely the act of appearance, but also the duality of W. E. B. Du Bois's "veil" and "double consciousness" at play in the Black performing body.[19]

In this book, I ask how the enfreaked Black subject in the nineteenth century was deemed abjectly valueless while simultaneously being rendered exponentially valuable as a performer through the contradictory logic of American slavery. These currencies of cruelty are measured in both the fiscal and social value assigned to Black subjects. For white enslavers, these enfreaked subjects were a source of profit and income, a designation the performers maintained within their families after emancipation. Yet the ways performers like the McKoys assessed and instrumentalized their worth both pre- and post-emancipation varied. Part of my project, therefore, is not just to evaluate the ways they negotiated the complex terrains of slavery and new freedom in the glare of the stage's spotlight but also how those negotiations continue to influence how we engage with the archives of slavery, disability, and performance.

As you trace the details of their lives, performance strategies, and archives, you may find yourself asking what makes the case of Millie Christine McKoy so noteworthy that I have dedicated the majority of my efforts to their archival remains. Outside of simply being the first case study I encountered in the archives that showed the intersections of enslavement, disability, and performance, the McKoys' archives also provide a complex portrait of the boundaries between legal freedom and unfreedom at the dawn of the twentieth century. Their work is also perhaps the most well-documented, if contested, evidence of an independent voice for the enfreaked and enslaved subject. And lastly, for better or for worse, the McKoys began my inquiries into the representations of enfreakment in the performance archive. Their self-fashioning, expert legal maneuvers, rebellions, and resistance have singularly shaped this work, informing not only the content of this book but the questions I have asked of the archive.

When writing this book, I've returned often to the bit of marginalia that opens this chapter. It has become something of a touchstone and talisman of my writing process, driven in no small part by writerly superstition. I have revisited the words almost every time I've sat down to write, in part because the idea of shared dreams and sensations is a fascinating and baffling one for those of us who live in solo bodies. But the greater motivation for me is the idea, the hope, and the imagination present in dreaming. Dreams hold within them an inherent desire for futurity that systems of ableism and enslavement look to at the very least dampen and at the very worst extinguish altogether. Dreams are evidence of imagining otherwise, an act of survival and resistance that spoke to me beyond the archives. We dream in futurity based on past experiences. Just like the McKoys' growing old together, which initially fascinated me, dreams were not supposed to be the lot of the enslaved. And yet they dreamed, in tandem, together as they always were in life. The McKoys are the spine of this book, and their stories animate this world. They started me on this journey over a decade ago, and I continue to walk alongside their archives with the full understanding that I may never truly understand everything necessary to tell this story, a story that is both settled and unsettled, overtold and underknown. I let their narrative, and their ingenious boldness and artistry, guide me.

1

Alternative Ledgers of Enslaved Labor

The Future Perfect and the Nineteenth-Century Performance Archive

An Unusual Demand

In 1882, nineteen years after the Emancipation Proclamation and seventeen years after the legal end of US slavery, American Black freak show performers Millie Christine McKoy made a strategic business and autobiographical transaction that linked their pasts as human property born into slavery in North Carolina in 1851 to their futures as independently wealthy performers and reportedly shrewd businesswomen. In her book *Millie-Christine: Fearfully and Wonderfully Made*, published in 2000, Joanne Martell offers a popular history of the famous enfreaked twins' lives, careers, and deaths.[1] While there are many issues with Martell's text, not the least of which is her unquestioning reliance on archival (auto)biographical programs that were authored in part by and for the profit of the men who alternately enslaved and employed the McKoys, it also provides key dates and archival references in the study of the twins' lives and decades-long performance careers. One example is Martell's retelling of a detail in the 1882 biographical program produced about the twins on behalf of Batcheller and Doris's Great Inter-Ocean Railroad Show. Writing about the twins' initial reluctance to join the traveling show and their subsequent business negotiations, Martell notes,

> Again she refused, but Doris persisted. He asked her lowest terms. "Seeing no other way out of the difficulty than to demand a salary so exorbitant that it would not nor could not be paid for a single feature in so vast an establishment as the Great Inter-Ocean Show she replied, "$25,000 for the season with traveling expenses for a maid and man servant." Twenty-five

> thousand dollars was the value set on Millie-Christine when the appraisal team of Bobo and Kirby had combed through Joseph Smith's Spartanburg estate. She had apparently kept that amount in mind all the years since. Imagine her surprise when Doris pulled a contract from his pocket, all filled out except for the salary. He wrote in the requested amount, signed his name, and handed the contract to her for her signature. She signed it.[2]

The veracity of the story, which is cited directly from a (auto)biographical program circulated by Batcheller and Doris's show, is not the necessary takeaway from this particular narrative of formerly enslaved labor. Rather, I am interested in the circulation of this potentially fictive narrative and the accompanying mythos in 1882, after the McKoys had gained access to their earnings as both adults and legally free subjects, because of the ways the McKoys expertly navigated the system of slavery to give both a descriptive and fiscal account of themselves.[3]

The program biography referenced by Martell would have been circulated in support of the McKoys' current and future performances, effectively providing a souvenir on which the show profited, as well as generating interest in upcoming shows. By announcing their appearance rate at an astonishingly high fee, and associating that fee with an appraisal from the days when they were enslaved, the McKoys' archive effectively disrupts other aspects of the (auto)biographical texts that claim that the McKoys were not only happy as the property of their final owner, Joseph Smith, but also considered members of the Smith family and household.[4] Instead, it subversively lays bare the reality of their position within the Smith house as formerly enslaved laborers whose presence earned a major profit for the Smith family and whose earning potential as laborers was evaluated and appraised as property within the estate. I argue that this self-appraisal, based on the past appraisal from the Smith estate, deploys the future perfect archival tense because it depends on a detail that will be a past event in the future. The appraisal makes plain the McKoys' projected worth, should legal slavery continue. Yet by the time they use this detail, it is a reality that exists both in the future of the McKoys as independently wealthy stage performers and in their past as enslaved laborers.

Here the McKoys' narrative, a narrative that they may have participated in the creation of, actively acknowledges their past position as enslaved laborers and property whose performance output and enfreaked bodies carried an inherent value from which the Smiths profited handsomely.[5] They then use this association to benefit themselves and profit from the fruits of their performance labor as actors. This is the counterintuitive exchange of values where the unfree enfreaked body is determined to be more valuable as an object of spectatorship even as it is rendered abjectly valueless or undervalued as a traditional enslaved or racialized laborer. I argue that it is an evaluation of this inverted system of appraisal that proves the salience of the McKoys' move to negotiate the price of their performance labor through an association with their former condition as enslaved people. But what is the archival future perfect tense, and how does it illuminate the lives and labor conditions of these nineteenth-century artists who performed under the fluctuating conditions of legal unfreedom?

This evidence of the negotiations they engaged in with the white sideshow proprietors is fascinating for a variety of reasons. First and foremost, it shows that part of the appeal of the McKoys' act postemancipation was a focus on their mental prowess, both onstage and behind the scenes. Although many of their (auto)biographies focus on their births and lives in the antebellum South, their act postfreedom both onstage and off centered largely on their skills. They coupled stories and information such as this anecdote with pastoral tropes of the Old South and old medical reports to create a performance persona that played on their past lives as enslaved women even while flaunting some of their newfound independence as free businesswomen. In this chapter, I will trace these strategic moves from the McKoys and others to demonstrate that they were not only arguing on their own behalf but rather creating alternative ledgers of enslaved labor through performance. By "alternative ledgers of enslaved labor," I mean systems of accounting that consider the fiscal value and worth of enslaved and disabled performers through the lens of slavery but do not rely entirely on the traditional bookkeeping of enslavers. This can include things such as the McKoys' strategically noting that they were once appraised as part of their former owner's estate as being worth $25,000 and then in turn using that figure to demand fair wages, in addition to other radical acts of self-evaluation. Alternative ledgers of enslaved labor look for evidence outside traditional sources used to determine the value of the enslaved, such as the slave master's ledger and the account books and bills of sale most often present in the archive. Instead, I turn my eye to the ways that the formerly enslaved, as well as enfreaked subjects with intimate connections to slavery such as the Bunkers, used the systems of evaluation once used to denigrate and devalue them as ways to enrich themselves and their families' postemancipation.

I look to these sources (stories like the foregoing one, an old personal ledger from the Bunker twins' archives, scraps of accounts of sale, etc.) to articulate this alternative ledger. These methods of self-evaluation of worth prove to be significant in my study of enfreakment and enslavement, two systems that worked to doubly devalue those who were born at the intersection of the identities associated with them. First, I turn to the connections between alternative ledgers of enslaved labor in performance and the future perfect archival tense. Next, I work through two letters written to the Freedmen's Bureau on behalf of the McKoys' parents, Jacob and Menemia, arguing that these letters can be seen as an attempt to claim reparations for their performance labor and lost wages. Then I theorize how the currency of children and the reproductive potential of these enslaved and enfreaked performers factored heavily into their performance strategies. I argue that children and the potential to have them were key to the ways these performers were viewed as enfreaked onstage. Next, I transition to discussing how the fights over ownership that took place both before and after emancipation eventually gave way to arguments over custody, a transformation that changed the legal language of enslavement from one of ownership to one of parentage. Then I explore the aural and oral fugitivity of these performers before concluding with an analysis of the future perfect's connection to alternative ledgers of enslaved labor.

The Archival Future Perfect

Archives hold a forward-moving connection to the past, demonstrating a desire for futurity through the preservation of history, which at its heart is our shared collective story. Performance also resists presentism in its analysis because it carries within it a multiplicity of past, present, and future tenses. It exists in the ephemeral present tense of the live act, the evocation of ghosts that ring with the past tense, and the acts of preserving and remembering these performances for future analysis and pleasure. All of these tenses exist alongside each other, crowding our understanding of how the act of performance is recorded in the archive. What accounts remain when historicizing the performance act, and how do we approach this circular timeline when telling the story of performances from years past? These were the questions that animated my initial inquiries into the lives and archival legacies of sideshow and freak show performers from the nineteenth century with intimate ties to American slavery.

Both the archive and enfreaked performance strategies contain within them the "future perfect" archival tense. These archives and performances both anticipate an unseen future, mirroring the desires and sensibilities of their creators and consumers. Archives are formulated around the desire of both the collector and the researcher, creating a system of subjective analysis that refuses objectivity (even as the historical record claims objectivity as a goal). Similarly, enfreaked performances are shaped by the ingenuity of the performers and the desires of the audience to witness difference and otherness onstage. This includes Millie Christine McKoy's famous duets, dancing, and signature act of speaking to two people at the same time, often in separate languages.[6] This also includes Blind Tom Wiggins's improvisational piano stylings, Chang and Eng Bunker's use of their families in their live shows, and Joice Heth's vocalizations and speech acts.

But how do these performance acts exemplify the future perfect historical tense? Perhaps it is contained within these performers' projected desire for a future history that has not yet been written, a history that could make space for their narratives of enfreakment and enslavement. Or maybe it is a self-awareness that their performance acts may indeed become historically relevant and important not just to their contemporary audiences but to audiences and scholars in the future. It was a desire to shape how they were narrated while they were alive and commemorated in death that dictated the performance strategies of the McKoys and their fellow performers. Even where there is a lack of evidence of financial and creative control by the performers themselves, there is evidence of financial and historical concerns raised by those who claimed (and in some cases seized) control over these performers and their acts. These additional figures were certainly invested in the earning potential of the performers, and that ties directly to the ways they appeared on the freak show stage. These concerns led to struggles over how and why performers like the McKoys entered and remained in the public eye for profit.

Letters to the Freedmen's Bureau

The year 1882 would not be the last time that the McKoys reportedly leveraged their past as a way of securing their financial futures and those of their family. By the time the performance program was being circulated with the remarkable story of their ability to negotiate their performance earnings (with the notable addition of a maid and manservant, themselves employees and laborers of the twins) through the lens of their history as enslaved laborers, the twins and their family were already well versed in navigating the connections between legal slavery, spectacle, and earning potential. The twins were born on the estate of a man named McKoy in 1851, one year after the passage of the 1850 Fugitive Slave Act. By 1870 they would purchase tracts of land near the plantation on which they were born, land that they would later build a house on and also allow their elderly parents to live on. The 1870 census notes "Jacob McKay" (their father) owned $250 worth of personal real estate and a personal estate valued at $150.[7] The strategic move to buy land near the plantation on which they were born opens up another facet of the twins' choices to continue to associate, in some regards, their future earnings with their past in bondage. Many obituaries and other newspaper articles indeed note the twins' decision to buy the land on which they were born as both an odd fact and an interesting triumph of their performance career.[8] There remains no physical trace of the McKoys' financial success. The home they built burned down, and all that remains are newspaper clippings and photographs noting their great earning potential as both enslaved and legally free performance workers.[9] In their last will and testament, the twins note a number of possessions, money, and land that they gift specifically to their sisters and nieces, furthering the line of inheritance through the women of their family line in the absence of biological children.[10] Yet the McKoy family's interactions with the legal system, slavery, and rights to performance earnings predate both the Census Bureau's 1870 evaluation and their 1882 playbill for Batcheller and Doris's Great Inter-Ocean Railroad Show. A letter uncovered in the archives of the Freedmen's Bureau not only supports these claims but also shows the relationship between ownership and custody, which I will discuss in the cases of the other performers I study in this chapter. The letter notes a claim that the twins' parents brought against the widow of their former owner, Mary A. Smith, on August 17, 1866, less than a year after the end of the Civil War in the United States.[11]

In the letter, Lieutenant Echelberry writes to General Allan Rutherford that he has met with "Jacob and Menemia McCoy (freed) and would respectfully ask if there can be anything done by the military authorities to help them get possession of their children." He goes on to note that Smith, who was the enslaver of Menemia and Millie Christine at the time of emancipation, "refused them their freedom, and by misrepresentations kept them in her service some time thereafter." Through threats, coercion, and concealment, Smith kept possession of the underage twins, requesting that Jacob and Menemia sign over their custodial rights to their children in exchange for "one fourth of all she made by exhibiting the children." The letter closes by saying, "Under these promises and threats, they signed the contract and Mrs. Smith kept possession of the children and has them now on exhibition in Barnum's Museum, New York City. Mrs. Smith has not paid any money for the services of the children and the parents are very anxious to get possession of them again, and they are not able to follow Mrs. Smith and appeal to the civil authorities on account of not having money. From the character that Jacob and Menemia have among those that know them, I think their statement true."[12] There appears to be the potential here to think of this move as an act of demanding labor reparations for the McKoys' time spent in Barnum's Museum in New York City. Here the distinction between custody of and ownership over the twins (both their enfreaked bodies and the earning potential of that unified body) remains in flux. Both the McKoys' biological parents and their former owner maintain that they have a right to ownership of the girls and their earnings and look to exert those rights through this custody dispute. The fact that the girls at this point are teenagers (merely fifteen years old) only serves to heighten the intensity of this legal battle. This comes at a point when, just a year prior, the twins began to change the shape of their act by refusing to be exhibited or examined nude in public,[13] instead focusing on acts of virtuosic aural performance such as speaking in two languages at once, reciting poetry, and singing in harmony, which is noted through multiple performance reviews in their archive.[14]

Although reviewers often deployed descriptive terms that utilized the language of scientific racism, their most striking commonality was their fascination with the twins' orality in its many forms. In fact, most reviewers undervalued everything outside of the twins' bodily freakdom except their signature act: displaying their polyglot skills in public by speaking separately, in two languages at once, and singing in harmony. I theorize that by refocusing the content of their act after emancipation to center on an improvisational orality that fully realized the potential of escaping archival capture through quotidian conversational skills, the McKoys skillfully engineered their own pointed fugitivity in a way that prevented them from achieving the fame of their more well-known counterparts such as Chang and Eng Bunker. Evidence in both the change in their act after emancipation and the letter to the Freedmen's Bureau on behalf of their parents points to the fact that the entire McKoy family deployed both legal and extralegal means that allowed them to eventually live and die as property owners in the state of North Carolina, the same state in which Menemia, Jacob, Millie Christine, and their reported seven siblings had all been born as human property.[15]

But this letter to the Freedmen's Bureau, while bold, was actually not the first time the McKoy twins' parents appealed to a higher legal authority against Smith. This is the same Smith who is spoken of so lovingly in their (auto)biographies as almost a second mother to them.[16] In an earlier letter to the Freedmen's Bureau dated October 26, 1865, the McKoys' parents attempted to appeal to the authorities for the return of their children and their earnings. The letter reads, in part,

> Col. Sir,
> I have the honor to submit for your consideration a matter between Jacob and Menevia his wife, Freedmen, and Mrs. Mary A. Smith, a relative of a pair of twin children, daughters of Jacob and Menevia. It seems that this Mrs. Smith a resident of South Carolina, living in an adjoining county to this State, and owning a plantation in Anson Co. N.C., owned as slaves Jacob and Menevia and the Twin children Milly and Christina. Jacob and Wife lived on the plantation in Anson Co N.C. The twins have been exhibited in Europe and other countries by Mrs. Smith or her agents and have made a fortune for her. They are similar to the celebrated Siamese twins, are 14 years of age and both female. The father and mother make

the following statement to me. That in the month of June last Mrs. Smith and a brother-in-law came to them saying that it was reported that the Negroes were free, but such was not the case, and that she wished to retain the children. The father refused saying that if they were not free, that he believed they soon would be. Mrs. Smith then told the parents that should it turn out that they were not free (and she knew they would not be) that she would make their lives a hard one unless they consent for her to retain the children, but if they would consent, that she would at the end of five (5) years give them their freedom as also the children. . . . A short time after Mrs. Smith and her friends went to Wadesboro, taking the parents before Capt Bennett, making a proposition to the parents to keep the children five (5) years, giving the parents the 1/4 of the nett proffits that might be derived from the exhibiting of the children paying them at the end of each year. No doubt but this was fraud practiced to get the children. . . . After hearing the parents' story I believe that the agreement was forced upon Jacob & wife. There is nothing in the contract giving the parents security or compelling Mrs. Smith to pay anything more than she sees proper. I am informed by White men that the children are valuable and that other parties would of advanced several hundred dollars for the hire of the children, giving the parents means of supporting themselves and a large family. . . . Their story is a plain and simple one, and if true shows a strong case of fraud on the part of Mrs. Smith and friends, and nothing to the credit of Capt. Bennett. . . . I enclose a copy of the contract held by the parents.

I am Sir most respectfully your obedient servant

John C. Barnitt,
Capt. and Asst Supt FMB. E Whittlesey,
Col and Asst Commr Raleigh, NC[17]

In the case of each letter, the McKoys' parents lay waste to any illusion that Smith was a benevolent maternal figure who nurtured and cared for the young twin performers. Instead, she's revealed to be hungry for the profits the girls provided while neglecting to pay them or their parents for their labor. Each letter, and the accompanying lawsuit that took place as a result of Jacob and Menemia's advocacy and legal savvy, serves as evidence that the McKoy family imagined alternative futures for themselves and were unafraid to use the courts to access these futures.

The audacity and courage of the McKoys' parents in their efforts to regain custody of their daughters is not lost on me here. They boldly call into question not only Smith's failure to uphold her contractual obligations but also her moral character with phrases such as, "Their story is a plain and simple one, and if true shows a strong case of fraud on the part of Mrs. Smith and friends." The McKoy family's letter also dares to question the legality and ethics of the original contract, saying, "There is nothing in the contract giving the parents security or compelling Mrs. Smith to pay anything more than she sees proper," even though it also expresses racist assumptions of who should be believed when it notes that "white men" have verified the twins' worth. This calls into question the legality of their agreement with Smith and makes way for their claims of lost wages.

Although the Freedmen's Bureau was a site of recourse for newly freed Black people, it was not a perfect institution. However, in cases like the McKoys', the Freedmen's Bureau administrators could make rulings on behalf of Black citizens. After lodging their complaints to the bureau through these two letters, Millie Christine's parents had a new contract drawn up in November 1865 that, among other things, demanded humane treatment for their daughters and monthly payments of their earnings. The contract was written by Ladd and Cartwright in New York City. That same month the bureau ordered Smith to appear with the twins for trial. But a telegraph from the bureau shows that Smith arrived alone without the twins. Under suspicions that she planned to transport the twins to Europe if she lost the case, Smith was then arrested. Clinton Cilley, an agent of the bureau, then ruled on December 3, 1865, that the twins be returned to the custody of Jacob and Menemia but that the contract they signed with Smith was in fact legally binding. The new contract drafted in New York was deemed unenforceable and unlawful. Cilley wrote in part,

> Salisbury, NC Dec 3rd 1865
>
> Col,
>
> . . . I have the honor to report that in the case of the twin girls, referred to me for settlement, I heard the parties Monday last and decided after as full an investigation as I could give the case that the children be

returned to their natural guardian, their father, holding back both contracts made by him, until he should see and answer with his daughters. They are aged 14 and should be able to think for themselves. Under the laws of this state the father has the right, by deed or will, to appoint a guardian or guardians for his minor children for any [term?] of years, except that the guardianship cease when the children arrive at the age of 21. Under this law, his first contract, giving the children to Mrs. Smith will be binding but before allowing it to be put in force I propose to have it made out differently so as to [see?] the children more firmly in their profits and rights. The 2nd contract made with help Ladd and Cartwright, would not be good in law in my opinion and in [?] of the ablest lawyers in this vicinity when I have consulted. These 2 gentlemen however very much incensed at my decision, I think understand, of appealing to you however it's our decision. I have yet made it to order present holder, Mrs. Smith, to give the children up to the parents, who have not seen them for 8 years. I [?] they will not be able to have it overruled.

Respectfully
Your servant
Clinton A. Cilley[18]

However, although he initially ruled in favor of the McKoys, Cilley later reversed his decision on December 9, 1865, less than a week after his initial ruling.

In his reversal, Cilley has Smith maintain custody of the twins but adds a stipulation to their original contract fining her $5,000 if she refuses to uphold her contractual obligations toward the McKoys. In his reversal Cilley notes,

Salisbury NC Dec 9th 1865

Col,
After considering the within case carefully, seeing both claimants' and the parents of the children and availing myself of the best disinterested legal advice in this part of North Carolina, and also after an inclusion reading of the statute law, I have decided to approve the contract made

with Mrs. Mary A. Smith, with the provision that she shall file her penal bond for $5000 five thousand dollars, the condition of the bond being that she shall pay the parents $5000 in case of non fulfilment of the contract on her part. The twins have already been in a school in reading for seven years. Under the laws, this contract is valid and can not be revoked in consequence of non fulfilment of the same by the guardians. I have revoked my order requiring the children to be restored to their parents being confident that they will be so restored as soon as the question of their possession is settled. I return all the papers sent me in the matter. Hoping that this decision will be approved and that the matter may be laid finally at rest.

I am, Col.

Very respectfully
Clinton A Cilley

This reversal highlights not only the limited avenues to legal recourse available to formerly enslaved families like the McKoys but also the ways the conditions of unfreedom were extended beyond the end of legal slavery. Although this represents a measured win for the McKoys (they did not regain custody of their daughters but still were able to have their original contract enforced), it demonstrates the lengths that the family was willing to go to in order to ensure that their daughters were well cared for and treated humanely after emancipation. The reversal of Cilley's decision represents an obvious setback for the McKoys and their parents. Yet it is the will to fight within a legal system that (until recently) had enslaved them all that fascinates me most. The McKoys were invested in the fact that their daughters were not only worthy of protection but legally entitled to it as both new citizens and minors. This assertion, while limited in its results, rings out in the archive even today.

But these encounters with the Freedmen's Bureau were not the McKoy family's first interaction with the complicated legal workings of transnational slavery. Neither was the twins' bold self-appraisal in their 1882 (auto)biography the first time they used their narrative methods to financially benefit from their ongoing fights for freedom and their parents' fights for custody. It was the currency of children that proved vital to the ongoing legal disputes over both custody and ownership that began in their childhood and lasted until they died in 1912. But to fully understand the vital role that childhood, ownership, and custody play in the lives of all six performers, I must consider the McKoys' historical and performance antecedents, Joice Heth, Chang and Eng Bunker, and Thomas "Blind Tom" Wiggins.

The Currency of Children and Reproductive Enumeration

The demands articulated by the McKoys' parents in their repeated letters to the Freedmen's Bureau and their multiple lawsuits demonstrate that they recognized not only the parental need to regain custody of their children after emancipation but also the fiscal value of their uniquely enfreaked daughters. These ongoing struggles for custody and ownership show that there was an inherent currency attached to children and children's labor both under slavery and after emancipation. This value was actualized for enfreaked children through acts of appearance and performances that highlighted their physically spectacular bodies and talents. But the currency of children extended not only to the enfreaked children but also to the children of the enfreaked (as is the case with Chang and Eng Bunker's children who joined their act after emancipation left the family in dire financial straits). In this section, I explore the unique value that these children presented in the enslaved world through bills of sale, ledgers, and narrative accounts. Through a continued ethnography of the performance archive, I explicate the pattern that emerges from the archival evidence to trace the ways that enfreaked childhood was represented and monetized by the adults in these scenarios. By utilizing the phrases *currency of children* and *reproductive enumeration*, I extend the analysis of scholars who have previously published about the financial value assigned to Black subjects and the reproductive potential of those subjects.[19] In doing this, I reveal the role that Black and racialized childhood played in the performances of enfreakment and slavery.

On my 2016 return research trip to the University of North Carolina at Chapel Hill, after I left the Hayes Plantation Library mentioned in the prologue, I was redirected to the reading room for archival materials. I began looking through the collection's boxes of materials on Chang and Eng Bunker. The first thing I found was a box of items from their archives largely comprising bills of sale and receipts. Although they are all now digitized and available online, I felt compelled to return to the scene of my first discovery about enfreakment, eager to learn what I could from the physical documents and ephemeral remains. I was immediately struck by the meticulousness of the twins' recordkeeping. I found everything from exact amounts paid for every performance, by month, day, and year, in an unbound logbook, to stacks of correspondence, receipts, and bills of sale. Preparing my body for a long day spent in solitary focus until I found evidence of the Bunkers as enslavers (the portion of their archive that would prove most relevant to my project), I was taken aback to discover that the second document in the second folder I opened was precisely what I'd come to see.

It was a faded but still legible bill of sale for "two negro girls" from September 29, 1845. The first is named "Mary aged 7½ years," while the second is named "Nicey aged 5½." Due to a stained crease in the center of the page, it is hard to ascertain whether Mary is seven and a half, five and a half, or one and a half, and Nicey's name could very well be Nicy.[20] Thomas F. Prather is named as the previous enslaver of the girls, and he swears to the fact that they are "sound and healthy" at the time of purchase. I spent time poring over this document, eager to glean what little I could about the lives of these two girls from this unsatisfactory source. This bill of sale is no more and no less than the sum of its parts. It tells me that the price paid was "four hundred and fifty dollars." It tells me all legal parties involved (the Bunkers and Prather, as mentioned earlier). It even tells me that the girls were considered "sound and healthy," although these terms are highly debatable given the conditions under which enslaved laborers were forced to survive.[21] Even its placement in the archive tells a story. Lost in a folder of sales receipts, it comes immediately after a receipt for one hundred acres of land sold for five dollars by the Bunkers to a man named David.[22] All property claims are filed and stored in their proper place. This reduction and truncation of two lives down to the barest of descriptions (price, age, and purported health) seemed immeasurably saddening to me. I drove myself to distraction reading and rereading the text of the receipt, but no new revelation came to me, despite my best attempts. In searching later, I came across a second bill of sale, this one dated November 20, 1855, and listing ten people to be sold.

Here I found a name that looked like "Nice," but in the transcription of the document found online, it is simply recorded as a question mark. The girl is reported to be sixteen years old, making her approximately the right age to have been the five-and-a-half-year-old from the bill of sale from September 29, 1845, around ten years prior.[23] I would like to ruminate on the vital punctuation of the question mark in the online transcription, a strange echoing of the unknowability of a girl I have alternately called Nicy, Nicey, and Nice, her name lost in the shuffle of archival transcription and inaccurate recordkeeping. It astounds me that the Bunkers have a noted variability in their recording of this name when the records of their expenses and finances remain otherwise painstakingly meticulous. One account book in the archive records every payment that the twins received in performance from 1833 to 1839, noting the source of the payment alongside the city, day, month, and year in which it was received.[24] Another, equally thorough ledger records all expenses from their dual households between 1832 and 1841.[25]

Everything is carefully recorded, including money spent on a range of items from food, to gloves, to daily allotments for postage. Yet nowhere in these two carefully supported ledgers are accounts of the expenses and financial gains related to the Bunkers' reported twenty-seven to seventy-five enslaved laborers (the numbers vary based on account).[26] Here the records of the girl named Nicey, her companion Mary, and the nine additional laborers named on the second bill of sale in the archive are joined by two copies of a photo that has survived of one of the Bunkers' many enslaved laborers in the archives at the University of North Carolina at Chapel Hill. The woman in the photo, unnamed except for the title "Former slave of Eng Bunker," bears a face that shows the weathering of time.[27] An inscription written on the back of one of the two copies of the photo that remain in the archive reads, "Born in 1799 this old colored lady lived until 1921—she was a wedding present to Mr. + Mrs. Eng in 1843. She was a house nurse to all their children."[28] She is remembered only within the category of property and her association with these famous enfreaked, othered, and raced bodies, and her name is not recorded or remembered. Rather, what is considered of note is her fantastic age and position as a "house nurse," placing her labor within the intimacy of the Bunkers' homes, specifically Eng's home. As with Mary and Nicey, her sole remembrance is her connection to the Bunkers' households as an enslaved laborer. And yet the specificity

Figure 1.1: "Former slave of Eng Bunker," photograph, ca. 1880–90, in the Chang and Eng Bunker Papers #3761, Southern Historical Collection, Wilson Library, University of North Carolina at Chapel Hill.

of her labor as a house nurse and her purported remarkable age of 122 cannot help but call to mind the story of Barnum's enslaved performer Joice Heth, the reported nursemaid of founding father George Washington who toured the country as a traveling enslaved "freak."[29]

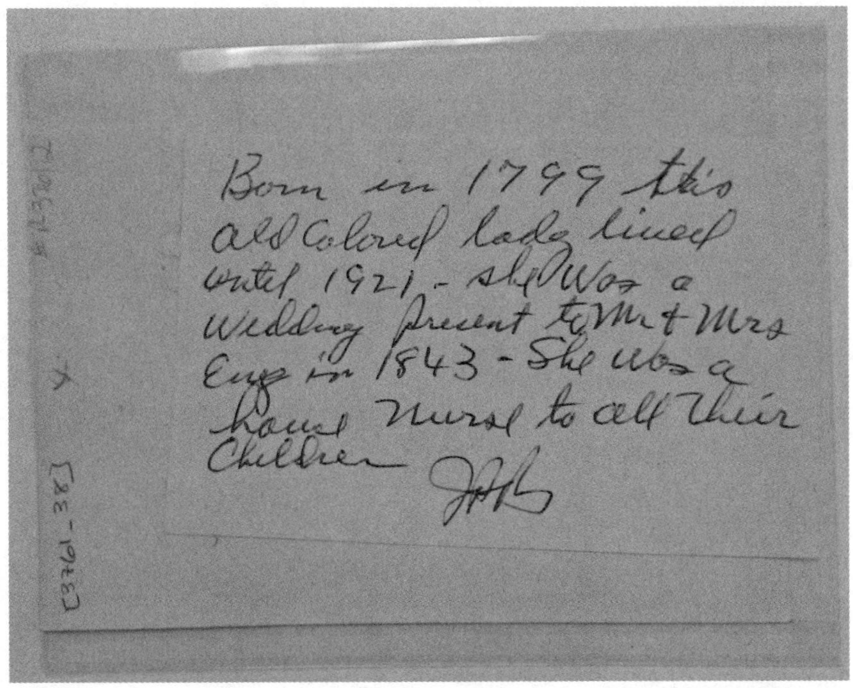
Born in 1799 this
old colored lady lived
until 1921 - she was a
wedding present to Mr & Mrs
Eng in 1843 - She was a
house nurse to all their
children

Figure 1.1: (*continued*)

Figure 1.2: Bunker family, 1870, Ronald G. Becker Collection of Charles Eisenmann Photographs, Special Collections Research Center, Syracuse University Libraries.

What stands as a curiosity of archival remembrance and fugitivity here is not only further evidence of what Uri McMillan has termed in regard to Joice Heth an "ancient negress" mythology but also the connection between the types of labor associated with this figure and the intimacy of the domestic sphere.[30] In fact, it was the labor of domestic women laborers within the Bunker household, caring for their families, and more specifically their children, that allowed for the Bunkers' successful rise to the North Carolina planter class in conjunction with their continuing performance as racialized freaks. It is telling that both photographs I have found of the Bunkers' enslaved laborers feature women. In the first, we see the unnamed "ancient negress." In the second, we see the Bunkers' large family, with eighteen of their twenty-one children, their wives, and one enslaved woman caring for a sleeping toddler.[31] It is this vital role as caregiver and nursemaid to the Bunkers' children (children who, in fact, became a focal part of Chang and Eng's act after the Civil War and the demise of the plantation economy drove them back onto the public stage) that proves the integral connection between enslaved labor and the viability and earning potential of the Bunkers' freak show act in later years.

The role that these women played was not purely functional but also narratively significant in the ways that the Bunkers were constructed as national figures, "American" performers who nonetheless remained othered and apart, and members of the planter class. Joseph Andrew Orser writes of the twins' rise and subsequent fall from wealth and the American cultural imagination in his monograph *The Lives of Chang and Eng: Siam's Twins in Nineteenth-Century America*. He notes that "the Siamese twins had long been used ironically as symbols of American nationalism," specifically citing a pamphlet published on the twins in the 1830s with a flying eagle carrying a banner that reads "E Pluribus Unum" and the phrase "United We Stand."[32] This tongue-in-cheek mockery serves as an unusual counterpoint to later documents that show the twins' features exaggerated in a caricature of stereotypical Asian appearance and others still that appear to present the twins as almost stereotypically Black or mixed race. Images of the twins' united bodies that depicted them as representative of the duality and division of the Civil War continued to circulate and haunt their act.[33] The McKoys', Heth's, and Blind Tom's acts were similarly associated with both the Civil

War and antebellum patriotism through the McKoys' depiction as stars in the American flag on their performance playbills, Heth's purported relationship to founding father George Washington, and Blind Tom's performances of fundraising concerts on behalf of Confederate troops.[34]

Indeed, it was a connection to the national imaginary, either as supposed perpetual children (in the case of the McKoys and Blind Tom) or as parents and caregivers (in the case of the Bunkers and Heth), that allowed for the continued success of these various performers' acts in both the antebellum and post–Civil War United States. For example, Heth's role as an "ancient negress" continued to be the highlight and selling point of her show. Of this role, McMillan writes, "I argue that Heth's role playing as a putative 'ancient negress' was intrinsically linked to particular conceptualizations of the past and national memory that were quintessentially American and, in themselves, performed. Heth's specific fundamental appeal to nineteenth-century audiences was her performative substitution for the absent personage of George Washington. . . . Heth's daily rehearsals before heterogeneous audiences as an embodied black maternal surrogate for a collective American memory, or what I term 'mammy-memory,' were in fact *performances*." McMillan goes on to note that "Heth was a social actor who manipulated her disabled and disfigured physical body to perform ersatz dramas of national memory," and yet that "the American past she ostensibly embodied was itself an imaginary mimesis."[35] I argue that these unnamed elderly women in the photographs in the Bunkers' archives perform a similar function in the archival memory of the Bunkers, whose own rise to fortune and fame was a constant negotiation through the pitfalls of nineteenth-century American racial politics and a hierarchy that was entrenched in the system of enslavement. I am interested in not only the duality of the twins' united bodies but also the ways it was incorporated into the national narrative of the duality of the Civil War, their own reproductive capability, and a rumor that they had traveled to the British Isles in 1868–69 to consult physicians about surgery for separation. How do these facts combine with their diminished status as freak show performers after 1865? And how does the surrogacy of these elderly enslaved women factor into the Bunkers' own carefully curated mythos as freaks?

Although there has been much said on the labor value placed on children, particularly Black enslaved or free children (namely in the

Figure 1.3: Illustrations of Chang and Eng Bunker, 1830 and 1829. Courtesy of the North Carolina Collection, University of North Carolina at Chapel Hill.

Figure 1.3: (*continued*)

work of Robin Bernstein and Camille Owens), as well as the emergence of childhood as a protected category for white children in the eighteenth and nineteenth centuries, the concept of the currency of children posits something different.[36] It theorizes that there was a unique value placed on children who were enfreaked as well as on the descendants of the enfreaked. They were envisioned as perpetual children on account of their disabilities and society's ableism (as was the case with the McKoys and Blind Tom and their respective parents' decades-long legal cases to regain custody of them). Coupled with the binds of enslavement, which falsely assumed Black subjects were incapable of legal, fiscal, or bodily autonomy, Black childhood added a layer of additional financially motivated oppression. In the case of the children of the enfreaked, the currency of children played out through the value and spectacle added to these performances, especially after emancipation. The twenty-one children of Chang and Eng Bunker were integral to their continued popularity and social relevance after emancipation and the fall of the Confederacy left them bankrupt. The appearance of and care for this massive brood, by the Bunkers, their wives, and the enslaved women on their plantations, as well as the archiving of their many descendants, continue to be relevant to the Bunkers' performance archives. At the University of North Carolina at Chapel Hill, the performance archives of the Bunkers are rife with images of family reunions stretching into the latter half of the twentieth century. Here the speculative value assigned to the reproductive potential (or presumed lack thereof) of enfreaked performers in the nineteenth century that played out through their performances and performance materials in the archive is representative of reproductive enumeration, or the evaluation of an enfreaked subject based on their reproductive potential (both real and imagined). For Chang and Eng, it was the focus on and amazement about the fact that they had so many children, coupled with innuendos about incest because they married sisters and presumably could not have sex privately. For the McKoys, it was that "medical men" focused on their shared genitals and reproductive organs and their presumed infertility. In each case, the question of sex and privacy takes center stage.

There were also complex negotiations of the value or perceived value of enslaved children, particularly disabled ones, during chattel slavery. In her article "Mothering the 'Useless': Black Motherhood, Disability, and

Slavery," Jenifer L. Barclay argues, "Because chattel slavery was a system designed to extract productive labor from individuals, those with disabilities were perceived as 'useless' by slaveholders even though they often provided labor and services that went unacknowledged (Boster 2013a). Slaveholders often considered them to be financially worthless and sometimes even 'chargeable'—meaning that the cost of their care was a financial liability. This calculated reasoning left disabled, enslaved children particularly vulnerable because slaveholders devalued them as property and privileged mothers' labor over their children's presumably irrelevant needs."[37] This reversal of the presumed racist logics of slavery, where a child becomes a "chargeable" ward of the plantation rather than a potential profit earner, marks Black disabled and enslaved children as unnecessary to the financial health of the estate. And yet what we see from the cases of enfreaked children and the children of the enfreaked like the McKoys, Blind Tom, and the Bunkers' children is that these children actually held the potential to be high earners precisely because they were disabled children. In the case of freak show performances, the ability to display themselves and appear in public counteracted the assumption that these enfreaked children were "useless" in any way, leading instead to a scenario in which the currency of children was of particularly high value. In these households children were not just surplus laborers or burdens; they were integral to the performance acts of the freak show.

By 1864 Chang's investments in land had skyrocketed to $6,000 and his investments in enslaved people to $9,500, while his brother Eng's own investments reached $1,000 in land and $17,500 in enslaved laborers.[38] However, these earnings were all but lost after the conclusion of the Civil War, forcing them to reluctantly return to the sideshow stage, with their children joining them onstage as informal additions to their act. Therefore, when they saw the diminishment of their estate postemancipation, they turned to the *currency of children*, their own children, as valuable performance laborers who could contribute to both the shock value and interest of their act. While it was Heth's role as a fictive "mammy" that drew audiences to her act, it was the Bunkers' enfreaked bodies, coupled with their ability to reproduce, that attracted audiences to their shows postemancipation. Around the same time the McKoys were decentering their performances away from the display of their shared genitals and the reproductive speculations that accompanied them, the Bunkers' focus on their own individual virility through the spectacle of their children brought them back to the freak show stage after semiretirement years earlier. Reproductive enumeration, or the speculation around and attendant fascination with the reproductive potential of enslaved, enfreaked, or othered bodies, remains crucial to my formulation of arguments about the currency of children. While the McKoys' were often displayed in their childhood for eager and paying white audiences and subjected to medical examinations at the hands of exploitative physicians (a performance strategy they recentered with other types of performance in their teenage years), the Bunkers' own reproductive potential and Heth's supposed caregiving connections to Washington remained focal parts of their acts throughout their lives. I argue that it is this speculative possibility, which calls on the combined power of the past, present, and future (in terms of past children born, present capability for children, and the future possibility for bearing more children), that creates the conditions of reproductive enumeration under which these freak show actors labored and performed.

Considering the integral role that children, child-rearing, and child-bearing played in these performers' relationship to freak show and enslavement, I turn my attention to the traditional ledgers that the Bunkers kept from 1832 to 1841 of monies expended and another of monies received from performance for the years 1833–1839.[39] For the Bunkers, it seems that no expense was too large or too small to record. Numbers vary from mere cents to hundreds of dollars, and in importance from taxes to expenses for handbills and other promotional materials and to mere buttons or pieces of thread. In their account book for monies received, they primarily note profits from performances and the dates and locations of their shows. While, as I noted earlier, there are no references to profits or expenses related to the Bunkers' enslaved laborers, there are exactly seventy-seven occasions on which they record having paid a Black laborer. The amounts range from a few cents to a peak of one dollar and fifty cents. There is a slight hiatus after February 1840 before a recording of one additional instance of them paying a Black laborer in January 1841. At the beginning, the ledger is both exactingly precise and overwhelming. Each entry bears the month, day, and year of the transaction along with the total amount and minor editorial notes from the twins such as exclamation points and parenthetical asides. But it is in the final pages of the ledger that the content takes a sudden turn. It becomes less detailed and clear, whole pages being left blank or even missing entirely. Then, on the 258th page of their ledger, after years of careful recording, is a page unlike any of the preceding ones. It records the names and birth dates of the Bunkers' children. In a different hand and with what I presume is a different pen, someone has written on the left-hand margin "white" or "col" (perhaps short for "colored") next to the name of each child. It is this unusual accounting for their children in a book of expenses that integrates them into consideration as part of the Bunkers' estate. Similar to the McKoys' pointed self-appraisal in Batcheller and Doris's playbill, the Bunkers are accounting for their children under the umbrella of property and performance.

This accounting for the Bunkers' children is notable for two reasons. First, it aligns them with the other property of the estate, acknowledging that children in the home were seen as both resources and loved ones. And second, the ledger sometimes notes which brother is the father of each child, perhaps because of the ambiguity surrounding parentage that played out in the popular media when reporters would insinuate that there was something inherently improper or "freakish" about the twins fathering children with sisters. The thinly veiled innuendo of incest or impropriety comes back to the presumed lack of privacy either brother would have during sexual acts. Therefore, the children seem to have been considered jointly owned or at least jointly claimed by the Bunkers, whose adjacent plantations mirrored in some ways their physical form. In her article "From Freak Show to Jim Crow," Edna Edith Sayers notes these marginalia next to the children's names when she writes,

> In fact, according to one recent biographer, Orser, an account book of Chang and Eng lists on one page the names and birth dates of "many" of the children born to Sarah and Adelaide intermingled with the names and birth dates, or just the years, of "some" of the black children enslaved to them. Some of these children were purchased after birth, while others were apparently born on the property. Again, records are spotty. A later hand has marked the recognized children with the word "white" plus a "C" or an "E" denoting the father, and some, but not all, of the other children with "col." ("colored"). Two of those children we know to have been purchased as children, and of the ten others marked "col.," Orser

> concludes that "one can only speculate about what they might be doing here" on this list.[40]

This mixing of the records of enslaved children with the children of Chang and Eng inadvertently denotes all of the children of the estate as property in some ways. By marking the racial identity and status of each child, the record keepers make a slight distinction between the two groups. But the intermingling of note-taking is telling nevertheless. It is this same negotiation over the terms of property, childhood, custody, and ownership that organized my research into the contentious and public custody battles that embroiled both the McKoy twins and Blind Tom.

The End of Legal Slavery: A Transition from Ownership to Custody

Building on the category of parentage that runs through the archives of Joice Heth and the Bunkers, this section focuses on childhood through a detailed discussion of the intersecting concerns of custody, ownership, and guardianship for Black freak show performers before and after the Emancipation Proclamation of 1863. While the national landscape saw a shift in the understanding and legal implications of freedom for Black laborers, other concerns such as childhood, race, and assumed mental capacity continued to factor into the road to freedom for Black sideshow performers.[41] The well-documented, public legal custody battles over both the McKoys and Blind Tom Wiggins not only contributed to the viability of their acts and the continuation of their onstage personae postemancipation but also served as case studies for the nexus of issues surrounding legal freedom for disabled Black bodies in the post–Civil War United States. Previously defined under law almost exclusively by the terms of ownership and potential labor output, disabled Black bodies were often rendered abject or valueless in the eyes of their white owners. And yet the virtuosity and earning potential of these same skilled bodies as sideshow and freak show performers caused their earning potential as stage performers to skyrocket far beyond that of a traditional enslaved laborer.[42] In fact, for many disabled people, entering sideshow and freak show performances in the nineteenth century was the most viable way of earning a living and maintaining their independence.[43]

While categories such as race, disability, and childhood in the nineteenth century were used to classify certain bodies as deserving of guardianship or ownership under the law, I would like to trace the way these unique trajectories intersected with the concerns of sideshow and freak show celebrity in the cases of Blind Tom and the McKoys. Postemancipation categories such as childhood and disability took precedence over racial markers in the court cases brought by the proprietors of various freak shows to maintain custody of these performers and, most importantly, continued access to their earnings. Mental capacity and disability often became synonymous with the argument that formerly enslaved performers were in fact perpetual children, incapable of managing their own financial affairs. These claims were often negotiated through the court system as rights over ownership in the antebellum South soon gave way to rights of custody and earning following emancipation and the Civil War. However, these terms of custody and guardianship, while distinct in their phrasing, often served to prolong enslavement for freak show performers, effectively creating illegal forms of ownership after emancipation and the conclusion of the Civil War.

Born in 1849 in Harris County, Georgia, by 1850 Blind Tom was sold to General James Neil Bethune of Columbus County, a vehement anti-abolitionist and early proponent of secession.[44] What ensued for the next thirty-eight years was a series of complicated court proceedings over rights not only to Tom but also to his vast earning potential after 1863. In 1864 Bethune convinced Tom's parents, Charity Greene and Domingo Wiggins, to sign an indenture agreement that designated Bethune Tom's legal guardian and gave him full access to his earnings. In exchange, Tom's parents received $500 annually and Tom received room and board, 2 percent of the net proceeds from his shows, and $20 a month of his vast income. The agreement was to last for five years.[45] During this time Tom gave many concerts, some of them in support of the Confederacy and organized by Bethune. Then, in 1865, an African American showman named Tabbs Gross sued Bethune for custody of Tom, eventually losing his case in Cincinnati courts.[46] In 1870 just before the indenture agreement was set to expire, Bethune had Tom declared mentally incompetent and assigned his son John as Tom's guardian. John married his wife, Eliza, in 1882, eventually filing for an annulment and shutting her out of his will in 1884 before his sudden death. In 1885 Eliza

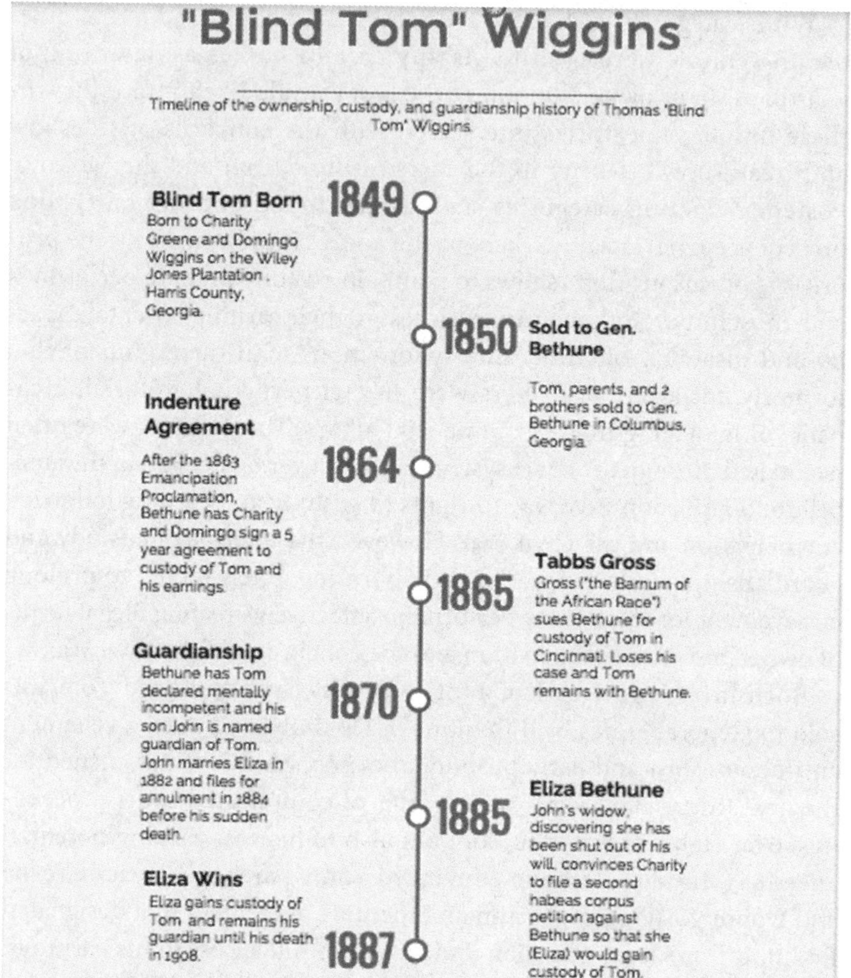

Figure 1.4: Timeline of the custody and guardianship cases of Thomas "Blind Tom" Wiggins, 1849–87.

Bethune convinced Charity, Tom's only surviving parent, to file a second habeas corpus petition for Tom, naming Eliza as his sole guardian. She won her case in 1887 and remained Tom's guardian until his death in 1908 at the age of fifty-nine in Hoboken, New Jersey.[47]

These custody battles were taking place not only on the courtroom stage but also on the public stage in various newspapers, which undoubtedly added to some of the spectacle of Tom's show. While the McKoys, born a mere two years after Tom in 1851 in North Carolina, share a similar narrative arc in terms of claims to custody and ownership, some of which I have detailed earlier in the chapter, their custody case remained an integral part of the fabric of their act and was detailed not only in newspaper articles but also explicitly in their playbills and promotional materials. By recording their legal battles selectively and narratively (rather than relying solely on newspaper publicity), the McKoys exercised increased control over the circulation and sale of information regarding their association with enslavement for their own benefit. The McKoys' own childhood custody battles both before and after emancipation were reproduced and mythologized in almost every version of their promotional materials and (auto)biographical texts, even after evidence shows that they were profiting from their act and no longer under the custody of Mary Smith.

Although several sources detail the twins' origins in North Carolina, perhaps the most extensive is a souvenir program and biography that was circulated on behalf of the proprietors of their traveling show. Published in 1883 and not attributed to any particular author, two versions of this biography are housed in the Beinecke Rare Book and Manuscript Library.[48] Additionally, the twins published an autobiography, reprinted in Linda Frost's *Conjoined Twins in Black and White*.[49] The sole major difference between the published biographies and the circulated autobiography is a switch from the third-person singular narration to a narration written in the first person (although both fluctuate between the singular and plural, as most materials on the twins do). Interestingly enough, the two versions of the biography are almost identical in content, showing that the same story was circulated as a generic template and that there was also a conscious cultivation of the twins' public image and personal narratives.

Only the autobiographical account, published in 1869, is credited to a direct authorial source: the twins themselves. However, considering that all of the content remains virtually the same as that of the published biographies, it seems highly unlikely that they were the sole original authors of the text. Speaking about the role their autobiography has played in modern interpretations of the twins' lives, Ellen Samuels notes in "Examining Millie and Christine McKoy: Where Enslavement and Enfreakment Meet," "I argue that contemporary attempts to recognize the McKoys' agency by treating this first-person narrative as an autobiography that speaks in their actual voice(s), and thus as a reliable historical source, have actually functioned to present the twins as collaborators in their own oppression." Samuels goes on to observe that the content of the autobiography falls into the category of "apologist slave narratives," seeking to promote its own form of supposedly "benevolent" slavery that is unsupported by contemporary historical evidence.[50] I agree with Samuels's assertion that uncritically utilizing this first-person narration as a site of agency unwittingly casts the twins as coconspirators and willing participants in their own enslavement. Yet coupling these biographical and supposedly autobiographical accounts with additional resources regarding the twins' enslavement, freedom, and varying legal statuses does elucidate that they were highly conscious of their status as physical commodities. As a result, these texts, which focus heavily on the twins' movements and legal statuses, show the permeability of the various sites of emancipation they traversed, as well as their own ability to manipulate and navigate these legal statuses to their own advantage.

The 1883 promotional biography begins by listing the eight known wonders of the world, with "Miss Millie Christine, the Carolina Twin," ranking in eighth place. The text itself is proclaimed to be a "Biography, Medical Description, and Songs" of the twins, effectively listing the three major selling points of their show. The biographical description goes on to note the twins' birth in 1851 on the plantation of a minor enslaver named Alexander McCoy (from whom the twins took their surname). Born to Menemia and Jacob McKoy, the twins would later go on to purchase tracts of land near the plantation on which they were born for their elderly parents. In turn, their father bequeathed this plantation to his children and grandchildren, with the stipulation in his will that the land could not pass to any other but his direct descendants.[51] The biography goes on to note that McCoy himself was a poor farmer, and when the twins were approximately fifteen months old he sold them to a man referred to only as Brower for $10,000. Because Brower was not in full possession of the cash amount, a Joseph Smith was then asked to secure the promissory note, after which Brower relocated the twins to New Orleans for a medical exhibit and freak show. Brower proved to be a poor businessman. He met an unidentified self-proclaimed Texas millionaire. The man claimed to be in possession of "large tracts" of land in that recently formed US state. However, the would-be millionaire turned out to be a scam artist and quickly absconded with the twins to Northern states where they were secretively put on public display.[52]

This initial saga, although rather bizarre in its details, is in fact rather commonplace when considered within the larger context of American slavery. The author relies on his audience's knowledge of institutional and legal slavery as it existed in 1853 (approximately two years after the twins were born) in order for this story to make sense. The mention of specific American states such as North Carolina, Louisiana, and Texas, all of which were slaveholding territories before 1865, works to strengthen these familiar tropes. That the twins were bartered for essentially two promissory notes, the first for $10,000 and the second for tracts of land estimated at $45,000 in value, speaks to the practice of slave owners hiring the time of their enslaved workers at a cost. Although neither note promised full ownership of the twins to the holder, these men were allowed at least a partial profit from the proceeds of their freak shows, in effect marketing their performance labor within the same paradigms of other physical labor of the enslaved. In the narrative of the biography, Brower's second note proves to be null and void, first because he never had full ownership of the twins to begin with; second, because he had not paid the full amount for them and was in fact indebted to the aforementioned Joseph Smith (who would go on to become the twins' legal owner and longtime exhibitor in real life); and lastly because the tracts of Texas land he was promised never materialized. Because the author chose to begin the twins' narrative with this complex web of assigned values and exchanges, the rest of their biographical account is notably marked by this system of bartering for flesh. The exchanges of slavery, coupled with the mobility of their bodies through various American states, mark the tension of this fluidity and the continuous ambiguity of their own legal status.

According to the narrative, when Joseph Smith is informed of the twins' kidnapping, he promptly pays the outstanding debt of $10,000 to McCoy, gaining full legal ownership of the disappeared girls. The author then notes this proviso in Smith's agreement with McCoy:

> He at once paid the purchase money in full to Mr. McCoy, and took from him a deed which made him the exclusive owner, under then existing

> laws, of the person of Millie Christine. The proviso, "wherever he could find her," was of course understood, and in order to quiet the mind of her mother and convince her that, whenever found, the child would be restored to her care, Mr. Smith at the same time purchased the father, mother and seven children, a transaction of course involving a large sum of money, all of which was dependent for its recovery on the recovery of Millie Christine herself.[53]

Although the author strives to mark this sequence of events as highly logical, this proviso, as well as the purchase of the twins' entire family, is in fact highly unusual. As Hortense Spillers notes in "Mama's Baby, Papa's Maybe," "The idea becomes useful as a point of contemplation when we try to sharpen our own sense of the African female's reproductive uses within the diasporic enterprise of enslavement and the genetic reproduction of the enslaved. In effect, under conditions of captivity, the offspring of the female does not 'belong' to the mother, nor is s/he 'related' to the 'owner,' though the owner 'possesses' it, and in the African American instance, often fathered it, *and, as often*, without whatever benefit of patrimony."[54] Therefore, Black women's bodies and those of their children were considered outside the legal and social protections of patriarchal coverture, creating a power dynamic whereby they were rendered more abjectly vulnerable to negative forces of sexual exploitation, while the Black men who fathered the children were discredited or discounted altogether. In many cases the unborn future progeny of an enslaved woman was also considered within the spectrum of ownership, falling into the hands of white masters and slave owners.[55] Therefore, if ownership over the child is not the inherent right of the enslaved mother, Smith's decision to claim legal responsibility for the twins' entire family is more closely related to his proviso that he should be able to recover the twins "wherever he could find her." It is at this precise moment the narrative diverges from the American context to take on a transnational scope. The twins' bodies were being passed from hand to hand in American slaveholding states, and even throughout Northern states that were obligated to return escaped enslaved people to their owners under the edicts of the Fugitive Slave Act of 1850 (passed scantly one year before the twins were born). However, the spectrum of international slave law further muddies the waters of their legal status.

The biography goes on to note that the twins were then secretly transported to Britain and were later discovered on exhibition in Glasgow, Birmingham, and finally London. According to the biography, Smith then transported the entire McKoy family, including Menemia, to London to reclaim ownership of the young girls. After he discovered them on display, the twins were returned to the care of their mother. In the biography the author ventriloquizes the ruling of the British judge presiding over the case, writing, "The child should be given into the custody of its lawful mother. If it was not the child of the defendants, then mother never bore a child. Every lineament, every feature, every look betokened it; every spectator in his inmost heart felt, yes, knew it to be her child, almost as certainly as though they had seen it every hour since its birth."[56] Because slavery had been abolished in Britain and its territories from 1833 onward, Smith's claims of ownership ended at US borders. The disavowal of the Black mother's ownership of her children that Spillers notes similarly ended at these same borders. Therefore, in Great Britain the children's legal status (and those of their parents, for that matter) was converted from enslaved to free. Yet the mandates of Smith's ominous proviso reign dominant here. By purchasing the twins' parents and moving them to London temporarily, Smith was able to circumvent British law and retain unlawful ownership of the entire McKoy clan. He then went on to transport them back to North Carolina, supposedly at the bequest of Menemia.

What this narrative actually recounts is a series of kidnappings and a small-scale illegal transatlantic slave trade, rather than the heroic rescue it is portrayed to be. When viewed in this light, the performance of the freak show and the performance of the courtroom become particularly vital to understanding these supposed legal maneuverings. The forum of the freak show provided the evidence needed by Smith and his hired private investigator to locate the twins first in the Northern United States and later in London. Without these performances and their subsequent publicity, not only would the twins have remained unfound, but they likely would have never been returned to the Smiths at all. The stage of the courtroom, with its own particular theatrics, is what the judge in the biography calls upon to give credence to Menemia's claims of maternal rights. By saying that "every spectator" in the courtroom can lay claim to Menemia being the twins' "lawful mother," the author plays into the theatrical nature of the courtroom performance to give credence to the Black mother's claims of legal custodianship over her daughters. After they returned to the United States, the entire McKoy family remained under the legal ownership of the Smith family until the official abolition of American slavery. However, even following the abolition of slavery and the departure of their parents and siblings from the Smith household, Millie and Christine remained with the Smiths for many years in a dubious legal status somewhere between enslaved laborers and employed performers.

In both the case of Blind Tom and the McKoys there is a fluctuating definition of the body and recognition of that body under the law. In her essay "Legal Slaves and Civil Bodies," Joan Dayan details how contemporary and historical notions of legality and the law in Western societies depend on the acknowledgment of the spirit or otherworldly. Dayan argues that by transferring the dominion of the spirit from religious bodies to the state, the law was able to capitalize on the idea of the spiritual to create civil bodies (those recognized within the law), legal slaves (those held forcibly under the rule of law), and felons (those rendered legally dead in the eyes of the law). Dayan's considerations of legality and the spirit or otherworldly help to center my research's ongoing questions about the fictions of legality in the archive and how these fictions are represented.[57] Both the McKoys' and Blind Tom's forays into the legal arena show the competing fiscal concerns that governed the lives of nineteenth-century Black freak show performers. In the case of Tom, it led to a lifelong custodianship that dictated and limited his potential for access to his earnings. On the other hand, the McKoys were able to deploy narrative self-appraisal (similar to the act of defiance they employed with Batcheller and Doris's in 1882) to guarantee continued interest in their shows through a connection to enslavement. It is precisely this connection and the ensuing disentanglement from the grips of legal slavery that make these custody cases significant in the study of nineteenth-century legal enslavement and performance.

Aural and Oral Fugitivity

As mentioned in the earlier section of this chapter on self-appraisal, the McKoys deployed a strategic fugitivity through their performance of aural and oral virtuosity after emancipation, such as singing in harmony, speaking two languages at once, or reciting poetry. Similarly, Joice Heth exercised what Uri McMillan theorizes as a "sonic of dissent" in her act with Barnum. McMillan writes, "The very sound of Heth's voice resisting, or what I am terming a 'sonic of dissent,' produced a form of embodied knowledge that momentarily troubled the slick schematics of the exhibit itself and its distinct circuits of spectatorship and performance. If the financial livelihood of Heth's exhibit doubly depended on her acquiescence to the whims of her owners, as well as the molding of her deteriorating corpse-like physicality into bodily evidence of freakishness and extreme old age, her resistant voice temporarily disrupted those norms."[58] While McMillan notes that Heth's outbursts created a rupturing of the "schematics of the exhibit," I argue that the McKoys' integration of oral and aural material into their acts created an opportunity for an escape from archival capture through the use of sound. While lyric sheets have been preserved in the backs of various playbills and programs, examples of their sheet music remain absent, creating a gap in our understanding of their performances. And yet I wonder if this absence, this gap, also serves as a way of understanding the impossibility of capture and exchange in the archive. I began this chapter with an exploration of the transactional nature of archival encounters. In the case of the McKoys' aural and oral fugitivity, perhaps there is a representation of an incomplete or broken transaction. The extraction is limited and, in turn, so is our ability to understand the objects that remain.

Similarly, in the archives of Blind Tom there are examples of multifaceted aural and oral performances that elude archival capture. In the 2004 encyclopedia *African American Lives*, John Davis notes Tom's almost indescribably complex performance routines:

> These mainstream pieces increasingly gave way to a series of sensational pianistic and extra-musical stunts. Among these stunts were Tom's flawless re-creations of original compositions played moments earlier by a local pianist onstage. Performances of complicated classical works with his back to the piano; on-the-spot improvisations of an accompaniment to any piece presented, even one he had never heard before; and simultaneous rendering of three different songs, one using the right hand,

> another using the left, and the third sung, each in a different key. Other program innovations were Tom's recitations of texts in foreign languages he could not even speak and famous political speeches of the era in the same rhythm and pitch pattern in which they were originally uttered. A final otherworldly touch was the verbal introduction by Tom of each of his own compositions in the third person.[59]

Similar to the McKoys and Heth, Wiggins utilized extemporaneous and impromptu performance techniques, coupled with a self-conscious self-articulation through the use of the third person to introduce himself, that defied simple archival capture through paper documents. Although his sheet music was widely circulated and consumed, the content of his act was nearly impossible to reproduce by anyone other than Wiggins himself (although, after his semiretirement, many imitators took to the stage purporting to be Blind Tom). In fact, Wiggins's choice to introduce himself in the third person in some ways mirrors the McKoys' own decision to refer to themselves with the first-person singular pronoun, not only in their (auto)biography but also in their promotional materials, interviews, and legal documents such as their will, as well as in their private lives with family members.

I propose that aural and oral fugitivity offer a disruption in our encounters with the archive and serve as an imaginative possibility for those whose voices are either overlooked or omitted, including the voices of the enslaved. While we often associate speech acts with power,[60] I wonder if there is a liminal or potentially decentralized power in not speaking, in remaining silent, or in filling the world with such rich and multilayered improvisational sound that it is at once indescribable and also unable to be reproduced. Can movements to say the names of survivors be met with equally contentious movements to subjugate the names of oppressors? It seems only fitting that this chapter's inquiries into performance, labor, and enslavement will end on these questions as they circulate in the contemporary moment, since these questions continue to haunt the descendants and researchers of slavery, not only at the margins but at the very heart of lived experience.

2

Slave Autobiography and the Performance Archive

It was because of the voracious interest in what the lives of people like these were really like that "freak" histories, pamphlets that recounted the biographies of these exhibited people, were produced and sold at exhibitions and performances of figures like Chang and Eng. These publications, or "show histories," attempted to satisfy the public appetite at the same time that they worked to create and whet it; a show history was as much an advertisement and an inducement to future viewings and show goings as it was then a souvenir. As well as these show histories, most major freak performers of the nineteenth and early twentieth centuries sold copies of their photographs as postcards, commonly known as carte de visites. . . . Today these bits of "freak memorabilia" continue to attract a pretty penny on eBay.
—Linda Frost, *Conjoined Twins in Black and White*

Correspondence

Millie Christine McKoy's "autobiography" remains today an unusual document, even within an archive that is notable for its density of materials and a personal "freak" history that has remained the subject of scholarly and artistic interest throughout the latter half of the twentieth and early twenty-first centuries. Since beginning my work on the McKoys, more than once I have been sent links to library search catalogs, auction houses, and even eBay (as Linda Frost mentions in the chapter epigraph). All of these emails are surprisingly similar, regardless of who sent them: "Have you seen this?" "Did you know about this?" "Your twins." "The price isn't too bad." I respond to all these messages with a kind thank-you and file them away under my ever-growing digital list of McKoy twins material that I can incorporate into my archival project or, perhaps, even afford to buy one day. I am no longer surprised by the increased interest in the McKoys' materials. After all, I am also part of this wave of production and reproduction. So it stands to reason that a natural result of increased interest in Millie Christine is also an increased interest in their "autobiography." I place the word *autobiography* in quotation marks here because as a document, its authenticity and purpose are a point of contention among scholars invested in articulating a mindful and truthful account of the McKoys' lives and work.

According to Joanne Martell's text on the twins, *Millie-Christine: Fearfully and Wonderfully Made*, their jointly composed autobiography was first written in 1869 after their owner's family, the Smiths, hired a new agent to promote their shows and to revive interest in their onstage act. Versions of the booklet have survived in the archives of the University of North Carolina at Chapel Hill, the Beinecke Rare Book and Manuscript Library, and the North Carolina State archives in Raleigh, as well as other locations across the country. A version on record at UNC Chapel Hill notes in all capital letters on the front page that the biography was "SOLD BY THEIR AGENTS FOR THEIR (THE TWINS) SPECIAL BENEFIT, AT 25 CENTS. PUBLISHED AT THE BUFFALO COURIER PRINTING HOUSE."[1] And according to Frost's monograph *Conjoined Twins in Black and White*, there are at least five distinct versions of the McKoys' autobiography. But these versions contain small alterations in detail, rather than complete rewrites of the McKoys' show history, and appear more as multiple reflections in a fun house mirror or trail of simulacra captured in nineteenth-century archival print.

However, despite the assurances Martell conveys (notably from a descendant of the Smith family named Dicksie Cribb, rather than the McKoys' own descendants),[2] the autobiography remains a highly contested document, especially concerning questions of its veracity. When the thirty-two-page show history first appeared in its diminutive size of four and a half by seven inches, published in Buffalo, New York, by Warren, Johnson, and Company, it seems to have had its intended effect. There was a subsequent resurgence in interest in the twins' onstage acts. Cribb also notes in her response to Martell that "Christine did all the writing; she was the correspondent. The other, Millie, crocheted and dictated to Christine what to write."[3] By consciously or unconsciously using the language of correspondence, Cribb evokes three relationships that indicate a level of complex intimacy between both of the twins and their paying public. The first is that of a journalist and her informant. In this relationship Christine is the journalistic hand while her sister Millie, crocheting and dictating their life story, is the informant. In this formulation Millie is in a position of power as the party with the supposedly "genuine" or eyewitness story of their origins, while Christine shares this burden of power by being charged with translating their conjoined story for the world. The second relationship that Cribb's statement evokes is that between ghostwriter and star. In this instance Christine is channeling the ideas of her sister Millie, writing the words that Millie has deemed suitable while also perhaps adding her own interpretive hand to the process. Considering the thesis of this book is invested in a critique of archival haunting and performance, the language of a ghostwritten show history holds a peculiar appeal. And the final relationship, and the one that interests me most from a scholarly perspective, is an epistolary one. In this lineage Christine and Millie are writing their memoir accounts from the point of view of a dual correspondence. For even though their lived circumstances of perpetual shared intimacy may make the epistolary form seem unnecessary (why write a letter to someone whose physicality and yours are so completely aligned?), the epistolary relationship captures the difficult terrain of the private, public, and intimate that enfreaked performers such as the McKoys were constantly negotiating onstage. The epistolary form also carries with it the implications of a conversational back-and-forth between the twins, both with each other and with their many audiences.

As mentioned previously, Frost asserts that, throughout the course of the McKoys' careers, at least five versions of the autobiography were printed and reprinted around the world. The first came in 1871 in London and was updated by their then show manager Judge H. P. Ingalls. In 1882 another version appeared during the twins' time touring with Batcheller and Doris's Great Inter-Ocean Railroad Show, published in New York by Torrey and Clark. Another three versions were published between the 1880s and the early twentieth century. In her monograph, Frost reproduces a version of the text that appeared sometime between 1902 and 1912 and was published in Cincinnati by Hennegan and Company.[4]

Adding to the lineage of Frost's five versions, in this chapter I will also do an in-depth close reading of show histories available at the Beinecke Rare Book and Manuscript Library, one that is connected to the versions that were printed for Batcheller and Doris's Great Inter-Ocean Railroad Show in approximately 1883 and other adjacent copies estimated to have been published between 1880 and 1883. Although these adjacent copies are listed as "biographies" and not "autobiographies," I include them here because they repeat and expand on almost the same details as the autobiography and are dated after the autobiography's publication. All of these versions, both those that were presumably written under the coercive instruction of the Smith family and those that came afterward when the McKoys had greater performance autonomy, abide by almost identical narrative structures and present the same biographical details, interspersed with notes of pastoral longing for the US South, despite its slaveholding past—a longing that was complicated for enslaved and recently freed Black subjects such as the McKoys, who often noted that North Carolina was home for them.

Rather than viewing the consistency of the McKoys' autobiography as an archival anomaly or a question of veracity versus coercion, I argue that the formulation of an epistolary relationship, where each version of the shifting autobiographical text is considered as a call-and-response letter in a long lineage of narrative versions of the McKoys, allows for a more capacious reading. The epistolary form, in which the McKoys are adjusting not only in their dual communication with each other but also in what is being conveyed as advantageous for their varying audience members and sideshow proprietors, shows that there are pointed and notable adjustments that demonstrate an awareness of audience. Additionally, a letter is a form that insinuates privacy between its intended writer and reader, while also acknowledging a shared constructed narrative between the two. This coupling of the private, public, and intimate demonstrates the ways that each seemingly minor change in the McKoys' narrative tactics was actually formed in response to a shift in their choices of self-presentation, rather than a complete reversal in the foundation of the performance acts. Therefore, the maintenance of the Southern pastoral and certain racist tropes was crucial to the McKoys' survival as popular performers in the latter half of the nineteenth century and into the dawn of the twentieth century. Although we see their performance labor shift from sexually exploitative displays pre-emancipation to singing, dancing, and the display of language skills postemancipation, the constancy of their autobiography in relation to their onstage resistance harkens to the larger trends of performances and show histories surrounding the lives of enfreaked performers that mirrored contemporary nineteenth-century international headlines.[5]

Alongside these almost identical autobiographies, I will also be examining descriptions and accounts of the McKoys written by external sideshow proprietors and satirists, namely the works of P. T. Barnum collaborator W. C. Coup (both his own 1901 biography and his advertising efforts around the McKoys for his Equescurriculum show in 1879), as well as French satirist Touchatout, who wrote a romantic farce in a text based on the McKoys that appeared in an 1873 issue of his circular *Trombinoscope*. By adding in the voices and texts of those who profited from the McKoys' narratives and stage shows without any attempt at the veneer of veracity represented by an "autobiography," I will explicate how the McKoys in some instances replicated and in others resisted the dominant narratives about their lives, performances, and bodies in order to participate in the often-exploitative economies of the freak show stage. For as Frost notes in the chapter epigraph, the purpose of these public show histories was "*to satisfy the public appetite at the same time that they worked to create and whet it*."[6] In order for them to remain viable as freak show performers and formerly enslaved women, the McKoys' autobiography was used to generate and sustain interest in them as a performance product. Therefore their show history both does and does not neatly align with other narrative autobiographical forms used by nineteenth-century Black writers. The aim of their text was not to expose the horrors of slavery, as was the case with Harriet Jacobs's *Incidents in the Life of a Slave Girl*. It also was not necessarily used to demonstrate the humanity of its narrative subjects, for as a version of their autobiography from the University of North Carolina at Chapel Hill's collection notes, they were consistently described as "two strange lumps of humanity" for which their owner Mr. Smith paid "the sum of $6,000."[7] Rather, the autobiography's many forms all walk a narrow line between satisfying, creating, and "whetting" public interest in the McKoys. As a result, it often re-creates racist tropes and narratives related to US slavery.

Rather than working to redraft or correct their narrative in their later life, the McKoys chose (to whatever degree we can speculate about the autonomy of those choices) to continue to re-create and distribute perhaps consciously fictitious information about their origins and movements under the conditions of US enslavement and postemancipation institutional racism. Evidenced by the unerring consistency among the various narratives, there was little narrative difference after the twins' wrested control of the *I*'s that had been fabricated on their behalf, adding more subterfuge to the original offense. However, as I mentioned earlier (and as Saidiya Hartman notes in her monograph *Scenes of Subjection*), perhaps it is the question of what *might* or *could* have happened, rather than what definitively happened, that organizes my concerns in this chapter. For example, why would the twins decide to continue the circulation of fictitious performative materials that painted them as happy participants in slavery in lieu of publishing a more "accurate" account of their lives in bondage? Both their formal enslavement and the conditions under which they were frequently forced to perform mirrored a system of exploitation that deprived the women of not only their liberties but their humanity. And yet although we know that toward the latter half of their lives Christine and Millie were able to gain some degree of financial control over their act, they still maintained the fictions cultivated by their enslavers. But to what ends?

By exploring the three aforementioned texts (the *Trombinoscope*, Coup's biography, and the McKoys' autobiography), I hope to explicate the process through which these documents perform a type of counterhistory of correspondence, a give-and-take of the McKoys' public, private, and intimate written lives in which the dominant structures and possibilities of what can and does constitute an enslaved narrative might be complicated. This offers a new structure in which the speech act of possessing and performing the *I* is not foregrounded as the primary functionality of archival inquiries into narrations of the afterlives of Black Atlantic slavery and performance. Instead, I will frame my readings of these texts as a challenge to the neatly articulated categories of first-person narration and unidirectional movement. The twins' geographical shift through both the tangible and invisible borders of international emancipation and their usage of their own mysterious and oft-fabled origins for financial and personal gains come to stand in for the sort of bodily protection and security that they presumably did not have in their lives as disabled sideshow performers before emancipation. Yet it is this contradiction and displacement of the roles of authority that form the twins' performance archive and what we may learn from their extraordinary experiences as Black female performers during the United States' slow and treacherous transition from enslaved to free labor.

Speaking the First Person: Unraveling the McKoys' *I*

Before we can truly understand the slippery and elusive nature of these various narratives, perhaps we should turn to a questioning of the very systems through which one is called on to account for oneself. Because the McKoys' rhetorical and performance strategies often utilized the singular *I*[8] on- and offstage, the autobiography's use of the singular *I* (and the addition of the prefix *auto-* before *biography*) requires closer evaluation. For if the McKoys are both *I* and *we*, how does this change the way we view their autobiographical writings? In their collection of lectures *Giving an Account of Oneself*, Judith Butler explores the routes through which we attempt to articulate the *I*. They write,

> Although we are compelled to give an account of our various selves, the structural conditions of that account will turn out to make a full such giving impossible. *The singular body* to which a narrative refers cannot be captured by a full narration, not only because the body has a formative history that remains irrevocable by reflection, but because primary relations are formative in ways that produce a necessary opacity in our understanding of ourselves. An account of oneself is always given to another, whether conjured or existing, and this other establishes the scene of address as a more primary ethical relation than a reflexive effort to give an account of oneself. *Moreover, the very terms by which we give an account, by which we make ourselves intelligible to ourselves and to others, are not of our making. They are social in character, and they establish social norms, a domain of unfreedom and substitutability within which our "singular" stories are told.*[9]

Butler presents their readers with an interesting conundrum. Although we often feel "compelled" or pressed to give a "singular" account of ourselves to one another, Butler's assertion is that this singularity is always already compromised from its inception. The system through which we read each other stresses singularity (one body, containing one unique or strange person) as the terms through which we are rendered legible to those consuming our narration. Therefore Millie Christine's own body, which was exceptionally singular in its strangeness but made plural because of the joint nature of its inhabitants, was already applying pressure to these norms of self-expression. Can the simple first-person *I* encapsulate the singularity of this story in its many iterations?

As Butler notes, while the act of self-narration has often been lauded as the pinnacle of self-expressive liberation, the oppression of societal norms remains. Operating under systems of oppressive legal slavery and the similarly restrictive modes of representation available to Black female performers of the latter half of the nineteenth century and early moments of the twentieth century, the McKoy twins possessed an understanding of these restrictions that is evidenced in their decision to maintain their partially fictitious autobiography after the dictates of American law had technically set them "free." Their correspondence expanded to capture not only a dialogue with each other but also a dialogue with their audiences operating under the weight of postemancipation realities of precarity for Black bodies. Yet despite the relatively unchanged nature of their story, the twins also actively pursued legal and other recourses to ensure their bodily, if not narrative, liberties. For instance, after the Emancipation Proclamation changed their legal status once more, at their request when they reached age fourteen, a medical doctor never again examined the twins with their clothes off during performances.[10] Clearly there is a separation here of the two types of "singularity" the twins represented. On the one hand, the rarity of their singular body is what made them viable and profitable sideshow performers and is a large part of what sustains the interest in their autobiographical text. On the other, their lack of a singular (in terms of number) body and consciousness put an immediate strain on their ability to account for themselves as one woman at all, precisely because they were and were not one person.

Although Butler provides a constructive lens through which to view the uses of *I* in giving an account of oneself, the analysis should also be extended to include theorists of Blackness and disability. In *Disabilities of the Color Line: Redressing Antiblackness from Slavery to the Present*, Dennis Tyler notes that slavery had a disabling and debilitating effect on Black subjects through the use of violence and retribution. To this end, Tyler establishes three key terms to explicate the relationship between anti-Blackness and disability: "In this book, *disability* refers to a restrictive system as well as an individual condition; *disablement* refers to the action of disabling Black subjects via systemic or physical acts of violence; and *racial injury* (or *racial injuries*) refers to the sometimes deadly and often disabling consequences—social, corporeal, and psychiatric—of racism."[11] This distinction between the ways that disability moves through the lives of Black folk as an active verb and adjective is relevant to my examination of the McKoys' use of *I* because it demonstrates the similar distinction I've made throughout the book between *enfreakment* and simply naming someone a "freak." Through their use of pronouns that confound and confuse our understanding of American individualism and bodily autonomy, the McKoys also acknowledge the ways they have been (to borrow Tyler's terms) exposed to disablement, disability, and racial injury. By aligning them narratively with systems that either avoided or refused to grant them the fullness of their dual Black identity, the McKoys' *I* stands defiant both on the page and in the ear. Their pronoun insists that the reader and listener view them on their own terms, regardless of the disablement they experienced as a result of their disability.

Other scholars have similarly wrestled with the use of singular versus plural pronouns in the works of enfreaked nineteenth-century performers, most notably in the case of Chang and Eng Bunker. In her book *Chang and Eng Reconnected*, Cynthia Wu addresses this duality and the resulting tension at the beginning of the book, writing, "In this book, I reference Chang and Eng Bunker in the plural form to reflect how they almost always functioned in civic life as separate individuals. When I discuss their combined 'body,' however, I use the singular to express their shared somatic existence and their deliberate comanagement of embodiment. This dislocation between personhood and corporeality sometimes produces jarring shifts from the plural to the singular subject in my prose, and I retain this tension because it performatively displays the paradoxes that *Chang and Eng Reconnected* is about."[12] Wu's approach to pronouns is meant to honor how the Bunkers operated in life while also complicating the narratives surrounding their supposed autonomy (and physiological lack thereof). Although the Bunkers, unlike the McKoys, chose to be addressed by the first-person plural *we* in most cases, Wu uses the *I* or the singular to express both their "somatic existence and their deliberate comanagement of embodiment." The tension between interiority and embodiment is present for all people but is uniquely complicated by the fact that these famed conjoined twins shared not only vital organs but a common embodiment that meant they were always enmeshed in each other's lives, despite the use of *we*. This constant copresence equally fascinated and alarmed paying audiences whose intrusive eyes and questions interrogated the Bunkers' and McKoys' assumed inability to gain access to privacy.

Speaking about the role their autobiography has played in modern interpretations of the twins' lives and uses of the first person to implicitly extol the benefits of benevolent slavery in the autobiography, Ellen Samuels notes in "Examining Millie and Christine McKoy: Where Enslavement and Enfreakment Meet" that considering this use of the first person as an accurate depiction of the twins' voices "and thus a reliable historical source . . . actually function[s] to present the twins as collaborators in their own oppression." Samuels goes on to observe that the content of the autobiography falls into the category of "apologist slave narratives," seeking to promote its own form of supposedly "benevolent" slavery that is unsupported by contemporary historical evidence.[13] I argue that by combining the concerns of critics such as Samuels with modern debates about the futility of searching for definitive "truth" in the archive, we can construct a reading of the McKoys' archival materials that recognizes the performance inherent in the reading act, as well as more overt allusions to scripting and performance within the text itself. These texts demonstrate a shift in the binary understanding that possession and replication of the *I* was a substitution for the freedoms they were meant to represent. Instead, we have texts that were circulated and shaped communally by participants in the American freak show circuits of the late nineteenth century, creating an environment in which audience expectations and the pressures of representation collide.

But how does Butler's configuration of the challenges of articulating a unified *I* interact with the McKoys' prolonged autobiographical correspondence? This correspondence is also in line with larger tropes and trends in nineteenth-century American freak shows to display enfreaked bodies that also closely aligned with national and international debates and headlines. Rachel Adams states,

> Not every freak was disabled. Sideshows also included people with extremely long hair or nails, tattoos, and women in pants, as well as non-Western people, and those with unusual talents like sword swallowing, fire eating, and contorting. Sideshow acts could also be inspired by current events. "I am speaking of America—the land of real humor, of ingenuity, or resource," reported journalist William Fitzgerald in 1897, "When some important political or other even agitates that great country, topical sideshows spring up with amazing promptness." Thus, at various points in the nineteenth century, suffragettes, Phillipinos [*sic*], Native American chiefs, and Africans were exhibited as freaks.[14]

But these show histories also existed in a world that placed primacy on the physically disabled enfreaked body, for as Adams also notes, "Born freaks—those with congenital disabilities—were the aristocrats of the sideshow world. The more unusual their bodies, the better chance they had to control their salaries and working conditions. . . . In the era before the welfare state, many people with severe disabilities turned to freak shows for economic support."[15] The McKoys' own autobiographical texts show an interplay between these two competing narrative impulses: that of the "born freak," whose physical bodies attract top billing and higher pay, and that of the headline freak, whose bodies are made to bear the weight of national and international spectacle because of the interest in their actions and activities. The McKoys' role as Black women and formerly enslaved laborers is evidenced throughout their autobiographical reprints and is often enmeshed and in conversation with Americana imagery that is meant to hark back to the transitional nature of life in the United States for newly emancipated Black subjects.

The 1883 promotional biography (which was published after the autobiography but contains almost entirely identical text, with the exception of the use of the third person instead of the first) begins by listing the eight known wonders of the world, with "Miss Millie Christine, the Carolina Twin," ranking in eighth place. Unlike the other sources, which will be discussed later in the chapter, this biography credits neither an author nor an illustrator on the front page. The text itself is proclaimed to

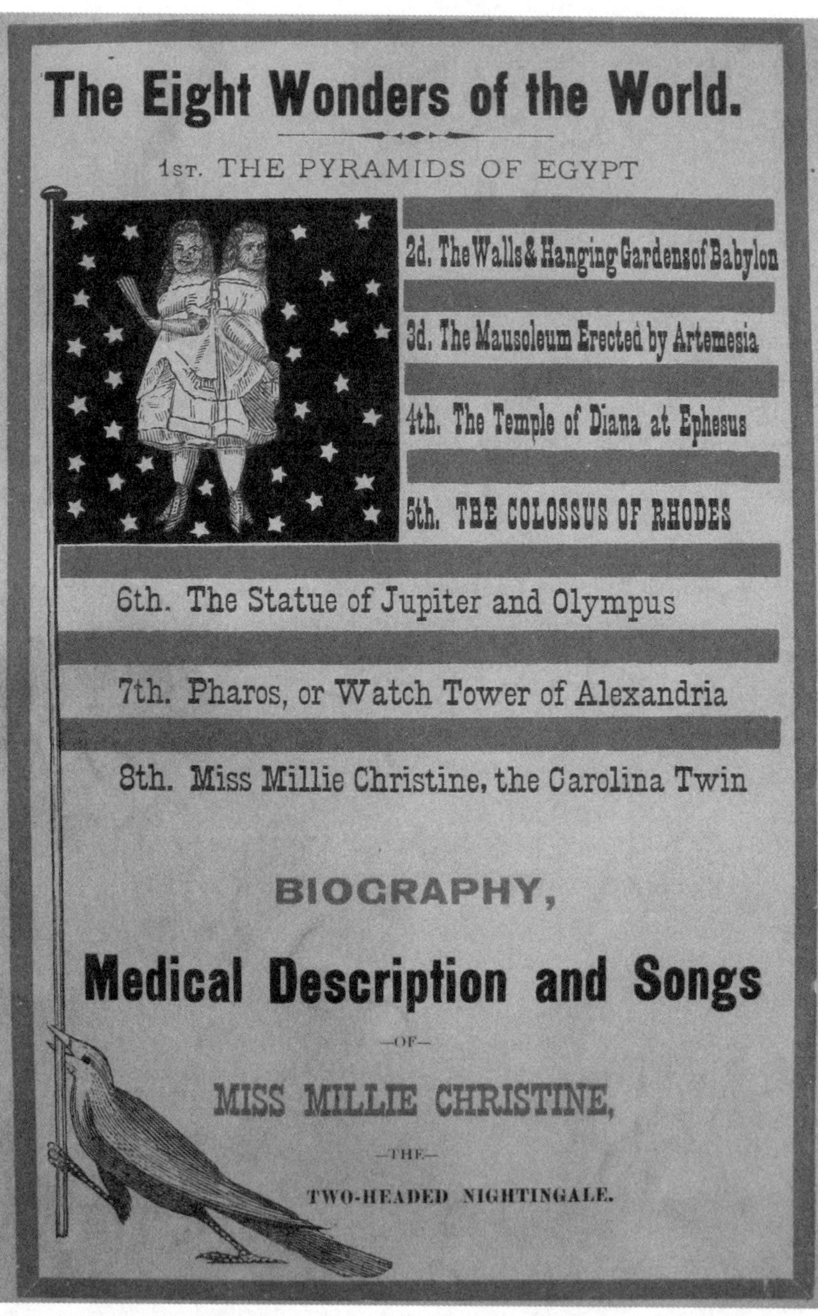

Figure 2.1: A copy of Millie Christine's biography, circa 1883. Beinecke Rare Book and Manuscript Library.

be a "Biography, Medical Description and Songs" of the twins, effectively listing the three major selling points of their show. The biographical description goes on to note the twins' birth in 1851 on the plantation of a minor slave owner named "Alexander McCoy" (from whom the twins took their surname) and that they were born to Menemia and Jacob McKoy. Notably, the twins are featured on the cover of the biography, standing within the blue square of the American flag.

The illustration depicts Christine and Millie here as children, although they would have been thirty-one or thirty-two years old at the time of its publication, effectively fixing them in the role of children in need of protection, a category that has never been comfortably inhabited by Black children's bodies.[16] Although they were frequently depicted as children born from the wellsprings of perpetual youth, the twins had a reported great fear of postmortem autopsy, exhibition, and exhumation, making public their desire not to be removed from their final resting place. Sadly, these wishes were not honored, and in 1969, fifty-seven years after their original burial, the twins' remains were moved to a more prominent place in their North Carolina cemetery at the behest of the Columbus County Historical Society and the North Carolina Department of Archives and History.[17]

Although the exact details of the twins' final request vary in other accounts,[18] it is clear that they had a palpable fear of bodily harm being exacted on them, even postmortem. We can only speculate as to the nature of the sexual and other exploitation these two women suffered at the hands of those who, by all accounts, worked to fix them in a state of perpetual childhood in order to continue reaping the profits from their successful touring show. The biography then goes on to note that McCoy himself was a poor farmer, and when the twins were approximately fifteen months old, he sold them to a man referred to only as Brower for $10,000, with the note insured by Joseph Smith (the twins' later longtime owner). The twins changed hands several times and were eventually kidnapped to the North, where they were secretly put on display.[19]

Smith went on to purchase the twins' parents and siblings while in search of the missing girls, who represented for him a lost investment. He began to search for them, advertising their missing status, and the biography states that "the proviso, 'wherever he could find her,' was of course understood."[20] Smith's ominous proviso was meant to encapsulate the entire land mass controlled by the United States, operating under the logics of the recently passed 1850 Fugitive Slave Act. And yet it is at this precise moment that the narrative shifts to take on a transnational scope that exceeds the boundaries of the United States and its growing internal divide. The twins' bodies were passed from hand to hand in American slaveholding states, throughout the Northern states, and later in Great Britain.

Harriet Jacobs's recounting of her own notice posted by her enslaver, Dr. Flint, in her narrative *Incidents in the Life of a Slave Girl*, published in 1861, takes a similar narrative form and operates under the edicts of a similar proviso to Smith's, showing the relative stability of the fugitive slave flyer as a form. The notice reads,

> $300 REWARD! Ran away from the subscriber, an intelligent, bright mulatto girl, named Linda, 21 years of age. Five feet four inches high. Dark eyes, and black hair inclined to curl; but it can be made straight. Has a decayed spot on a front tooth. She can read and write, and in all probability will try to get to the Free States. All persons are forbidden, under penalty of law, to harbor or employ said slave. $150 will be given to whoever takes her in the state, and $300 if taken out of the state and delivered to me, or lodged in jail.[21]

Notice that Jacobs's now famous notice not only is interested in her recapture but also takes time to list her known skills, such as reading and writing, a common feature of posters circulated for the return of escaped enslaved people (presumably so that if these people attempted to gain employment in their former trade, they might be easily identified). This format of listing physical attributes alongside skill sets is mirrored not only in Smith's "proviso" but also elsewhere in the twins' archive. Often the biographical pamphlets and newspaper articles circulated on their behalf focused at length on the twins' outward appearance. And yet there was still an attendant fascination with their intellectual capabilities. The twins went on to receive what could only be termed a formal "lady's" education. Although accounts vary, they were said to speak anywhere from four to as many as seven languages, played several instruments, sang duets in harmony, danced, and were able to speak on different subjects to different people simultaneously (with some accounts claiming they spoke in two different languages at once).[22]

The unknown author of Christine and Millie's biography draws on the well-known edicts of the Fugitive Slave Act in a way that performs the legal ramifications of capture without addressing the humanity of its intended prisoners. In the biography and autobiography, the authors tell the tale of the McKoy twins finally being returned to their rightful mother in dramatic terms. In the scene there is an insidious intimacy with which the white male bodies of Smith and an unnamed judge supplants the figures of both biological parents. Yet strangely enough, the McKoys, Menemia, and Smith appear in court not to question the legitimacy of the paternal claim that Joseph Smith asserts as his legal right but rather to manipulate the parental rights of Menemia. If, under the edicts of US enslavement, Menemia had no legal or natural right to the safe return of her children, the same is not true of the fictionalized retelling depicted in the biographies. Again, we see an appeal not only to the court (as represented by the character of the judge in the biography) but also to the unnamed spectators present in court that day. By having the judge state that "every spectator in his inmost heart felt" that the twins must belong to Menemia because of their incredible facial similarity, the text romanticizes the role of the Black mother while also delegitimizing her right of control over her children. The story ends with the McKoy twins returning to North Carolina with their mother and Smith.

The reader cannot help but realize that, by concluding the story of their kidnapping with a homecoming to antebellum North Carolina with Smith and Menemia, the text's anonymous author appears sympathetic to a regime of Southern white supremacy and racial subjugation. Yet could there ever truly be a homecoming for these two women who were so horribly exploited and abused under the blind eye of North Carolina's legal system? Although this moment of return is represented as a triumph in the McKoys' fictionalized biography, the story's conclusion with a return to business as usual (or rather to North Carolina) flattens any hope the reader might have that the twins escaped entirely from the systems of oppression that haunted their performance lives. And yet, even with this unsatisfactory ending, there is still room for addressing the McKoys' many acts of personal agency as they looked to build a new understanding of the legal mandates that shifted them from property, to children, to adult women over the first two decades of their life. It is in these acts of agency that we can begin to imagine new, more expansive, and emancipatory ways of recounting the lives of these two remarkable performers in order to further unveil the nexus where slavery and performance meet.

The previously discussed excerpts from the autobiography place the twins' physical and legal status firmly in the realm of quotidian performance. Even away from the formal mandates and strictures of the public stage, the staged and performed nature of the legal arena and the fugitive slave flyer provide an informal stage of sorts for the twins' highly visible and valuable bodies (as both enslaved women and marketable performers), with a maternity suit and not a paternity suit taking center stage. Yet in this moment it seems that the text's literary referents extend beyond the boundaries of slave narratives such as Jacobs's and Frederick Douglass's or even sentimental abolitionist propaganda. That Millie and Christine's own narrative structure in this moment focuses so closely on Menemia's encounter with the British court and the power of the gaze (even turning to those waiting in the courtroom to verify the claims) seems to suggest that conscious efforts were made to appeal to the audience's desire for salacious spectacle and theatrical performance over verisimilitude.

In these instances, the McKoys' lived subject position is called on to provide continued interest in their onstage personae as conjoined twins and formerly enslaved laborers. Their physical duality is drawn on to metaphorically bear the weight of international debates about statehood and slavery. In the case of the United States and their domestic performances, the demise of US slavery is called into focus through the itinerary of their travels, both from plantation to plantation and owner to owner. Away from the formal mandates and strictures of the public stage as hypervisible and valuable bodies, their return to the realms of legal manipulation sees them occupying the highly performed arena of the courtroom and the fugitive slave flyer. Both of these public platforms are built around the conversational models of correspondence because of their communal and communicative nature. The courtroom and the fugitive's flyer both indicate the contested legal and public domains that were commissioned to help maintain the permeable boundaries of slavery. Both of these spheres and their documents are evidence that the physical markers of race were insufficient to maintain the geographical confines of enslavement, especially in light of the changes in laws surrounding slavery, which were not uniform across international or state boundaries in the latter half of the nineteenth century. And yet, in the case of formerly enslaved freak show performers such as the McKoys, traveling and crossing state and national borders was an essential part of their onstage performance labor. Therefore, some of the correspondence shifts in their wandering and evolving autobiographies reflect this crucial reality. For them, mobility and performances of modernity worked hand in hand.

Humor's Double Edge

Some of these shifts, in terrain, travel, and pronouns (from the plural third person of the biography to the singular first person of the autobiography), are evidenced in later printed versions of the twins' texts. A humorous report opens a version of the twins' autobiography that would have been published and circulated anywhere between 1902 and 1912 under the umbrella of Hennegan and Company in Cincinnati. In it, H. G. Thompson of the Southern California Railway Company's Passenger Department writes to H. K Gregory (the assistant general passenger agent) the following memorandum:

> TO CONDUCTORS, Los Angeles to Santa Ana, San Bernardino via Orange, San Bernardino to Redlands, and Redlands to Los Angeles:
> It is customary for Millie Christine, the dual woman, to require but one ticket. Please be governed accordingly when Millie Christine is making a trip over any of our lines as above indicated.
>
> Yours truly,
> H. G. THOMPSON

Following this note are several other memorandums: one refunding the twins $4.71 for an extra fare, and one, sent to all conductors, simply stating,

> TO CONDUCTORS:
> It is customary to carry Millie Christine on one ticket.
>
> Respectfully,
> A. F. PILCHER, Agt.

This quite literal squabble over the cost of the ticket not only serves as an eye-catching introduction to the twins' autobiography but also shows the ways that narrative moments of physical and fiscal evaluation often intrude on the edges of the twins' archival materials. Although the memos are dated 1895, the question remains about the twins' identity as either one remarkable human or two, which, when coupled with their identity as formerly enslaved Black female performers, recalls such notorious practices as the three-fifths compromise.

Yet this textual opening also mirrors the twins' own rhetorical strategies, in public and reportedly in private, of referring to themselves as one person using the singular first-person *I*.[23] The title of the autobiography, *The History of the North Carolina Twins: Told in "Their Own Peculiar Way" by "One of Them,"*[24] shows the continuous struggle over the McKoys' terms of personhood. This conflict lies at the heart of the systems through which the McKoys were evaluated as fiscally viable performers. But these rhetorical moves were equally a measure of protection and also a marker of grave harm. The twins often wielded their singular identity, both on- and offstage, as a sign of unification and shared strength in negotiations and methods of performance, while sideshow proprietors emphasized their conjoined and singular bodies as a site of invasive exploration.

Equally of note here is the content of these satirically placed memos, coupled with their descriptions of the train lines in California where conductors should charge the twins one fare. The twins are billed, especially following US emancipation, as cosmopolitan, worldly, educated, and virtuosic. And in the case of their performances and of other nineteenth-century freak show performances I study, traveling was an essential part of the act, as performers moved from town to town and country to country, accompanied by claims that they had met with foreign dignitaries and spurious assertions about refined living and associations with gentility meant to downplay performance labor and mythologize the enfreaked body. These are the hallmarks of the archival accounts.

Traveling is explicitly linked to the McKoys' improvisational linguistic performance styles in a memorial article published in the Whiteville *News Reporter* on December 10, 1925: "Mentally they were two separate individuals, with intellectual faculties entirely distinct, with wills independent but fortunately much in harmony. They could talk to each

52 **Biographical Sketch of Millie Christine**

SOUTHERN CALIFORNIA RAILWAY COMPANY. PASSENGER DEPARTMENT.[3]
H. G. THOMPSON, Gen'l Pass. Agt.
H. K. GREGORY, Ass't Gen'l Pass. Agt. Los Angeles, Cal., Jan. 30, 1895.

TO CONDUCTORS, Los Angeles to Santa Ana, San Bernardino via Orange, San Bernardino to Redlands, and Redlands to Los Angeles:

It is customary for Millie Christine, the dual woman, to require but one ticket. Please be governed accordingly when Millie Christine is making a trip over any of our lines as above indicated.

Yours truly,

H. G. THOMPSON, G. P. A.

THE PENNSYLVANIA RAILROAD CO.
PHILA., WILMINGTON & BALT. R. R. CO.
ALEXANDRIA & FREDERICKSBURG RAILWAY. CO.
CAMDEN & ATLANTIC RAILROAD CO.
NORTHERN CENTRAL RAILWAY CO.
BALTIMORE & POTOMAC R. R. CO.
WEST JERSEY RAILROAD CO.
OFFICE, 233 SOUTH FOURTH STREET.
PASSENGER DEPARTMENT.
J. R. WOOD, Gen'l Pass. Agent.
GEO. W. BOYD, Asst. Gen'l Pass. Agent Philadelphia, June 10, 1894.
Subject: Refunding extra fare.
J. P. SMITH, Esq., Grand Central Hotel, New York City.

DEAR SIR:

Referring to your call at this office a few days since I enclose herewith order No. 25286 on our Treasurer for $4.71, covering refund of extra fare paid

3. It is unclear exactly why these notices appear in the McKoys' biography; while they function as further authentication of the sisters' anomalous physiology, they also may well have had the practical intent they declare—to assure conductors that the sisters only require one ticket to travel, the text therefore in particular circumstances acting as both show history and traveling pass. These railway notices in fact pepper the text, appearing at the beginning, again at the middle, and at the end. For ease of reading, all of them have been moved to the beginning of the text, starting here.

Biographical Sketch of Millie Christine 53

from Washington, D. C. to Philadelphia, June 4th, by Millie Christine, the dual woman, in connection with one first-class ticket between same points, which the conductor lifted on the ground that two fares were necessary to cover passage.

Please sign and return enclosed form of receipt, and oblige,

Very truly,

GEO. W. BOYD, A. G. P. A., Wash.

BALTIMORE & OHIO SOUTHWESTERN RAILROAD.
PASSENGER DEPARTMENT.
CITY OFFICE, SOUTHEAST CORNER FOURTH AND VINE STREETS.
O. P. McCarthy, General Passenger Agent.
CHAS. H. KOENIG, District Passenger Agent. Cincinnati, O.,
April 13, 1892.

CONDUCTORS B. & O. S. W. and connecting lines:

This is to certify that Manager Smith has purchased three (3) tickets, Cincinnati to New York, in connection with Millie Christine, the dual woman, this person being included. It is customary to require but one ticket for her passage. Kindly be governed accordingly.

CHAS. H. KOENIG, D. P. A., B. & O. S. W.

TREASURER'S OFFICE, T. H. GIBBS, Treasurer.
COLUMBIA, NEWBURG & LAURENS RAILROAD COMPANY.
Columbia, S. C., Sept. 8, 1893.

CONDUCTORS S. A. Line and connecting lines:

This is to certify that J. P. Smith, Esq., has purchased three (3) tickets from Columbia, S. C. to Lincoln, Nebraska, in connection with Millie Christine, the dual woman, this person being included. It is customary to require one ticket for her passage.

B. F. F. LEAPHART, Ticket Agent. C. N. & L. R. R.

54 **Biographical Sketch of Millie Christine**

BURLINGTON, CEDAR RAPIDS AND NORTHERN RAILWAY.
LOCAL FREIGHT AND TICKET OFFICE.
A. F. PILCHER, Agent. Sioux Falls, So. Dak., Oct. 5, 1895.

TO CONDUCTORS:

It is customary to carry Millie Christine on one ticket.

Respectfully,

A. F. PILCHER, Agt.

SOUTHERN RAILWAY CO., Office of Division Passenger Agt.
R. W. Hunt, D. P. A.
S. H. Hardwick, G.P.A., Washington, D.C.
W. H. Taylor, A.G.P.A., Atlanta, Ga. CHARLESTON, S. C.,
December 13, 1902

To Conductors—It is customary for Millie Christine, the dual woman, to travel on one ticket. Please be governed accordingly when she is traveling over the Southern Railway.

Yours very truly,

R. W. HUNT, D. P. A.

ATLANTIC COAST LINE, Traffic Department.
T. H. Emerson, Traffic Mgr.
H. M. Emerson, G. F. & P. A. WILMINGTON, N. C., December 10, 1897.

To Conductors—Millie Christine, the dual woman, is transported over these lines for one ticket, notwithstanding the fact that she has two heads.

Yours truly,

H. M. EMERSON, G. P. A.

BALTIMORE & OHIO RAILROAD, Passenger Department, J. H. Cowen & O. C. Murray, Receivers.

Biographical Sketch of Millie Christine 55

S. D. Hege, D. P. A
H. R. Hoser, Ticket Agent, 619 Pennsylvania Ave. WASHINGTON, D.C.,
June 9, 1898.

Conductors B. & O. R. R.—This is to certify that Manager Smith has purchased four tickets, Washington, D. C., to Zanesville, Ohio, in connection with Millie Christine, the dual woman, this person being included. You will accept one ticket for the passage of Millie Christine.

Yours truly,

J. N. SCHRYVER, G. P. A.
Per S. B. H., D. P. A.

PLANT SYSTEM OF RAILWAYS.
B. W. Wrenn, P. T. M. SAVANNAH, GA.,
November 22, 1900.

To Conductors—It is customary for Millie Christine, the two-headed woman, to travel on one ticket. You will please govern yourself accordingly.

Yours truly,

B. W. WRENN, P. T. M.

SEABOARD AIR LINE RAILWAY.

To Conductors—It is customary for Millie Christine, the two-headed woman, to travel on one ticket. You will please govern yourself accordingly.

Yours truly,

A. O. MACDONALD, A. G. P. A.

ATLANTIC, VALDOSTA & WESTERN RY. Traffic Department.
Smith D. Pickett, G. F. & P. A. JACKSONVILLE, FLA.
November 30, 1900.

To the Conductors, A. V. & W. Ry.—It will only be necessary for Millie

Figure 2.2: Printing of the McKoys' autobiography, in Linda Frost's *Conjoined Twins in Black and White*.

56 Biographical Sketch of Millie Christine

Christine, known as the dual woman, to present one ticket for her passage over our line.

S. D. Pickett, G. P. A.

Southern Ry. Co. Office of Trav. Pass. Agent.
W. A. Turk, G. P. A., Washington, D.C.
C. A. Benscotter, A. G. P. A., Chattanooga, Tenn.
J. C. Lusk, T. P. A. Selma, Ala., January 11, 1901.

To Southern Railway Conductors—It is the custom for Millie Christine, the dual woman, to travel on one ticket. Please be governed accordingly.

Yours very truly,

J. C. Lusk, T. P. A.

The Missouri Pacific Ry. Co., St. Louis, Iron Mountain and Southern Ry. Co. and Leased, Operated and Independent Lines.
August Sundholm, P. & T. A.
G. E. Richie,
Guy E. Thompson, Ass'ts, S. W. Cor. Markham & Louisiana Sts. and Union Depot. Little Rock, Ark., February 19, 1899.

Conductors S. L., I. M. & S. Ry. and Connecting Lines—It is customary to carry Millie Christine on one ticket.

Respectfully,

August Sundholm, P. & T. A.

Norfolk & Western Ry. Co. Norfolk & Richmond Vestibuled Limited, Fastest Train in the South, Virginia and Ohio Line, West and Northwest.
C. H. Bosley, D. P. A.
John E. Wagner, C. P. & T. A. 838 Main St., Richmond, Va.
W. E. Hazelwood, P. A., 95 Granby St., under Monticello Hotel, Norfolk, Va.

To Conductors Norfolk & Western Railway Company:

Gentlemen—For your information, I beg to advise that the manager of

Biographical Sketch of Millie Christine 57

Millie Christine, a dual woman, is in the habit of only purchasing one ticket for her. This custom has been adhered to and recognized by all lines.

Yours truly,

W. E. Hazelwood, P. A.

Nashville, Chattanooga & St. Louis Railway.
W. L. Danley, Gen'l Pass. and Ticket Agent. Nashville, Tenn., Oct. 20, 1892.

Conductors N., C. & St. L. Ry.:

This is to certify that Manager Smith is authorized to purchase *one* ticket good for ten seats Nashville to Atlanta, in connection Millie Christine, the dual woman, this person being included. It is customary to require but one ticket for her passage. Kindly be governed accordingly.

W. L. Danley, G. P. & T. A.

Chicago, Milwaukee & St. Paul Railway Co.
Office of Division Freight and Passenger Agent.
425 Pierce St., Iowa Savings Bank Building.
Sioux City, Iowa, Sept. 30, 1895.

To Conductors:

It is customary for Millie Christine, the two headed woman, to travel on one ticket. You will please govern yourself accordingly.

Yours truly,

E. W. Jordon, D. P. A.

The Philada. & Reading Railroad Co. Wilkesbarre, B. Station, Jan. 22, 1893.

To Conductors:

It is customary for Millie Christine, the dual woman, to require but one ticket. Please be governed accordingly.

S. S. Chase, C. T. A.

58 Biographical Sketch of Millie Christine

Old Dominion Steamship Co. S. S. "Jamestown," Oct. 4, 1897.

The dual woman, Millie Christine, travels on this steamer on one ticket as one person.

Ford Kuiskene, Purser.

Louisville & Nashville Railroad Co.
Passenger Department, 114 North Fourth Street, St. Louis, Mo., Feb. 4, 1889.

Conductors of L. & N. R. R. and connecting lines:

This is to certify that J. P. Smith, Esq., has purchased three (3) tickets St. Louis to Columbia, S. C., in connection with Millie Christine, the dual woman, this person being included. It is customary to require but one ticket for her passage. Kindly be governed accordingly.

Very truly yours,

John W. Mass, D. P. A.

Central Railroad and Banking Company of Georgia.
H. M. Comer, Receiver. Macon, Ga., Nov. 3, 1892.

Conductor No. 1:

It is customary for Millie Christine, the dual woman, to require but one ticket. Please be governed accordingly.

J. C. Haill, G. P. A.

Northern Pacific Railroad Company.
Thomas F. Oakes, Henry C. Payne. Henry C. Rouse, Receivers.
Traffic Department.
I. A. Nadeau, General Agent. Seattle, Wash., July 28, 1895.

Biographical Sketch of Millie Christine 59

Conductors:

It is customary for Millie Christine, the dual woman, to require but one ticket. Please govern yourself accordingly.

I. A. Nadeau. Gen'l Agent.

Figure 2.2: (*continued*)

other, carry on two different subjects with two different persons and even in two different languages for she spoke several languages acquired during her travels in various countries. Beginning these travels when quite young and being very intelligent the acquisition of these Romance languages was not a difficult task." However, the McKoys' travels were also marked in their childhood by being falsely imprisoned and captured by various white men looking to profit from covert sideshow performances. So the levity in this story of train fares, as well as modern attempts to celebrate them as early pioneers of a Black cosmopolitan identity, also recalls those other coerced transports. It is also worth noting that the previously mentioned story of their singular train ticket in the autobiographical text took place when the twins were being displayed by Batcheller and Doris's Great Inter-Ocean Railroad Show, a performance that folded the concepts of interocean or international travel and the looming figure of the railroad into the title of the show. Therefore, the addition of details relating both to railway travel and to an international case of kidnapping and legal boundary crossing would amplify the marketability of the twins for ticket holders.

Touchatout's *Trombinoscope* about the McKoys also utilizes humor, although not entirely along the same routes.[25] In contrast to the McKoys' own autobiographies, which speak in great detail about their origins and performance lives, the *Trombinoscope* presents an alternative, hypersexualized image of the performers with an emphasis on a romantic farce. Published in 1873, Touchatout's weekly and semiweekly circular focused on the lives of notable French public figures, with an emphasis on satirical humor. Dozens of issues of the *Trombinoscope* were later bound and republished in complete volumes. The cover would notably sport a highly caricatured drawing of the celebrity or public figure in question, with an eye for rendering these beloved figures both ridiculous and unseemly. Touchatout's livelihood was derived from the writing and circulation of these documents. Although he sometimes referenced himself in issues of the *Trombinoscope*, his primary function was that of a scholar, editor, and satirist. His concerns lay with the explication and exploitation of the talents of others. By focusing on those who were already popularly known in the public sphere, Touchatout guaranteed his newspaper's audience and cemented his role as a notable showman

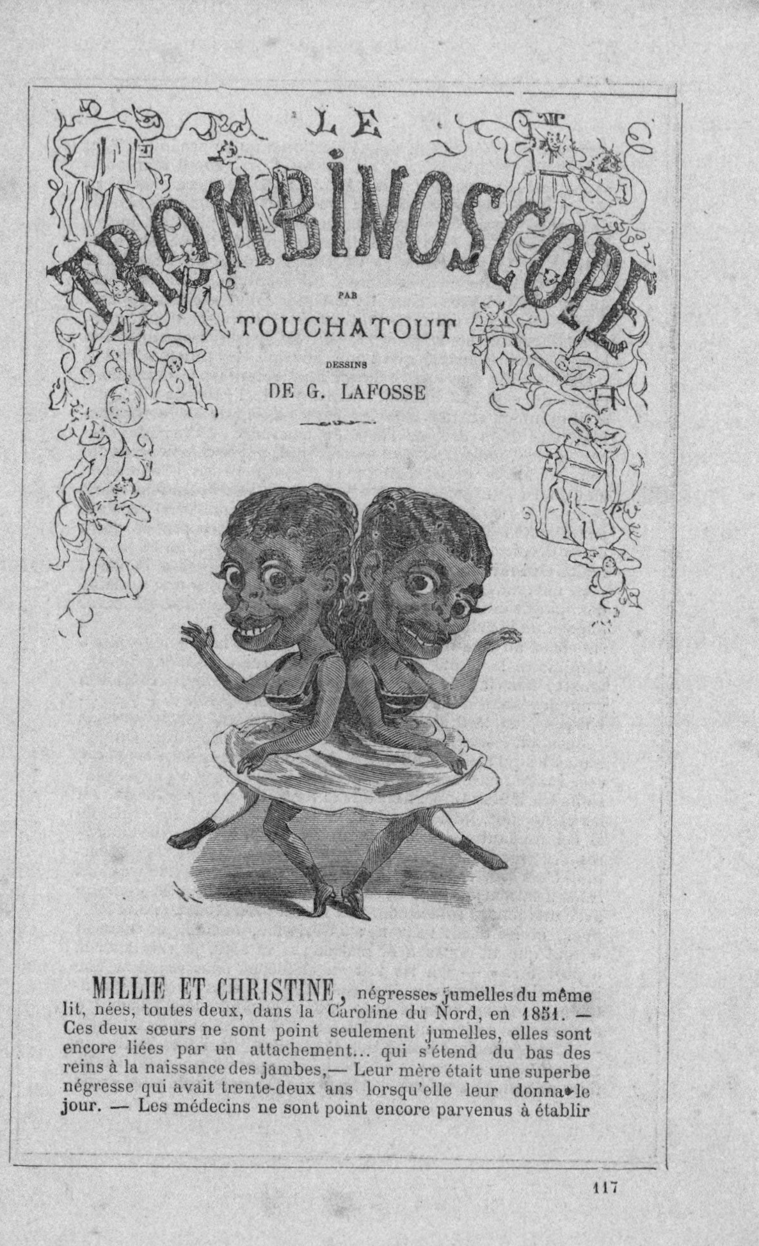

Figure 2.3: Cover of the 1873 *Trombinoscope* on the McKoys. Beinecke Rare Book and Manuscript Library.

and wit. Here we see the conscious efforts of performative fiction making at work.

On the cover we are shown a caricatured and highly altered illustration of Christine and Millie. Although their short stature and dark skin are represented with a greater degree of accuracy than on the cover of their biography and autobiography, the proportions of their limbs, torso, and faces have been altered to emulate those of a more elongated and rounded figure. Their waists have been cinched, their heads have been enlarged, and their lips are considerably inflated. Their cheekbones are higher, and their hair is straightened into flowing waves down their back. Both twins are sporting sizable bosoms made visible by the plunging necklines of their matching tight-fitting dresses. The hems of their skirts rest high above their knees, billowing outward to suggest flirtatious movement from vigorous dancing. Each twin is balanced on her outermost leg while the two limbs that are foregrounded are kicking high into the air in their best imitation of the French can-can girl style. We see the hands of the performers carefully lifting their billowing skirts to reveal longer expanses of stocking-clad feet. The caricature is credited to a "La Fosse," a departure from the logics of anonymity and false attribution that frequently obfuscate readings of English-language biographies and autobiographies.

The story detailed in the *Trombinoscope* differs wildly from those of the twins' many autobiographies. By detailing their childhood kidnapping from the antebellum South to the US North and later England, the anonymous authors of the English biography solidified a pattern indicative of the unidirectional movement often replicated in enslaved people's narratives. Depicting them as fixed in a state of perpetual and dangerous girlhood, the biography does not develop to include the particulars of their lives after around age thirteen or fourteen, instead concluding with lyric sheets and doctors' reports. It is an abrupt about-face, since the opening years of their lives in the antebellum South are recalled in such great detail.

But the *Trombinoscope* is operating under a different set of expectations and conditions. Freed from the strictures of the American viewing public and their focus on the McKoys' lives in slavery, Touchatout's biography focuses instead on what the girls had denied their audiences access to since they were fourteen years old: their genitalia and answers to questions about the boundaries of personhood and Black female sexuality that the precise nature of their conjoined bodies raised. By diverting the twins' story from the familiar terrains of childhood and a US-centric model that re-creates the North-South divide as a site of potential irrevocable rupture for Black female subjects, the *Trombinoscope*'s satirical mockery exposes some of the workings of the previous biography's obsession with melodrama and the disturbing romanticism of enslavement that haunts so many of the other texts.

Opening with the story of the twins' birth in North Carolina, Touchatout foregrounds the problem of their birth as one of *literal* accounting—namely, were these twins two women or one person? Writing of a humorous tale of the confusion created by the twins' arrival into the world, Touchatout explains, "When they were taken to declare their civil status, there was a conflict. Millie was in very good health, but Christine was a little bit feeble."[26] Notice two significant differences between Touchatout's story and those of the anonymous biographers. He establishes that the primary concern of those who initially delivered the twins was not whether they should be considered one woman but rather that they were ill-prepared to receive two babies at once. This is also the first instance that Touchatout tries to establish independent personality and physical traits for the two sisters. This departure is significant. He writes of the women as two sisters competing for the love of the same man. Although their bodies are united, their motivations, expectations, and desires are shown to be almost entirely autonomous. He makes a point of addressing each sister by her first name, using the pronoun *she* or *it* to refer to each one in turn. He goes on to elaborate on this theme of two people trapped in one physical body when he details their early life. Millie is depicted as healthy, responsible, proud, and dependable while Christine is portrayed as passionate, mischievous, sickly, and often ill tempered.[27]

Although Touchatout's narrative resists the seduction of the Southern plantation romance, which was reliant on a sort of nostalgic idealization (such as that present in the texts on the twins that originated in the United States), he doesn't entirely resist the urge to titillate his readers with stories of a whirlwind romance with an unnamed young Black man. The man is said to have fallen in love with the sweeter-natured

Millie. Although they were determined to be together, Christine soon found herself admiring her sister's lover. Operating under the assumption that a woman's primary function and attraction to her husband is her ability as a reproductive and sexual engine, the "punch line" of Touchatout's joke, so to speak, is the twins' conjoined genitals. In his opinion, this will forever bar them from entering into romantic relationships because it is, to him, impossible or inconceivable. Therein lies the humor. He notes the ludicrous nature of this particular conundrum when he says, "The small malignant god had aimed for only one heart, and, without wanting it, it had pierced two. Christine had also died of love for the betrothed of her sister! . . . Christine had a good heart, she proposed to Millie the division of the beloved object; she offered even to favor her sister on every February 29th of the leap years. Millie refused with pride."[28] Deliberately mocking the idea that a romantic partner could be shared between two women with only one set of genitals, Touchatout's observation is meant to intrigue his audience. Although there is no documented evidence within the archive itself that either of the twins ever had romantic relationships or engaged in sexual acts, this satirical rendering of the potential struggles they would face attempted to broach the tricky subject of the twins' transition from infantilized girlhood to hypersexualized adulthood. Gone are the innuendoes and attempts at a mocking modesty. Instead, they are replaced with a depiction of two sisters who are bound for life and still desperately human and competitive.

After attempting to seduce the lover of her sister using subterfuge, Christine eventually gravely offends Millie's lover, thus ruining the engagement. Touchatout concludes the story of the three lovers with a tale that reeks of tabloid-style exploitation. Sneaking from their bed in the dead of night without waking Christine, Millie attempts to drown her sister in a nearby creek, causing Christine to retaliate with vigorous hair-pulling.[29] Of course, there is the underlying understanding that any harm one sister could potentially cause to the other would be futile, since Millie could not possibly kill Christine without causing herself fatal bodily harm. After briefly mentioning that the twins were appearing for the month of November at P. T. Barnum's circus at the Champs-Élysées, Touchatout goes on to end his article with a searing condemnation of the twins' performance act, writing, "In physique, the sisters Millie-Christine are two quite graceful young girls.—Their talents of approval have been jaded by reporters.—Their music and their choreography are less than mediocre.—They sing little beyond mid-range and do not dance much higher than the *ground*."[30] In this final indictment of the twins' talents, which US-based sources lauded as exceptional with all of the offensive undergirding of anti-Black racism, Touchatout unapologetically mocks their physical stature and vocal range. In his satirical rendering, the story of the twins is more of a draw for his readers and for circusgoing audiences than anything they could possibly perform onstage. He even adds a "complimentary notice" on the final page that projects the twins' romantic trajectory into the future. He writes that they married Chang and Eng Bunker and together they had 118 children, "all of which are held by the part of the body and forming a human chain with no end."[31]

Extending the anxieties about the nature of Millie and Christine's sexual potential and human personhood to their most hyperbolic degree, Touchatout's final joke imagines a future in which the McKoy twins are married and begin a family. He even notes a fake time and date of their death, sarcastically projecting that they would live into the early part of the twentieth century. Here the sisters are catapulted from the treacherous confines of nineteenth-century Black girlhood to become fully functioning women with desires, autonomy, and dreams. Sadly, it seems that this potential futurity is only conceivable to Touchatout and his audience as a twisted joke, with Christine and Millie bearing the brunt of the criticism. But what if this were not the case? Couldn't the image of a chain of human babies, laid side by side like paper dolls, also be used to demonstrate the unstable and multiple natures of self-representation? Could these replicating biographies and correspondences be a paper chain, looping one into the next without an end? Although their shows and performance materials operated under a system of exploitation whereby Black bodies became more spectacular or "worthy" of performance only through suffering, I would dare to suggest that the McKoys might have been able to negotiate their own terms of emancipation through their performance acts and the circulation of their narratives. These possibilities allowed them access to a new mode of engagement with their audiences that complicated the forces that sought to continuously enslave them, ultimately providing new avenues of self-representation.

This chain also brings me back to the chain-mail nature of the humorous opening of the McKoys' autobiography, which features the literal paper chain of letters from conductor to conductor, throughout California and the country, instructing all conductors about how to appropriately charge the sisters one fare. In addition to the theoretical frameworks of correspondence (from McKoy to McKoy and McKoy to audience), this display of letters demonstrates the centrality of the epistolary form in the McKoys' formulation of self-narration. Like the sisters, the letters are mobile, expressive, and communal. They are private and public, moving from the private spheres of the conductors to the public spheres of the McKoys' autobiography. The reprinted letters also travel along the train lines the McKoys were supposed to follow, creating a sense of spatial awareness that is linked to their act. The humor in the correspondence of the autobiography is related to a punch line that involves their singular body being entitled to one train fare into the foreseeable future, whereas in the world of the *Trombinoscope*, any kind of normative future for these nonnormative bodies is laughable and implausible. So while the McKoys' autobiography uses scripted racial prototypes in their self-narration, it falls within the realm of contemporary texts like the *Trombinoscope* while still attempting to subvert these expectations through the epistolary form.

"Merchant's Gargling Oil Linament" and the Equescurriculum: The Narrative Boundaries of Animal and Human

The McKoys' wandering autobiographical texts bore a connection not only to their shifting legal status as enslaved laborers but also to their status as Black performers in the latter nineteenth century and early twentieth century. These texts were used to draw attention to their conjoined Black bodies as well as to highlight the nature of Blackness on the freak show stage. Freak show performances often called on the alignment of the enfreaked bodies on display (often in their own separate tent that required an extra entrance fee from audience members) with other styles and forms of entertainment housed within those same shows. Rachel Adams explicates this contradictory form of engagement in her monograph *Sideshow U.S.A.*, where she notes that purveyors of nineteenth- and early twentieth-century American circuses often dictated and subsequently manipulated the terms of freakdom to suit their fiscal needs. Adams writes that while those with disabilities were often targeted as being "true" or "authentic" freaks because of their perceived physical difference, this did not preclude the inclusion of those whose freakishness was dependent on other factors, such as perceived racial or ethnic difference, xenophobic assumptions, and alterable or performed traits.[32] Adams notes the rise in popularity of the late nineteenth-century "wild man" sideshows. Featuring Black and brown men in "savage" dress, these shows were intended to display the uncivil nature of the exotic other. Adams states that for white audiences, "those most anxious about their own status as citizens applauded the reassuring vision of nonwhite bodies that absolutely could not be assimilated."[33]

A similar technique was used when the McKoys were featured in W. C. Coup's Equescurriculum. Coup circulated an 1879 visiting card in support of the twins' appearances in his show, and some of the alterations made to their physical appearance in the ad are evidenced in versions of their autobiography that were circulated around the same time as his shows. In his 1901 biography *Sawdust and Spangles: Stories and Secrets of the Circus*, Coup recalls his life as a purveyor of American circuses and freak shows during the latter half of the nineteenth century. Although he started as an independent connoisseur of human oddities and animal attractions, perhaps he is still most well known as an early business partner of another, more widely known, American circus man: P. T. Barnum. Born in 1837, Coup died in 1895, a full six years before his biography could be published. Supposedly conceived of in collaboration with Coup and constructed from accounts of his colorful circus tales, *Sawdust and Spangles* seems to offer insight into the mechanisms deployed by Coup in the marketing of his own human and animal oddities or "freaks." Focused almost entirely on the performers themselves, with little revealed about Coup's own origins, the text reads more like an extended promotional flyer than the retelling of a man's life. Page after page is filled with the particulars of all the acts Coup used to manage. Details of their performances, their histories, their skills, and their past proprietors line the pages of what is supposed to be Coup's farewell to the performance world. But he remains a showman throughout. He exchanges his own desire for self-narration with biographical accounts of "the other" (his performers), choosing instead to follow the oldest showman's trick in the book: Give the people what they want.

Detailing his career in entertainment, Coup's biography features a litany of acts from his past performances, focusing on the veracity of his performance oddities and the skill of his performers while simultaneously defaming his contemporaries as frauds with subpar talents. It is in the introduction of this archival oddity that I found my first working definition of one of Coup's many inventions: the Equescurriculum. The author of the biography describes this supposedly unique performance innovation as follows: "Started out on the road with the 'Equescurriculum,' an entirely novel and original exhibition consisting of trained bronchos, performing dogs, goats, giraffes, etc., and troupes of Japanese acrobats. Each year new attractions were added to this show, and, in 1879, the New United Monster Shows were organized by Mr. Coup and developed into one of the largest consolidated circuses in the United States."[34] In this passage, Coup, ever the showman, is described as having reestablished the rules of viewing bodies categorized as "freakish" and therefore nonhuman. This litany of circus attractions is laid out carefully, moving from more familiar domestic animals common throughout the United States (e.g., broncos, goats, and dogs), to what can be termed "exotic" animals (e.g., giraffes), before finally culminating with his advertised "troupes of Japanese acrobats." This is not the only source that draws a connection between animal flesh and the flesh of human sideshow performers. Another version of the twins' biography, also published in 1883, features advertisements for a "Merchant's Gargling Oil Linament." The ad is reproduced in the margins of every single page, making a clear connection between the human bodies depicted in the biographical sketch and the animals the liniment claimed to cure. Similarly, the linearity of Coup's 1879 visiting card and the elision of the difference between trained animals and trained racially othered bodies encapsulates the contested nature of the circus space, where the boundaries of "freakishness" are mandated by the terms of the purveyors and marketers, and the boundaries of human and animal are represented in the proximity of the performance spaces and in the advertising on the margins of the written accounts. Audience members are asked to view the slope between the animal and the human onstage

Figure 2.4: Visiting card from Coup's Equescurriculum, 1879. Beinecke Rare Book and Manuscript Library.

as a slippery one, while also being called to account for their own fascination with this elision by advertisements that claimed humans could be cured by the same means as a horse or other farm animal. This is also notable because while they are consuming the labor of the enfreaked body before their eyes, they are also reminded of their supposed biological connections with animals associated with farm labor (namely horses, for the sake of the metaphor inherent in the name Equescurriculum). And Black bodies, both enslaved and newly freed, enfreaked and able bodied, are added to this constellation of labor in the performance and domestic spheres. Because of these multiple ways of viewing the enfreaked body and the various lenses through which "freakishness" might be attributed, measured, and subsequently consumed, Coup's framework offers insight into the terms of American freakdom for performers in his Equescurriculum. They were, first and foremost, racial others, excluded from the full category of human engagement. As well trained as his performing dogs, they represent the added promise of Orientalist exoticism being offered up in its most transparent form.

While Coup had one intention in displaying the McKoys and other enfreaked performers alongside animals (specifically horses), the line between the human and animality remains blurred for today's reader for reasons not altogether connected to Coup's original intent. On the relationship between Western ideology and the nonwhite human subject, Alexander Weheliye drawing on Sylvia Wynter writes,

> Since colonial policies and discourse are frequently grounded in racial distinctions, the colonized subject cannot experience her or his nonbeing outside the particular ideology of western Man as synonymous with human, or, as Fanon writes, "not only must the black man be black; he must be black in relation to the white man." The colonial encounter determines not just the black colonial subject's familial structure or social and physical mobility and such, but colors his or her very being as he-or-she-which-is-not-quite-human, as always already tardy in the rigged match of the survival of the fittest. Conversely, in this ontological face-off, the white colonial subject encounters herself or himself as the "fullness and genericity of being human." However, he or she only does so in relation to the deficiency of the black subject and indigenous.[35]

In this formulation, the Black subject is in constant comparison with the Western configuration of the human, which is squarely cisgender, male, heterosexual, and white. The fact that the McKoys do not neatly align with many of the aforementioned categories places their humanity into question by the standards of Western modernity. Their union through their shared genitals places their gender and social identity in question, as it is not easily explicable along binary lines. Because they do not fit neatly into the category of the human as defined by these constructs, it is essential that we look to other formulations of the relationship between the animal and the Black subject in order to rearticulate the ways the McKoys were marketed and viewed.

In *Being Property Once Myself: Blackness and the End of Man*, Joshua Bennett begins his introduction, fittingly titled "Horse," with an analysis of the interspecies relationship between Black subjects and nonhuman subjects. Bennett begins by looking at the opening of Frederick Douglass's 1845 autobiography *Narrative of the Life of Frederick Douglass*, where Douglass writes, "I was born in Tuckahoe, near Hillsborough, and about twelve miles from Easton, in Talbot County, Mary land. I have no accurate knowledge of my age, never having seen any authentic record containing it. By far the larger part of the slaves know as little of their ages as horses know of theirs."[36] Explaining the relevance of this interspecies connection, Bennett writes,

> This moment of all too fraught proximity between the enslaved black person and the nonhuman animal—positioned here as *twin* captives, affixed by modernity's long arc—demands our attention. What Douglass names is a kinship forged in the midst of unthinkable violence, kinship born of mutual subjugation, yes, but also the shared experience of opacity mistaken for emptiness. Here, Douglass foregrounds animal perspective as a means to convey the impossibility of personal history for the enslaved. A slave's past cannot be recalled because there is no socially recognized, generally honored means by which to recall it—no system to record one's emergence into the world, one's entry into the proper chronology, and cosmology, of the human.[37]

This "shared experience of opacity mistaken for emptiness" is what concerns me most for the sake of this section and my analysis of Coup's

Equescurriculum. Although enslaved and free Black subjects were often relegated to the status of an animal in order to devalue and dehumanize them, Bennett's assertion of a shared opacity and subjecthood is significant because it demonstrates the elasticity of terms like *animal* and *human* and the interrelated nature of these terms. By aligning himself with the horse in his autobiography, Douglass makes a more expansive *I* that stretches to include not only other Black enslaved subjects but also nonhuman subjects. Therefore, although Coup attempted to relegate them purely to the status of the nonhuman, the lines between human and animal are not as strictly defined as someone like him would like to assume.

The border between the animal and the human has been probed and deconstructed by scholars such as Mel Chen. In their work *Animacies: Biopolitics, Racial Mattering, and Queer Affect*, Chen writes,

> What happens when animals appear on human landscapes? In spite of their regular co-occurrence with humans, nonhuman animals are typologically situated elsewhere from humans, as in the linguistic concept of an animacy hierarchy, a scale of relative sentience that places humans at the very top. This presumed superiority of humans is itself duratively supported and legitimated by "modern" states in a transnational system of (agricultural) capital. Yet to consider the biopolitical ramifications wrought by these separated categories is extremely complex, since "humans" are not all treated one way and "animals" are not uniformly treated another way. This is why the statement that someone "treated me like a dog" is one of liberal humanism's fictions: some dogs are treated quite well, and many humans suffer in conditions of profound indignity.[38]

Of particular significance is Chen's assertion that the treatment of animals and humans often appears blurry when analyzed closely. Although Coup's ambition in his marketing was to represent enfreaked and nonwhite subjects in animalistic terms, he actually tapped into a complex system of relationality that doesn't always neatly align with the assumption that humans are good and animals are bad. In fact it parallels Douglass's claim that he was no more likely to know his birthday than a horse, drawing on the fact that some horses would be treated better than Black subjects, even though their functionality under enslavement was similar. Therefore Chen's argument that "some dogs are treated quite well, and many humans suffer in conditions of profound indignity" draws greater attention to the ways that the treatment of humans and nonhumans is not fixed.

In one of Coup's visiting cards sold as souvenirs and advertisements during the twins' public appearances, dated around 1879, the twins' appearances have been notably altered. Their hair is pinned back, displaying long necks and elongated, European features, and the twins' bodies are depicted as curvaceous. They have been made significantly taller. Gone are the white, prim, ruffled dresses of childhood displayed in the biography and autobiography. Each woman is daintily clutching a fan between the tips of her gloved fingers, and they are both facing their audience in a decidedly seductive pose. With their ankles bared by one hand suggestively lifting the outermost hem of their skirts, there is no question that they are being portrayed in an overtly sexualized and flirtatious style. Boldly calling on the reader to imagine the hidden pleasures of the twins' "1 body" to be displayed "every afternoon and night," the visiting card advertisement draws on well-publicized beliefs about the supposedly lascivious and hypersexualized nature of the Black female body. Coup's portrayals highlight the fluidity of flesh, horse or human, sexualized, or invisible. Like in Touchatout's account of the twins, there is little to no room for variability or subtlety. But even though they lack the intense focus on attempting to produce details of the twins' lives that manifest their inner thoughts and autonomy, all of these texts share something in common: a fixation on the McKoys' bodies. The true correspondence is always between the singular and subjective self, the self that is housed within or in relation to our bodies, and another.

Writing to the Dead

In the texts that were published under the guidance of the twins' surviving family members in conjunction with white reporters, it was noted that the McKoys were afraid of being autopsied. I go into greater detail about this story in chapter 3. The twins remained fearful of an autopsy being performed on them like that performed on their freak show predecessors Chang and Eng Bunker, whose bodies have also been preserved to this day in the Mütter Museum in Philadelphia. In

Figure 2.5: Marker near the McKoy twins' grave in North Carolina.

order to avoid this fate, they had family members maintain watch over their graves for many years. By the time the twins were reinterred in 1969, their bodies were so badly decomposed that they had to be placed inside a smaller box and resettled. The decision to draw them nearer to the road and to mark the location of their final resting place as a historical site within North Carolina seems to have revived an academic and artistic interest in these performers, their legacies, and their lives. It is worth noting that the majority of works (my own included) on the twins' lives are dated after their 1969 reinterring, which served as an effective rebranding of their legacies. They were moved to the edge of the cemetery facing a road that has been renamed in their honor. To this day a highway marker declares, "Black conjoined twins born near here, 1851. Exhibited in U.S. and Europe. Died in 1912. Grave is five miles N." They were "exhibited" but did not perform.

A dual headstone also marks their final resting place, with elegies written in dedication to the McKoys neatly divided under two names: one that reads "Mille-Christine" and the other "Christine-Mille." In each case Millie's name has been altered. It names her parents as Jacob and "Monemia," noting that she "died October 8th and 9th, 1912, fully resigned at her home, the place of her birth and residence of her Christian parents." When viewing a photograph of this headstone, it occurs to me that in form and narration the McKoys' story is still a varying correspondence. They are given two names, with their last name given with a different spelling closer to that of their original owner, McCoy. They are called the child of Jacob and "Monemia" but listed as dying at the homes of their "Christian parents," which could stand for their biological family or their enslavers. They are noted as pious and God fearing, and "a real friend to the needy of both races." But there is no mention made to their former life in bondage, with the focus shifted instead to their "life of much comfort." Just as the roadside marker continues to mark the McKoys as an exhibit and not as performers, their floating autobiographies and biographies straddle this same divide. Although the authorship and intention remain contested, these texts often serve as the backbone of scholarly and artistic interventions into the McKoys' lives. And in attempting to negotiate their fictions, we continue to effectively reenter their narratives into the courts of public opinion and scholarly fact-finding.

It is telling that the McKoys' final gravestone contains a scripture from Psalm 92:13, which reads, "They that be planted in the house of the Lord shall flourish in the Courts of our God." Perhaps it is a willful misreading, but the dual meaning of "courts" here strikes me as particularly significant. Not only are the courts the final place where the McKoys have been resettled, but the term can (in another context) refer to the courts and justice system that they and their family spent a lifetime navigating. The insinuation that there is a higher court than the one of man where the final judgments of the McKoys will be made seems particularly significant in light of their lifelong battles for freedom. That

Figure 2.6: The McKoys' dual headstone. North Carolina.

they will flourish and thrive outside the earthly courts of the South that alternately sided with them and against them seems to be a promise the McKoys' family took to their grave. There is a sadness to this final declaration of growth, bringing to mind the "jes grew" narratives of Black girlhood in *Uncle Tom's Cabin* and its attendant legacies. Like Topsy, the McKoys were left to grow among thorny and treacherous circumstances that denied them the protections of childhood. Instead, they were bartered and traded, from legal slavery through custody cases to eventual limited financial and legal freedom. But here the tragedy of Topsy is turned on its head as the viewer imagines a future of growth and prosperity for the McKoys related to their unwavering Christian faith.

But the addition of the prefix *auto-* in the autobiographies still operates as a site of self-reflection, working backward to reference the McKoys and their audiences, who are the essential components of their narrations. They are in conversation with each other, dueling inside the strictures of enfreakment and enslavement that sustained their performance practice. And we are in conversation with them, as we continue to generate works that function as letters to the dead, a sort of necromancy that attempts to work through their subject positions in their stories in search of a definitive reply that will never come.

3

Autopsy and Enfreakment on the Nineteenth-Century Stage

Sir enclosed you will find the receipt for bringing the bodies of Papa and Uncle from Salem. . . . My mother and Aunt was very sorry that we did not bring the lungs and entrails of our fathers with the bodies home, and as we did not bring them, you can keep them, until further orders from the families.
—C. W. and J. D. Bunker to Harrison Allen, April 1, 1874[1]

God created black people and black people created style.
—George C. Wolfe, *The Colored Museum* (1988)

The Negro's universal mimicry is not so much a thing in itself as an evidence of something that permeates his entire self. And that thing is drama.
—Zora Neale Hurston, "Characteristics of Negro Expression" ([1934] 1970)

Nowhere is the archival future perfect more present in the archives of the enfreaked than in the autopsy, display, and disposal of their bones and flesh. What became of the bodies of these entertainers once the spotlights dimmed and the glare of public attention turned elsewhere by the mid-twentieth century? As their stories and performance legacies faded into obscurity, their bodies remained as a tangible reminder of the harms and highs of the freak show stage. For Joice Heth, Chang and Eng Bunker, and the McKoys, autopsy (a fate that their predecessor Sarah Baartman was submitted to) was both a harsh reality and an ever-present fear. Heth and the Bunkers, like Baartman, were ultimately subjected to autopsies that were made public to either paying audiences (in the case of Heth) or readers of scientific journals (in the case of the Bunkers).

Although Heth's remains were ultimately discarded, the Bunkers' remain on display in Philadelphia's Mütter Museum. There is evidence that, as a direct result of what happened to the Bunkers, the McKoys spent their lives in constant fear of the same fate: being autopsied for those who cared more for their enfreaked bodies than their humanity. This caused the performers to spend their lives trying to control and ultimately determine what would happen to their remains in the archive when they died. In this chapter, I will detail how these intersecting stories of death and survival were recorded and examine evidence of a future perfect awareness of the performers' legacies by both the performers and their surviving family members.

The future perfect is evident in the ways that these performers (namely the Bunkers and McKoys) and their families negotiated the lasting legacies of their remains in the public eye. Learning from the practices that had been forced on performers like Heth and Baartman, as well as the rising prevalence of forced autopsies in the nineteenth century, the Bunkers' and McKoys' kin expertly engineered the final display of their remains in a way that has cemented their legacies in popular culture today. The Bunker family's decision to allow their patriarchs' remains to stay in Philadelphia (as noted in the first epigraph of this chapter) effectively ensured that they would remain in the public eye and in American popular culture for decades to come. In contrast, the McKoy family's decision to honor Millie Christine's final wishes and avoid autopsy altogether resulted in them truly being able to retire from the freak show stage in death as their stories faded into obscurity alongside their remains.

In 1863 *Harper's Weekly* published an image of a man they identified as "Whipped Peter," an alias for a formerly enslaved person from New Orleans named Gordon. His portrait, titled *The Scourged Back*, was taken up swiftly by abolitionists who argued that the brutality evidenced in the network of thick keloid scars on his back served as concrete proof of slavery's past atrocities and present evils.[2] The image continues to circulate today as a reminder of slavery's brutal afterlives, Gordon's keloid wounds displaying one of the many physical manifestations of how enslavement's torture was compounded on the bodies of its victims. And if we consider enslavement both a system of labor and a methodology of advanced torture, then the black keloid was the return on investment, or perhaps it was a sign of compounded interest from oppressors. Slavery was an economy built on routinized cruelty. But even though there is finality in the wounding of Gordon's photographic and actual flesh, there still remains a conditional projection of uncertainty about the events and labor system (chattel slavery) that produced his scars. This uncertainty isn't because Gordon and his photograph survived. Rather it is because his body resisted being engulfed by the sum totality of Black death. Even in the archive, a structure and device not of his choosing, Gordon is able to look at us sideways over his shoulder and examine us just as we are examining his keloid grooves. He sees us from the corner of his eye as we face him head-on. He is wounded but exercises this autonomy in his archival entry. And he has all the style of a Black side eye, even in attempted abjection.

This two-way looking glass of history is echoed in the title and content of Carrie Mae Weems's 1995 archival photography project *From Here I Saw What Happened and I Cried.*[3] Weems features Gordon's infamous picture, an example of one of slavery's physical afterlives, superimposed with the following uppercase text:

> BLACK AND TANNED
> YOUR WHIPPED WIND
> OF CHANGE HOWLED LOW
> BLOWING ITSELF—HA—SMACK
> INTO THE MIDDLE OF
> ELLINGTON'S ORCHESTRA
> BILLIE HEARD IT TOO &
> CRIED STRANGE FRUIT TEARS

In her choice of image and text, Weems has identified a Black groove and followed its path through nineteenth- and twentieth-century American popular culture, a structure that (like enslavement) was often built on the backs and by the hands of Black subjects. She traces its legacy from Black bodies treated and toughened like leather under the systems of chattel slavery, to Duke Ellington's orchestral overtures, and into the echoing resistance of Billie Holiday's "Strange Fruit" cries (1939). It is all always there, always a present pulse that Weems's hand is keeping

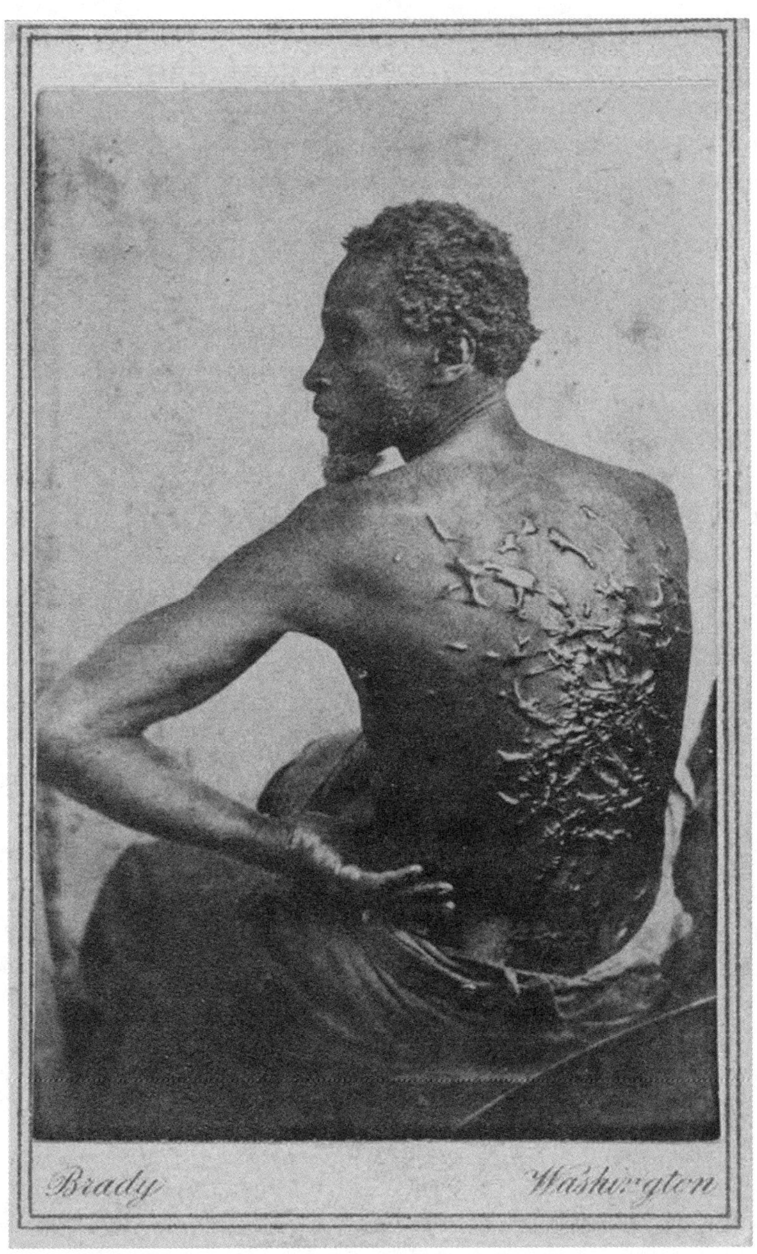

Figure 3.1: Gordon, also known as "Whipped Peter," 1863. Library of Congress.

time with. And yet it is also all set in the historical past tense. Weems's rendering of Gordon contains two distinct perspectives: the "what happened" of the historical past and the amorphous "here" that is at once Gordon's nineteenth-century glance, Ellington's and Holiday's early twentieth-century sonic rise, and Weems's 1995 artistic lens; and the shifting standpoint of every subsequent viewer who encounters these traumas in these works. Weems's past tense but present location are at once capacious enough to uphold the weight of these multiple standpoints and also porous enough to allow for the brutality of Gordon's past. It is a past that gave him both the raised scars on his back and the initial wounds full of blood that caused them.

Gordon's famously wounded skin seems to be evoked again in Signature Theatre Company's 2017 production of Suzan-Lori Parks's 1996 play *Venus*. At the beginning of the performance, Zainab Jah (the actress portraying famed nineteenth-century freak show performer Sarah Baartman) steps nimbly into a padded flesh-tone bodysuit created by costume designer Emilio Sosa.[4] She pivots slowly for the crowd, which includes both the ensemble onstage and the audience in the theater, using the excess and abundance of the bodysuit to exaggerate the shape of Baartman's famed naked body and the textured grooves of her imagined and overexposed skin. For it was Baartman's physical dimensions and racialization as a Black woman (although she was never legally enslaved) that led sideshow proprietors in the mid-nineteenth century to bill her as the "Hottentot Venus." It isn't just the weight and shape of the suit but its texture that draws the eye. Its ridges and movements are slowly revealed as a chaotic chorus of voices in the ensemble swiftly orbit around Jah's and Parks's Baartman. The ridges and folds of her padded exterior are pelted on all sides by the angular rapidity of the ensemble's speech. Like Weems's portrayal of Gordon, this moment is driven by a collapsing of past, present, and future actions surrounding the memorialization and performance of slavery.

The legacies of unfree performance have been traced throughout the genealogy of Black studies from Zora Neale Hurston's early anthropological interventions quoted in the third epigraph to the work of scholars such as Saidiya Hartman, Daphne Brooks, Farah Jasmine Griffin, Joseph Roach, and Hortense Spillers.[5] I attempt an alternative accounting of enslaved labor that encapsulates the performance of nineteenth-century freak show autopsies and the archival practices surrounding the preservation of these histories.

For at its roots, enslavement was a labor system. And the places where it did intersect with the praxis of Black performance brought two distinct types of labor systems together: stage labor and enslaved labor. The challenge of articulating these connections and interstices is that both slavery and performance, as labor praxes, dictate that we invisibilize the labor of Black actors. Even in her facetious articulations of a Black performance history and theory in *Negro: An Anthology* edited by Nancy Cunard (1934), Hurston calls "drama" the inherent state of the Black person and not their carefully cultivated practice of self-protection.[6] And what Hurston calls drama George C. Wolfe names as Black "style." In each case, the author indicates that it is some ineffable thing that's inherent to Black expressive culture. Yet, I am also aware that there can be an implication that style is either inherent to one's structure or entirely absent. But I assert that style is an active praxis born out of the scenes of slavery, an invention of early modern Black subjects looking to influence the creation of American popular culture in the face of unimaginable cruelties.

This is why I pulled from George C. Wolfe's oft-quoted witticism in his satirical *Colored Museum* that "God *invented* black people" and, in turn, "black people invented style." Because although the project of racial terror is to keep people so paralyzed in the present that they cannot accurately recall the past or adequately prepare for the future, there is evidence in the archives that Black performing enfreaked bodies have always defied these odds through their carefully cultivated staging of the future perfect archival tense. I borrow and expand the term *enfreakment* from Ellen Samuels's "Examining Millie and Christine McKoy: Where Enslavement and Enfreakment Meet."[7] Samuels offers the framework of "enfreakment," or the *process of becoming* a freak body, as a substitution for the loaded term *freak*. I agree that the term is critical to complicating the terms of *object* and *subject* in nineteenth-century racialized freak shows because it is invested in performance and process rather than in concretizing freakdom as a fixed state of being.

The archival practices surrounding both enfreakment and enslavement are dictated by a future perfect archival verbal tense. When used appropriately, the future perfect expresses that which will have been or "describ[es] an event yet to happen."[8] It is the unwritten history of the unarrived future. The anticipatory nature of the archival practices of slavery is deeply invested in dictating this unseen future history. This mirrors the archival anticipation embedded in nineteenth-century freak shows' investment in accounting for enfreaked bodies through public autopsy.

The archival structures of enslavement and enfreakment on the nineteenth-century stage are deeply invested in accounting equally for the physical flesh of the performer *and* the performer's labor. This creates a system of whereby the unfree enfreaked body accrues high value as an object of spectatorship and performance in life onstage and in the archive after death, even as the terms of bondage and death render that same body abjectly valueless as a traditional enslaved laborer. These practices are demonstrated in the nineteenth-century public autopsies of freak show performers, which combined showmanship with the archival obsession to rigorously account for the bodies of the enfreaked and enslaved. This dual obsession is represented by *the grooves of the flesh* and the types of archival documents favored by enslavers and freak show proprietors to record the textures of the lives and performances of the enfreaked. The groove can extend to encompass the scars, stitches, paintings, soundscapes, woodcuts, body casts, visiting cards, printed texts, and surgical cuttings used to mark and account for the autopsied bodies of freak show performers. It carves a path through history that our eyes and fingers frettingly trace. In this way, the groove is the physical manifestation of the future perfect tense. It stands either as evidence of resistance to enslavement and enfreakment or as a sign of excess flesh that resists simple accounting. The past tense and present archival grooves of three sets of freak show performers from the nineteenth century, with intimate connections to the system of US legal slavery, reveal the intricate textures of historical harm. These performers are Chang and Eng Bunker, Millie Christine McKoy, and Joice Heth. Each of these enfreaked performers stood at the intersection of freakdom and enslavement, whether it was as slave owners or as the enslaved.

Born near Bangkok, Siam (current-day Thailand), in 1811, Chang and Eng Bunker toured the world as traveling freak show performers. By the time of their 1874 autopsy, they were world-famous medical anomalies. Although they adopted the name Bunker, it was their racialized association with their home country of Siam, along with their conjoined torsos, that gave them their famous moniker as the original "Siamese Twins."

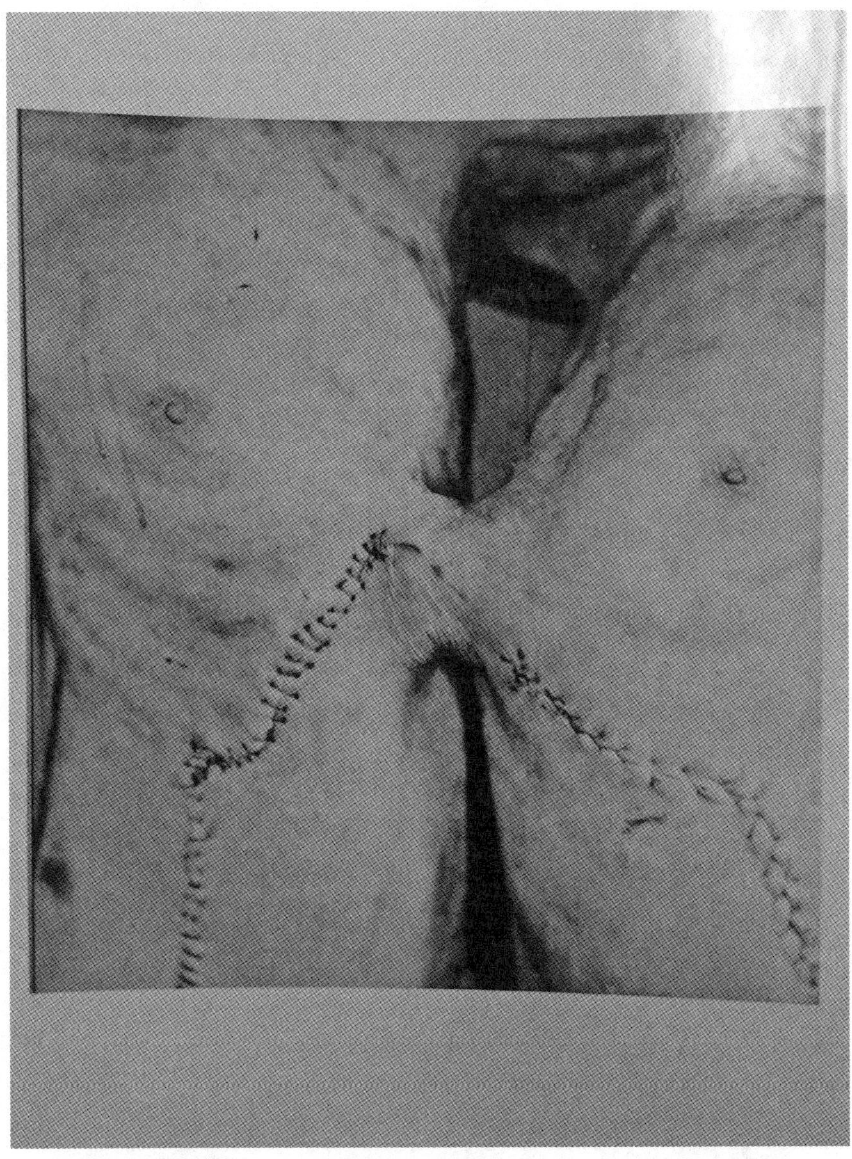

Figure 3.2: Autopsy photo of Chang and Eng Bunker, 1874. North Carolina Collection, University of North Carolina at Chapel Hill.

Their rise to stardom in the late nineteenth century not only added a phrase to the English lexicon but also raised the profiles of freak show performers worldwide as politically and fiscally savvy business people. After marrying two white Southern sisters in 1843, the Bunkers eventually raised two large families (Chang had ten children, while his brother Eng had eleven). After marriage the Bunkers retired from the freak show stage to become enslavers on two adjacent plantations in North Carolina, only to return to the public eye in 1868 when they went on tour with their children, a financial necessity prompted by the demise of legal slavery in 1865 and poor investments in the short-lived Confederate currency. The twins' conjoined livers and a plaster cast of their bodies remain on display at Philadelphia's Mütter Museum. Although their entries into the archive are as freak slave owners and not as freed slaves, I take up the Bunkers' archives here because the extended performance of their autopsy continues their enfreakment to this day. The contentious acquisition of their dual bodies noted in the first epigraph of this chapter demonstrates an archival instability around questions of legal autonomy for enfreaked nineteenth-century performers, regardless of their status as enslaved laborers or enslavers.

The archives of conjoined twins Millie Christine McKoy share a number of biographical similarities with the Bunkers'. As fellow North Carolina residents whose life spanned from 1851 to 1912, they were born into slavery and spent their life straddling the line between legal unfreedom and liberated Black subjects. They also had a traumatic medical examination of their conjoined genitals conducted in 1871 by a William Pancoast, one of the physicians who later assisted in the autopsy of Chang and Eng. During his exam of the McKoys, Pancoast created a woodcut of the twins' shared genitals that was widely distributed in the Philadelphia-based *Photographic Review of Medicine and Surgery*, an image that extends my theory of the groove. This invasive examination, conducted just three years before Pancoast would famously assist in the autopsy and preservation of the Bunkers' corpses in an equally textured method (a plaster casting), led the twin sisters in later life to assert that they had a "horror of autopsy."[9] Pancoast's and his associates' preferred methods of capture involved heavily textured and grooved systems of recording so as to account for every inch of the enfreaked flesh that they sought to preserve.

The McKoys' fears surrounding autopsy were not entirely unfounded. The Civil War and the following years saw the convergence of two things: the rise of autopsy in the medical profession and the proliferation of dead bodies as a result of combat. In *Medicine, Science, and Making Race in Civil War America*, Leslie A. Schwalm writes,

> It was not only the living Black body that Northern white medical men appropriated in their wartime pursuit of racial knowledge. The war's violence—as a military conflict, as a medical catastrophe, as an armed assault on a slaveholding republic—yielded a bounty of corpses. White medical personnel eager to take advantage of the wartime bounty of cadavers would claim, dissect, and disassemble thousands of Black war dead, both soldiers and civilian refugees from slavery. Regimental and contract surgeons, hospital stewards, and other medical employees performed tens of thousands of post-mortem examinations on soldiers and civilians, Black and white, who died from wounds and disease. The war abruptly expanded access to hands-on anatomical knowledge, regarded as the hallmark of medical professionalism. During the war as before it, surgeons and hospital workers made ample and focused use of the human remains of African Americans.[10]

In the passage, Schwalm notes the particular attention that was paid to the remains of Black civilians and soldiers, who provided the medical community with corpses to conduct experiments and perform autopsies. But the legacy of autopsying unwilling Black subjects dates further back than the American Civil War. The McKoys' and Bunkers' predecessors Joice Heth and Sarah Baartman were both subject to autopsies that were either ticketed and fully public (in the case of Heth) or made public through museum displays and scientific publications (in the case of Baartman). Baartman, who was born in present-day South Africa around 1789, was brought to Europe and exhibited in the mid-nineteenth century under promises of compensation that never arrived. Baartman, who was famed for her physical appearance (more specifically her backside), suffered an untimely death around the age of twenty-six, followed by an autopsy and display in the Muséum d'histoire naturelle d'Angers, after which her body was relocated to the Musée de l'Homme in the 1930s and finally repatriated in 2002 to South Africa. But the years of displacement and mistreatment of Baartman's remains continue to tell the story of a legacy of exploitation and neglect at the hands of so-called medical men and scientists.

As a result of their fears, the McKoys deployed legal means, specifically a will, that entrusted their estate (including cash and a plot of land) to various family members; and extralegal means (namely, the use of euthanasia in their deaths[11] and the directive that their family members maintain a constant vigil over their shared graves) in an effort to subvert the abjection of nineteenth-century autopsy and archival capture. They effectively performed their own version of an archival future perfect partial fugitivity.

The performance of P. T. Barnum's Joice Heth as an "ancient negress" was driven by an evaluation onstage of her deeply wrinkled and grooved skin, her diminutive stature, and the false claim that she was 161 years old and the nursemaid of President George Washington. In 1836, her autopsy was conducted before a paying audience. (The McKoys' and the Bunkers' deceased bodies were examined in private.) Audiences paying to view Heth's autopsy were in fact paying to see the final performance of a freak. Heth's grooved body stood as a fantastical placeholder for President Washington, continuing to enact the values of the future perfect archival memory in death.[12]

It is in the future perfect archival tense that we can trace and cautiously attempt to predict the intentions of both enslavers and enslaved. The future perfect is there in what enslavers and the enslaved choose to place in the archive after the fact and what they choose to withhold. Each contribution to the archive creates the history of their unseen futures (unseen to them, but perhaps experienced by us in the present tense). The moment of tension evinced in the physicians' decision to retain the "lungs and entrails" along with a grooved plaster cast of the Bunkers, despite the ambivalence of their families and that expressed in the letter written by C. W. and J. D. Bunker, creates a ripple of uncertainty in the historical narratives of enslaved and enfreaked lives. This ripple is present also in the McKoys' successful withdrawal from the archive after death by avoiding autopsy and in Heth's entry (despite her bodily disposal) into the archive after her public autopsy.

These grooved casts, woodcuts, speech acts, and pliable bodies are as much the stuff of history as the paper documents recording dates, city names, and tour routes. In each moment, there remains the tension built on a future perfect awareness by historical enactors that all of this enfreaked ephemera from early American popular culture one day "will have been" history. But how do we plot history with performance once it arrives?

Act I: A Trip to the Mütter Museum

As I enter the impressive front doors of Philadelphia's Mütter Museum, I am overwhelmed by the density and length of the line. Although I know that the Mütter's strange collection of human flesh is a popular attraction, I am still surprised that the crowd snakes its way around the ticket desk and through the lobby before spilling onto the sidewalk. The crowd, me included, is curious to inspect the museum's macabre repertoire. A sign attached to the front of the building notes that the College of Physicians of Philadelphia founded the Mütter in 1787, while another proclaims that this site is a national historic landmark. A plaque in the foyer lists a host of recognizable donors, including Andrew Carnegie, the Vanderbilt family, and the Campbell's Soup Company. I see another sign that prohibits photography throughout the collection.

I weave my way past a variety of human body parts before I finally arrive in front of the display I've come to see: a plaster cast of the torsos of Chang and Eng Bunker. The cast shows in vivid detail the ridges of their skin and the thick band that made their racialization as "Siamese twins" synonymous with their status as conjoined twins. Their autopsy was conducted by Harrison Allen, a professor of comparative anatomy and zoology at the University of Pennsylvania, assisted by William Pancoast of the same institution. Both men were members of the College of Physicians of Philadelphia when they conducted their autopsy on the twins in the Bunkers' North Carolina farmhouse on February 1, 1874, before taking their remains to Philadelphia for further examination. Their plaster cast and the remains of their livers make up their prominently featured display on the ground floor.

Duncan F. Cameron posits that there are two configurations of the museum, the temple and the forum.[13] The temple is a sanctified space where a rarified class protects and displays knowledge to a receptive but subordinate population. The forum, on the other hand, offers debate by welcoming different viewpoints. I'm surprised upon entering the Mütter Museum that it is more of a riotous forum than a sterilized temple. This seems counterintuitive considering the corporeality of the museum's collection of human remains. Before I arrived, I had assumed the subject matter of the Mütter would make people feel more cautious and removed from the displays rather than encouraged to actively engage. As I walk to the Bunkers' plaster cast, one of the museum's most popular attractions, I take a moment to observe the adjacent cases.

I see a jar with a small whitish blob identified as a tumor removed from the jaw of US President Grover Cleveland. Human organs are sliced lengthwise and displayed with the indifference of meat in a butcher's window, their subtle inner machinations unnaturally exposed to the eye. One toddler points to a fetus floating in a jar, calling it a "baby doll" before his mother quietly corrects him. There are two children's bodies carefully splayed out in a display, their gaping arms unconsciously mirroring the Vitruvian man's. People stop to stare, point, and guffaw. But perhaps most unsettling is the number of visitors on this summer day who appear apathetic to the humanity of the subjects on display, barely pausing to glance at the various body parts before moving on.

The spectacle of human remains in the Mütter Museum naturally raises the question of origins. More specifically, it raises the question of how the museum came to be in possession of such a vast array of human remains and body parts. Although the floor plan of the museum is typical in that it encourages the flow of traffic in specific directions in order to control the press of the crowd, the museum is also highly unusual in that we are not just looking passively at something like visual art or natural history. We are called to look at something much more visceral and fleshy: our own insides. As I stroll through the collection, I find that my typical museum posture (interested but not gaping, lingering but not holding up traffic) feels somehow wrong to me. I get the sense that I'm in an interstitial space somewhere between a museum and a graveyard, the latter of which calls for a certain amount of deference and respect that is different from the respect paid in the museum.

Founded originally as a teaching museum for physicians, the Mütter was rebranded as a public attraction during the late nineteenth and early twentieth centuries. Over time it developed a reputation as an offbeat tourist attraction, an identity that it still maintains today.[14] As a placard in the museum notes, "A body of parts: examples of the human body—healthy, diseased, abnormal, or injured—were collected by medical museums so that medical students, and now you, could learn about what it means to be human by looking at real examples." In doing so, the text suggests that to be human is to be a collection of anatomical parts.

Even more curious is that, though the Mütter advertises the Bunkers as one of its main attractions, it is not in possession of the full remains of Chang and Eng's spectacularized enfreaked bodies. Rather, its website boasts a "plaster death cast" of the twins from the waist up that was molded by physicians during their 1874 autopsy. The plaster exoskeleton of the Bunkers holds a materiality of what used to be and yet still is because it replicates the skin, grooves, and wounds of its human subjects even as it maintains an unsettling status as an object of spectatorship. The Bunkers' cast is an example of spectacularized otherness through enfreakment and performance; as an object, it continues to perform daily before crowds of museumgoers. And yet it also provides proof that the archival practice of accounting for enfreaked subjects, their bodies, and their labor remains as unstable as the Bunkers' physical bodies, which have now disintegrated, leaving behind incomplete archival traces as a simulacrum for flesh.

In her reading of Rosamond Purcell's photograph of the plaster death cast of the twins, *Chang and Eng* (1990), Cynthia Wu notes the naturalizing effects of the photographic lens and the reflective properties of the glass case surrounding the cast. She explores the directness of Eng's inanimate gaze, the illusion of multiplicity afforded by the plexiglass case, and the almost liveness of the cast itself. In her reading, the Bunkers "are keeping watch or holding vigil to remind museum staff and visitors that they, too, have an interest in these dialogues about medical knowledge."[15] Wu's reading of Purcell's photograph is curiously akin to my experience of viewing the cast in person. Standing in the center of the lower floor in a 360-degree glass case, the torsos have been lifted to meet the gaze of the average viewer. Like the rest of the glass in the Mütter's displays, the case surrounding the Bunker twins is highly reflective, so that as I look at the cast of the bodies, I'm also looking at a reflection of myself and the other spectators around me.

This strange doubling makes viewers hyperaware of their own role in viewing the almost fleshy cast of these famous twins. While the viewer looks upon it, the object appears to also be looking back at the viewer in a closed loop of gazing that is at once unnerving and also hypnotic. Just as the twins are themselves a double, and then doubled again in their reflection, viewers are also engaged in the act of doubling, looking at themselves looking at something else, consuming their own images as they consume the dual reflections of the Bunkers' bodies. This feedback loop of viewing creates in me a feeling of unearned kinship with the twins. It reminds me of the experience of going to an open-casket funeral. There is something unnerving about the fleshy stillness of a corpse that reminds the viewer of the person whose spirit used to inhabit this body. Every time I've encountered a corpse, there is a small and superstitious part of me that imagines that the body can be reanimated, even though I recognize the impossibility of this.

Up close to the cast, viewers can see the scars from the postmortem autopsy performed on the twins in 1874. They can see the thick band of skin that connects one body to the other. They can see the definition of the bones that make up the twins' rib cages, the small puckering of four nipples, and the tight, strained expressions on their faces. They can see the jutting vertebrae and shoulder blades, flexed as if the arms were retracting away from them. They can see individual strands of hair, the folds in the dual necks, the wrinkles next to two identical pairs of eyes, the strain of shoulders, and the tension in the muscles just visible under the thin protection of skin. This is an autopsy for the eyes, preserved forever in plaster and put on display.

Below this reflective case, in a large, squat jar of preserving fluid, are the Bunkers' conjoined livers. Presumably the contents of this jar are a part of the missing "entrails" mentioned in the first epigraph of this chapter that the Bunkers' sons instructed Allen to keep, "until further orders from the families." And yet the lungs are not on display. This directive still hangs in the balance, a future perfect note that the instructions of the twins' families about their bodily remains are contested and could change at any moment. The entrails and lungs could in theory be called home by their descendants, who today number in the hundreds instead of dozens. The anticipatory tense of the "further orders" that may or may not ever materialize holds these objects suspended both in the jar and in time. These livers also are the final vestiges of the twins' bodily tissue, preserved alongside their plaster cast, presumably to metaphorically show us the "heart" of their conjoined bodies, represented by the vital organs they shared.

Although the modern display of the Bunkers' flesh may seem an unusually long continuation of a nineteenth-century freak show autopsy performance, it is not unprecedented. When thinking about the role of medicine in the dehumanization of the racialized body in performance, one must consider the autopsy story of Sarah Baartman. After her death in 1815, a dissection was performed on her remains, which were displayed in Paris's Musée de l'Homme until 1974, along with a plaster cast. Her remains were repatriated in 2002. In her text *Monstrous Intimacies*, Christina Sharpe writes, "One can read the redemptive conferral of subjectivity to Baartman (and through her to coloured, black, KhoiSan people) itself as a retroactive and redeeming subjection analogous to objectification. That is, subjectification = objectification as Baartman once again is overwritten with multiple histories and used in the service of a number of national and political agendas that involve not the emergence of history but its repression."[16]

It is crucial to recognize that, as Sharpe points out, subjectification can in fact be equal in outcome to objectification in terms of the process of how audiences and researchers alike have engaged the remains of these performers' bodies. What are the possibilities and limitations of the subject and the object? How do these histories and remnants—cut up, preserved, and displayed for entertainment—represent both the end and beginning of a fluctuating spectrum?

When the Bunkers were taken away for autopsy in 1874, their families requested that all incisions made during the autopsy be made on the twins' backs so that they could be buried as intact as possible. Some accused the twins' widows of callously wanting to display their bodies in a countrywide tour, although these allegations were never substantiated.[17] Instead their bodies were cast, their organs removed, and a series of photographs taken. Then the bodies were returned.

The photographs of their remains, still in the archives of the University of North Carolina at Chapel Hill, show the twins' bodies covered in raised stitches down the front of their torsos, evidence of postmortem wounding that directly disobeyed the desires of their families. The grooves of these unsanctioned stitches are a reminder that despite their later status as enslavers, the Bunkers' ascension to the planter class was always precarious because of their enfreakment and the proven instability of nineteenth-century slavery. They still held a precarious status in the economic ecosystem of Southern slavery, at once able to ascend beyond the Black bodies they subjugated and yet still subjugated by the more firmly established white planter class who, in private, considered them "a couple of little, ugly, tawny fellows, in features resembling the African quite as much as the European."[18]

Although the Bunkers were briefly able to leave the freak show stage to retire as enslavers, the collapse of legal slavery left their large families in dire straits. Both before and after the Civil War, the Bunkers were displayed as symbolic figures of a national "American" identity onstage, even while they remained othered within the hierarchies of racialized freaks. In his monograph *The Lives of Chang and Eng: Siam's Twins in Nineteenth-Century America*, Joseph Andrew Orser writes of the twins' rise and fall. He notes, "The Siamese twins had long been used ironically as symbols of American nationalism," specifically citing a pamphlet published on the twins in the 1830s with a flying eagle carrying a banner that reads "E Pluribus Unum" and the phrase "United We Stand."[19] This tongue-in-cheek mockery serves as an unusual counterpoint to later documents that show the twins' features exaggerated in a caricature of Asian appearance and others still that present the twins as stereotypically Black or mixed race.

Images of the twins' united bodies that depict them as representative of the duality and division of the Civil War continued to circulate and haunt their act.[20] Meanwhile, the textured cast of their grooved stitches was displayed well into the twenty-first century; similarly, the plaster cast made of Baartman upon her death was displayed in France into the twentieth century. Presumably, both exhibits were established with the intention of remaining forever in the public eye. And yet Baartman's eventual repatriation in 2002 shows the archive's inability to account for the shifts in value, labor, and nation that were often marked on the bodies of nineteenth-century freak show performers, even after the end of legal slavery. The future perfect flux of the Bunkers' organs is explicitly tied to the question of US slavery and emancipation (the historical events that first enriched and then bankrupted them in conjunction with their onstage act), just as Baartman's repatriation is linked to the afterlife of legal slavery displayed on the nineteenth-century stage. And yet neither the Bunkers nor Baartman was ever legally enslaved, proving that the winding rhizomatic roots of unfreedom can take hold even in soil that is merely adjacent to slavery's gardens.

Act II: The McKoy Twins' Archival Fugitivity

The Bunkers' archival themes of national memory and US identity through the period of emancipation are echoed in the performances and autopsy narrative of Millie Christine McKoy. Standing around or under five feet tall and conjoined from the base of their spine down through their shared hip and singular vagina, anus, and reproductive organs, the McKoys were put on display soon after their birth. After having their labor as performers leased to various showmen in the United States by their first owner, the McKoys were involved in a highly publicized legal battle in Britain after they had been kidnapped and forced to appear in public. They were eventually returned to the man who would be their final owner, Joseph Smith. They spent almost the entirety of their sixty-one years as a musical singing duet, medical sideshow exhibition, and American freak show act.[21] Yet what continues to drive my research on the McKoys is not only the physical realities of their shared lived experiences but also their incredible performance versatility and strength. Reviewers describe an act that combined singing; dancing in lockstep, back-to-back and in time; and playing musical instruments (at least one photo features Christine holding a small custom-made guitar while her sister Millie delicately holds a piece of sheet music).[22] The reviews also refer to the invasive public examinations, conducted by doctors, displaying their conjoined vagina. This part of their performance was eliminated after emancipation changed their legal status from enslaved to free.[23]

The performance playbills for the McKoys, which form a sizable amount of their archived materials, are written in the common style of late nineteenth-century sideshow acts, with doctors' reports appearing alongside accounts of Christine and Millie's most popular performance trick: conducting two separate conversations about two very different topics at the same time in order to prove that they were not one person. Additionally, they performed songs in harmony (according to their autobiography, Christine was marketed as a soprano and Millie as a contralto), spoke to patrons in five languages, and often used the "refinements" of ladies holding a private concert to attract customers to their shows.[24] Nevertheless, this intellectual multiplicity was often undermined in the marketing of their spectacular freak bodies. One poster for W. C. Coup's Equescurriculum (a traveling animal act and freak show) even goes so far as to describe them as having "2 heads, 4 arms, 4 legs, 1 body."[25] The "1 body" more than hints where the essential female body and self is to be found.[26] Yet by refocusing their act after emancipation on their ability to speak separately, the McKoys skillfully engineered their own celebrity away from what gave fame to Chang and Eng: the juncture of their conjoined bodies.

In fact, there is evidence that the McKoys deployed both legal and extralegal means to ensure that their bodies, ostensibly their most valuable assets, would not remain in the public spotlight posthumously. This careful negotiation of the terms of legal personhood by Black performers in the period immediately following US emancipation is exemplified by the McKoys, whose lifespan straddled not only slavery and emancipation but also the critical decades of Reconstruction and the dawn of the twentieth century.[27] This time span marks not only the end of legal slavery but also a period of rapid change for Black subjects in the United States. Freedom was slow to emerge for these newly freed subjects, as extralegal racial terror became the order of the day. But these performers negotiated often hostile terrain that sought to dehumanize them by engaging in performances that challenged expectations about the Black and white racial binary. Even so, Black enfreaked performers were unwillingly caught in the archive's piercing gaze.

In 1871 William Pancoast published an article based on his examination of the McKoys in the Philadelphia-based journal *Photographic Review of Medicine and Surgery*.[28] It was a journal centered on its spectacular images of the enfreaked body, and Pancoast's article on the McKoys was no exception. Photographs of fatty tumors and twisted joints grace the pages next to detailed reports of medical examinations and their often-dubious conclusions. In fact, it is the allure of the photographs that seems to mark this journal as unique, illustrating firsthand for its viewers the wonder of unmitigated access to the bodies of the patients featured within its folds and building on an already budding public interest in autopsy that Michael Sappol traces in his monograph *A Traffic of Dead Bodies*.[29] Pancoast simply titled his article "The Carolina Twins," referring to the twins' most commonly used stage name. While the titles of other reports in the journal name the ailments themselves, ranging from "horny tumor" to "malformation of fingers and toes" to "inherited syphilis," in Pancoast's article the twins themselves—their existence, their bodies, and their privacy—are offered up as medical maladies.

Even considering the heavily documented intervention of medical men in their early lives, when the twins were often put on display and examined nude for eager audiences, Pancoast's report still represents an anomaly. The first medical man to examine the twins' genitals after age fourteen, Pancoast, in his 1871 report—when the twins were twenty years old—claimed a twisted medical "victory." In "Examining Millie and Christine McKoy: Where Enslavement and Enfreakment Meet," Ellen Samuels writes of the twins' six-year refusal to be seen nude,

> This decision provoked strong reactions from doctors in the United States, Britain, and France. Medical reports for the next six years expressed reactions ranging from chagrin to rage that the twins "would not allow me to see them naked, nor place my hands under their clothes to examine the pelvis" (Lee quoted in Martell 2000, 113), that they would not permit examination of "the genito-urinary organs" (Fisher 1868), that they would not consent "to a vaginal examination" (Jackson 1869, 415), and that "despite all our insistence, it was impossible for us to observe the most secret parts of the body" (Tardieu 1874, 37).[30]

Pancoast himself expressed frustration at what he perceived as the twins' persistent modesty. Desperate to capture what so many before him had failed to, he proceeded to take the photograph that is featured on the first page of his article in the *Photographic Review of Medicine and Surgery*. Of the photo he writes,

> After great persuasion and with the kind assistance of my friend Dr. F.F. Maury (owing to the modesty of the twins and the natural reluctance of Mrs. Smith),[31] the accompanying photograph of them was taken. They clung to their raiment closely, as may be seen, and it was only by earnest entreaty that they were willing to compromise by retaining the drapery as photographed. The expression of their countenances shows their displeasure, as their features ordinarily express great amiability of character.[32]

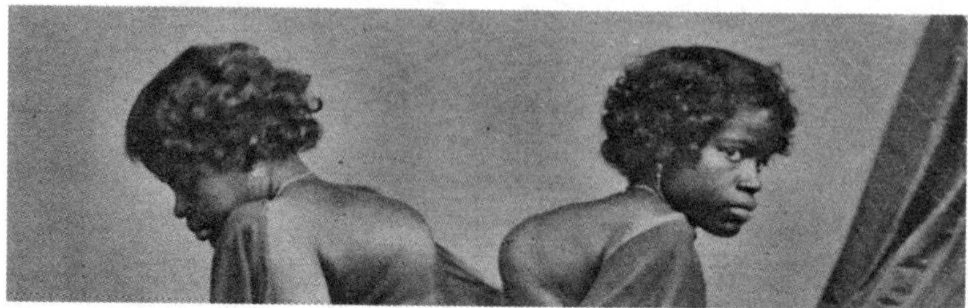

Figure 3.3: Partial photo from William Pancoast's 1871 report "The Carolina Twins." Printed in the *Photographic Review of Medicine and Surgery*, vol. 1.

The coercion by Pancoast and his associate Maury is evident in this passage as they work against the twins' wishes and even the wishes of their final enslaver, Mary Smith. We can only wonder what the "great persuasion" and "kind assistance" of Maury and Pancoast entailed, but perhaps in studying the twins' expressions, we can gain greater insight into the transgression represented by the photograph. Here I mirror Samuels's gesture of cropping the photo, showing only the McKoys' expressions and not their full bodies, as the picture was taken under duress. Through reading this photograph, we can begin to make educated guesses about the twins' reaction to having their photo taken in a state of undress after years of fiercely fighting for and protecting the privacy of their enfreaked bodies.

While Samuels does an excellent reading of Millie's fiercely defiant expression, her eyes glaring sideways into the camera clearly, directly, and unafraid, I would like to turn now to Christine. By all accounts she was the shier and more reserved of the two sisters, and her eyes are downcast, turned away from the unwanted invasion of the photographer's lens, keeping her counsel, emotions, and interiority separate from those of her sister. It is this Janus-like performance, the looking away while also looking back, the shy and the defiant, the reserved and the brash, the unafraid and the timid, that encapsulates what researchers have found so fascinating about the McKoy twins' archive. How do we begin to tell the extraordinary story of these women, who fought so hard to maintain their bodily integrity and privacy, but whose exceptional bodies and talents could not escape the focus of the archival spotlight? We see their two heads here, each defying in the way that she sees fit as they both protect their one shared singular body.

Millie and Christine's Janus-like performance mirrors Gordon's expression in the abolitionist photo displaying his keloid scars that Weems used in her work. All three subjects exercise the sideways glance of the enslaved. At once protective and subversive, this sideways glance (a phrase I borrow from twentieth-century anthropology) allows the enslaved and enfreaked subject to engage with the viewer and the camera while also maintaining a performative gesture of submission that makes the photographer feel unthreatened even as he is being observed. This practice is a type of resistance enacted by the enslaved when in circumstances beyond their consent or control. They have eyes on us, just as we hope to control the terms of our engagement with their subjugation. The enslaved person's sideways glance is a performance of resistance in the face of unimaginable terror. Under the alias assigned to him, Gordon became "Whipped Peter," his medical condition becoming synonymous with his identity to *Harper's* readers, just as Pancoast's phrase "the Carolina Twins" created a collapsed identity for the McKoys.

However, Pancoast's report contains another, yet more invasive image. Within the journal's pages, we see a picture of a woodcut of the McKoy twins' most famous attraction: their conjoined genitals. I will not reproduce the woodcut here, as it seems to have been made without their knowledge or consent and the same technique of cropping that I deployed for the previous photograph of the twins would be ineffective in minimizing the harm of the image. Pancoast describes using a coercive process to construct the woodcut, similar to the process he used to take the photograph: "When called to examine the so-called abscess, I caused them to lie down upon the bed. In lying upon their backs, Chrissie was upon my right and Millie on my left, both limbs on each side drawn up. They lifted up the inside limbs as far as they could, but I was obliged to push them gently up still farther. I found only one vulva, deeply placed between the four limbs. The above wood-cut, drawn by the artist, Mr. Faber, from my description, represents the appearance they presented."[33] Again, we see Pancoast calling on an unseen but named male assistant, this time an artist named Faber, to document and spectacularize the twins' singular body. Yet here I will take a page from Samuels's reading of the report, in which she theorizes that "an 1871 medical article by Dr. William H. Pancoast, despite being both 'demeaning and dehumanizing' (Frost 2009, 23), may actually offer a richer and more reliable source for tracing the sisters' assertion of identity and resistance than the purported auto-biography found in the *History*."[34]

Rather than viewing the 1871 woodcut as the triumph Pancoast touted, it serves as another important instance of defiance on the part of the McKoys. Here we see a wavering in Pancoast's attempted panoptic gaze: He is forced instead to rely on his description from memory and the artistic skill of Faber to construct a crude woodcut of the subjects of his invasive curiosity. In fact, the woodcut can be read as a failure on the part of Pancoast to carry out his plan of complete and unmitigated access to the twins' spectacularized bodies. This simple act of refusal is represented in the crudeness of the woodblock print itself, a form comprising ink, contrast, and relief to create images from a carved block of wood. As Pancoast was forced to work from a recollection rather than utilizing the camera's photographic precision, the woodcut can be read as the product of McKoys' assertion of privacy and autonomy.

The legal and extralegal means the McKoys deployed to avoid autopsies like those inflicted on the Bunkers and Baartman effectively continued this resistance through the projection of the future perfect archival tense. Several reporters charged with composing the McKoys' obituaries repeated the same fact: The McKoys had an almost deathly fear of postmortem autopsy. This fear is noted in a 1925 article about their lives, which states,

> They had a horror of an autopsy or of their body being dissected, and asked that it be cremated. This not being practical, and the idea being new to the colored people of that vicinity, the relatives instead carefully guarded the grave for many weeks. They might have sold the body for, to them, a fabulous price, but be it said to their credit that no thought of such desecration entered their simple, faithful hearts. There are three sisters and one brother still surviving. They labor and live in frugality on their small farms and on anniversaries place simple home-made wreaths on the grave of this twin sister.[35]

From their appearance on the world stage as young children, the twins were constantly in the public eye. Their terms of personhood were indelibly linked to their consumption as public figures, a reality that they were certainly aware of. As a result, the twins were noted to be fearful of being made into a medical exhibition postmortem. In *Millie-Christine: Fearfully and Wonderfully Made*, Joanne Martell writes of the twins' fears of death and burial,

> The twins had wanted to be cremated. They'd been horrified when Dr. Pancoast shipped the Siamese Twins to Philadelphia for autopsy. Even after family members swore they would never let that happen, the sisters had cause for worry. As Millie grew sicker, rumors circulated that graverobbers were scheming to dig up the twins for a sideshow exhibit. When he learned that the sisters were fretting, Joe Smith promised he would hire a guard to stand watch day and night. . . . Joe's watchman and Millie-Christine's family kept an eye on the grave for nine long months. It lay peaceful and undisturbed.[36]

Despite the bucolic scene of eternal Christian rest that Martell paints here, she goes on to recount a later disturbing disregard of the twins' final wishes. As she aptly phrases it, "Millie-Christine played one last public engagement." In 1969, at the request of the Columbus County Historical Society and the North Carolina Department of Archives and History, their bodies were exhumed and their remains were taken out of their ornate custom-built double coffin and placed in a "one-by-three-foot pine box," then moved to a more prominent location of the cemetery for display.[37]

The day Fred McKoy, a direct descendant of one of the twins' siblings, approved this invasive exhumation, he effectively reopened their old performance, one that by all accounts they hoped to lay to rest after their retirement back home to North Carolina in their later years. The fact that a full fifty-seven years after they were buried, what remained of their bodies (three rings, a piece of spinal cord, a scattering of bones, and swatches of the dress they were buried in) was dug up in front of a public audience confirms their original fears.[38] And yet this moment of bodily invasion does not stand for the totality of the twins' experiences as African American freak celebrities. Even in death, the twins' physical selves took center stage.

By circulating the story of the twins' fear of being autopsied in local newspapers, a story that their siblings restated after Millie succumbed to the complications of tuberculosis and Christine was euthanized, the McKoy family as a whole showed their legal savvy, deploying the same methods of legal ownership that plagued the system of enslavement into which they were all born. Yet their story is not entirely redemptive, nor should we, as Saidiya Hartman warns in "Venus in Two Acts," romanticize what was ultimately archival violence.[39]

Instead, I look to the twins' final remains as an example of their attempts to preempt the archival future perfect through an expert fugitivity. By the time the twins were reinterred in 1969, their bodies were so badly decomposed no autopsy could be performed. Instead, they were placed inside a smaller box before being reburied. So while they were able to subvert to a certain degree the archival future perfect of an autopsy performance through resistance and bodily decay, they were still reintroduced to the public eye in 1969 through a historical society dedicated to making monuments of the past when they were reburied closer to the road with a historical marker. In some ways their archival fugitivity temporarily ensured that in death they would be liberated from the confines of their conjoined bodies and remain in relative obscurity. Yet the instability of the archival future perfect was still enacted on their bodies once they were reinterred. So while the plaster casts of Baartman and the Bunkers share a common groove with the woodcut of the McKoys, the woodcut, alongside the McKoys' physical disintegration, must also be viewed as enacting an archival escape, however fleeting.

Act III: The Evaluation of Joice Heth's Ancient Skin

The enfreaked bodies of the McKoys and the Bunkers served as symbols of the rupture of legal slavery signaled by US emancipation in 1863 and the close of the Civil War in 1865. Conversely, P. T. Barnum performer Joice Heth's narrative begins and ends in captivity, her body and performances firmly bound by the terms of a contractual unfreedom. By the time she had reached old age, she was owned by the then relatively unknown Barnum, who began displaying her deeply wrinkled and aged body in 1835, after she had passed through the hands of at least two previous sideshow proprietors. When she died one year later in 1836, the value of her body sharply skyrocketed, before quickly plummeting again. The price of tickets to see her public autopsy, conducted by David L. Rogers, was twice the normal rate for her display while alive. In life, viewers could see her at Niblo's Garden in downtown New York.

In "Mammy-Memory: Staging Joice Heth, or the Curious Phenomenon of the 'Ancient Negress,'" Uri McMillan notes that the all-white audience at this infamous "pleasure garden" paid an additional 25 cents (12.5 cents for children) for the privilege of viewing Heth's act. After her death, the price doubled: When Barnum staged her public autopsy, he charged 50 cents per customer.[40] In death, Heth became an object of performance, her value as a performer transferring directly to her corpse. Here I am drawing on McMillan's definition of "performing objecthood": "*Performing objecthood* . . . is a process that enables black women to transform themselves into art objects. Performing objecthood is a world making, one that envisions the capacity for agency in, paradoxically, becoming and performing as an object."[41]

When Rogers completed his public examination of Heth, he proclaimed to a crowd of fifteen hundred gathered in the City Saloon, New York City, that she could in fact be no older than eighty. This debunking effectively severed Heth's ties to George Washington as well as rendering the affective "mammy-memory" she represented moot.[42] Her perceived value as a subject of archival interest shifted. While alive, her grooved and wrinkled skin, alongside her connection to the American national memory through Washington, rendered her enslavement and enfreakment absolute. But once autopsy's incisions severed the mythos of both her age and her connection to Washington, her body was not deemed worthy of enshrinement in the archive like the Bunkers' and Baartman's. If the truth about her age had been known while she lived, her value as a freak show performer would have been sharply lower.

As McMillan notes, "In life and death, as a coerced performer and an inanimate object, Heth's disfigured body was prodded, laughed at, displayed, discredited, dissected, and ultimately disposed of."[43] Heth was "ultimately disposed of" by those who stood to profit heavily from the fiction of both her public persona and her severely disfigured body. It is this careful staging of the narrative fiction made real by her wrinkled skin that was at the heart of Heth's act, rendering her valuable to those who exploited her unpaid labor. But this could continue only if Heth's true origins, which apparently had nothing to do with George Washington, remained hidden. This archival instability, combined with the disintegration of her body, marks the future perfect condition of Heth's archives and autopsy.

Because there remains a level of uncertainty surrounding Heth's origins, the disproven story of her life as Washington's "mammy" remains as a placeholder for her narrative. The future perfect for Heth lies in the fact that as of this moment, the danger of conferring a retroactive subjectivity to an enfreaked historical figure persists. Although physicians ultimately determined that Barnum's story about Heth could not be true, multiple aspects of Heth's tale mirror the future perfect instability. More than merely an antecedent to more well-known and widely studied performers such as the Bunkers and the McKoys, Heth should not be cast merely as a foremother. This would reinstate her narrative as a historical antecedent, rather than as an enfreaked performer in her own right. The autopsies of performers like Heth and Baartman, which preceded US emancipation (and in Baartman's case the abolition of British slavery in 1833), show that enfreaked bodies rendered abject revealed much about national consciousness. And because we are still reckoning with the future perfect tense and the relationship of the archives of slavery to the formation of nation, we must continue to wrestle with these enfreaked remains.

In the cropped picture of the McKoys from Pancoast's 1871 article, the split nature of the McKoys' stares represents a Janus-like performance. Janus is known for his association with the dual nature of time, both a beginning and an end. The expressions on the faces of the McKoys, alongside the grooves of the Bunkers' stitches, Baartman's plaster cast, and Heth's ancient skin, show the dual nature of the future perfect archival tense in enfreaked performance: The future perfect looks both ahead and behind to predict *what will have been*. At once turning away from and looking back toward, these nineteenth-century freak shows, autopsies, and medical interventions continue to bear the weight of an unknown historical future. It is a future that, undoubtedly, we will continue to struggle with in order to find ways to articulate the unsettled bones of these archives. We are still self-consciously acting on how to tell the stories of unfree labor, racial memory, and enfreakment. Even as the stories begin to form a somewhat solid picture or begin to feel firmly cast, they continue to shift as the narratives of slavery, enfreakment, and performance remain in a future perfect state of fluidity. We are caught in the gazes of enslaved performers, just as they are caught in the creases of our collective consciousness.

4

Aural Fugitivity in *Zong!*, *Olio*, and *Curio*

I 'member w'en I's jes' a li'l gal a-hearin' bells in d' night. D' ol' folks say dat some 'r' d' run-a-way niggers from uder plantation. Dey put bells on d' slaves, wel' [weld] dem on so dey kaint gittum off 'n' dey kin hear dem iffen dey git 'way in d' woods.

[I remember when I was just a lil gal hearing bells in the night. The old folks say that some are the run-a-way niggers from other plantations. They put bells on the slaves, weld them on so they can't get them off and they can hear them if they get away in the woods.]

—Amy Domino, former Alabama enslaved laborer, quoted in Shane White and Graham J. White, *The Sounds of Slavery*

How do voice and its antithesis, silence, shape the stories we are told? It is telling whose voice and silence are allowed to tell the stories of those who have been lost in the annals of the archive. By *silence* here, I mean the purposeful absence or withholding of sound and articulation.

In the epigraph of this chapter, a former enslaved laborer from Alabama named Amy Domino recounts the soundscape of repeated enslaved fugitivity. That soundscape is characterized by bells piercing the air as enslaved Black people who had previously attempted to self-emancipate ran to freedom once again. For Domino, the sound of the bells signaled both the attempt at and the failure of freedom, possibilities welded shut like the devices clanging around the ankles of the enslaved. This sound of coupled truncated fugitivity and captivity became one of the major catalysts for my 2018 performance piece and 2023 short film, both titled *Curio*. In them I ask, What are the sounds of slavery onstage, and how does the excessive pathologizing and medicalization of the

Black fugitive or free body contribute to these soundscapes? Although the bells remembered by Domino were heard on the terrifying landscape of the cruel plantation, my interest in the bell in both iterations of *Curio* stemmed from my own inquiries into the lives and nineteenth-century performances of enfreaked, enslaved performers, most especially Millie Christine McKoy.[1]

The McKoys' performances before emancipation consisted of semi-public medical examinations and publicity materials that centered on the nature of their attachment, which ran from their hips through their shared genitals. This included doctors' notes and claims of authenticity that were printed in the backs of their promotional programs and still exist in the archive today. In contrast, their performance strategies both under slavery and after legal freedom consisted of ways to center their vocality, speech acts, and musical abilities in order to decenter the previous exploitative focus on the medicalization of their physical bodies. Yet there is evidence in the archive that even under the binds of legal slavery, the McKoys and their family spent a good portion of the twins' childhood embroiled in both public custody and kidnapping claims, as well as private extrajudicial attempts to secure their earnings from their performance labor after emancipation, which I detailed in chapter 1. Because this evidence of complex fugitivity also relates to the performance strategies the McKoys adopted after slavery that centered mental prowess, polyglot skills, and song over their former physical exhibitions, I am terming this performance technique *aural fugitivity*.

Through aural fugitivity, the Black enslaved performer is able to gain conditional freedom from an all-encompassing archival capture by using sound acts that defy accurate archival recording. This chapter will couple an analysis of the McKoys' aural fugitivity with an excavation of three texts (M. NourbeSe Philip's poetry collection *Zong!*, Tyehimba Jess's poetry collection *Olio*, and my piece *Curio*) in order to answer the opening questions about voicing and silence in the archival remnants of the enslaved while also looking at ways that these archives have been transformed and interpreted for modern audiences through performance. The McKoys' aural fugitivity took the form of lyrics that exist in the archive without music (which served as the basis for *Curio*), as well as their improvisational speech acts that so delighted and astonished audiences that they apparently failed to be recorded. Through the use of improvisational and ephemeral speech and sound acts, the McKoys were able to maintain a fugitivity rooted in their uniquely untraceable and hard-to-define sound. Similarly, both Philip's and Jess's poetry utilizes complex negotiations with sound and silence to offer potentially liberatory avenues for commemorating those whose lives were overwritten or dictated by the bounds of slavery. Both the poetry and the McKoys' articulations and music served as the catalyst for my own artistic and scholarly exploration of the sounds of slavery onstage, leading me to contemplate the best ways to stage nineteenth-century aural fugitivity for a twenty-first-century audience.

To this end, *Curio* never allows the audience to become completely lost in the pure pleasure of visual observation and performance of the enfreaked body that defined the McKoys' act before emancipation. Rather, every aspect of the staging and script is designed to highlight the qualities of aural fugitivity that the McKoys took part in onstage. Since the McKoys were enslaved until emancipation but constantly either passively (as children) or actively (as newly freed young women) engaged in an ongoing struggle for freedom, I looked for ways to stage the aural fugitivity they perfected under slavery and continued to refine even after legal freedom. I realized early in the writing process that merely faithfully restaging the McKoys' shows would not illuminate the strategies of aural fugitivity that dictated the terms of their pre- and postemancipation performances. All the archival evidence that remains of their performance strategies exists in incomplete fragments: reviewers' praise of their singing voices, reports of them speaking to two people at once to prove they weren't one person, claims that Millie was an alto and Christine a soprano, evidence that they always used the singular first-person pronoun when referring to themselves, and lyric sheets that survive in their coauthored (auto)biographies sans music, with the indication that some of the songs were written expressly for them and instructions that audiences should sing along. As previously mentioned, their surviving sister Clara Yeoman always referred to Millie Christine as a single person, mirroring their preferred form of address in life.[2] It was out of these fragments of information that I began to interrogate how I could create a soundscape that encompassed both the complexity of the McKoys' performed world and also the social and legal conditions of aural fugitivity that were evident in their biographical information. Building on Daphne

Brooks's "spectacular opacity" and Uri McMillan's "sonic of dissent," the theory of aural fugitivity looks to how hard-to-record and hard-to-define sound acts that refuse all-encompassing archival capture are antithetical to the attempted panoptic gaze of slavery's meticulous recordkeeping and exist in the archive as an act of refusal by enslaved or otherwise oppressed performers.[3] Therefore, the fragmentary nature of the McKoys' performance archive should be honored and spotlighted in any attempts to re-create or restage it for contemporary audiences.

But aural fugitivity as both a performance strategy and a method of intracommunal secret keeping and survival is not limited to the archives of the McKoys and my contemporary reimagining of their works. Alongside the work of the McKoys and my own piece *Curio*, I also investigate the poetics of Tyehimba Jess in his 2016 Pulitzer Prize–winning collection *Olio* and M. NourbeSe Philip's acclaimed 2008 collection *Zong! Olio* tells the story of the generation of African American performing artists that arrived on the cultural scene in the late nineteenth and early twentieth centuries (with the collection including notable poems about the lives of the McKoy twins and Blind Tom Wiggins). In it, Jess uses experiments with form (namely, pages that unfurl like programs and sheet music, graphic design, and a form he's dubbed "syncopated sonnets") in order to narrate the performance legacies of enfreaked and formerly enslaved artists. *Zong!*, on the other hand, recounts a much grislier and far less celebratory tale of the 130 enslaved Africans who were callously thrown overboard from the eponymous slave ship *Zong* in 1781. Their murders became the basis of the 1783 case *Gregson v. Gilbert*, when insurers refused to pay for the "loss" of human property. Philip excerpts her collection directly from the transcripts of the trial, creating a type of erasure poem and reimagining of what the archival record leaves unexplored.

Although the choice of these three pieces may appear incongruent at first glance considering their differing subject matter, time periods, and themes, I've brought them all into conversation here because *Olio* and *Zong!* serve as an inspirational basis for *Curio* both thematically (in the case of *Olio*) and methodologically (in the case of *Zong!*). The McKoys, Blind Tom, and other performers like them are featured in *Olio*, and incorporating music into *Curio* factored heavily into my thinking as I devised my own musical reanimation of the McKoys' archives. In a different vein, M. NourbeSe Philip's decision to repurpose and directly lift text from the archival remains of the *Zong* legal case influenced my decision to use verbatim quotes from the McKoys' archives as dialogue in both the stage and film versions of *Curio*. This methodology allowed me to play with the official record while also confronting the absences and inconsistencies of the archives surrounding the McKoys' lives and performances. Both *Zong!* and *Olio* provide a conceptual underpinning for ways to approach the legacies of slavery in the twenty-first century through verse and performance. The mixed temporality of these sources mirrors the future perfect in practice because each text is a modern interpretation of a past-tense fragility, a realization of a future-perfect unfolding in the twenty-first century. Therefore, I take up an analysis of both *Zong!* and *Olio* here in order to evaluate the ways that aural fugitivity runs through the archives of the McKoys and the world of *Curio*.

Each collection invites the reader to think of the complex roles that sound and silence play in the history of enslaved labor. Both Jess's and Philip's poetics embody the type of deliberate withholding and aural obfuscation that is present in the sonic worlds of the enslaved. Drawing on incomplete and sometimes deliberately absent archives, each poet utilizes strategies that manipulate sound and silence in equal measure. Outside of the ways that these poems perform on the page, each poet engages in a more conventional live performance practice with these works that draws them into conversation with enfreaked and enslaved performance histories. Jess, for example, recorded *Olio Live* for Audible Books and is in development for a concert performance of *Olio*'s poems on Millie Christine in collaboration with composer Janice Lowe.[4] And Philip, who is also a skilled performance artist, often brings *Zong!* to audiences around the world as a performer, having performed the piece over sixty times.[5]

Each of the three central texts discussed in this chapter offers a performative reimagining of the archival remains of slavery. My hope here is to put my own creative inquiries as they relate to this book alongside the works of Jess and Philip, which were instrumental in my thinking as I developed my piece, first for the stage in 2018 and later as a short film in 2023. Each work seems to demand the same question of its audience: Whose voice and silence shape the stories of slavery? To that end, every one of these three works begins with a provocation and an invitation to the reader or audience. I open *Curio* (both the stage production and the film) with a bit of marginalia from an 1885 photo of the McKoys that has become central to my writing practice as I've developed both this book and the companion performance pieces: "I conversed with this/these person-s and found her quick and of pleasant manner. Both at times have identical dreams."[6] I found this line provocative for a variety of reasons. First, it focused on the McKoys' mental prowess, abilities, and connection over the purely physical reports that are more common in their archives. Second, it opened me up to the possibility of *Curio* being a site of dream space and imagination, rather than a faithful retelling of the McKoys' biographies and (auto)biographies, which often prove to be unreliable. And lastly, it invites the audience to enter and imagine this dreamscape alongside me as a writer and director.

To this end, I eschewed a more faithful restaging of the McKoys' performances and evidence in the archive that indicated more conventional approaches in favor of a "critical fabulation" that was in service of the methods they employed during their lives.[7] Namely, I chose to stage a historical and theoretical intervention by replacing the instruments there is evidence they played in life (e.g., the piano and the guitar) with a set of handbells when I had their lyric sheets set to music. I was drawn to the bells for a variety of reasons. First, their use in torture devices like the ones described in the epigraph meant that they were already a part of the accounting and property loss prevention methods well documented in slavery. These torture devices, as essential to the mechanisms of slavery as the plantation owner's ledger and the whip, had an accompanying auditory function different from other methods of control: to make fugitivity heard when it could not be seen. Second, combining a fictional element like the bells with a historical fact like the lyric sheets allowed for a bridge between a faithful restaging and a complete reimagining. It allowed me to take what I could glean about the McKoys' aural performances and to fill the voids where I could not know (namely, the sound of the music that would have accompanied them in real life). And lastly, because the bells were played onstage in *Curio*, and later transformed into a bell rack worn by the actresses playing the McKoys, they never allowed our audiences to become completely comfortable in the visual realities of the enfreaked and enslaved Black body onstage. The bells decentered physical awareness in favor of repurposed sound.

Figure 4.1: The bell rack. Courtesy of the WPA Slave Narratives online archive.

In collaboration with undergraduate performers at the University of Pennsylvania (Duval Courteau, Aria Proctor, Breyasia Scott, and Hannah Spear, along with student composer Elias Kotsis), scenic designer Sara Outing, and our director Dr. Rosemary Malague, I staged *Curio* first at the University of Pennsylvania in April 2018 and again that same year in August at the Edinburgh Festival Fringe. The result was a process born of mutual interrogation and creative discovery that helped to reimagine the worlds of enslaved and enfreaked performance around aural fugitivity. After live theater came to a sudden halt in 2020 as a result of the COVID-19 pandemic, I looked for new ways to continue developing this piece with a new creative team (namely, Brian Inocencio,

Figure 4.2: Cover of the handbill for the 2018 stage production of *Curio*. Courtesy of the University of Pennsylvania Theatre Arts Department.

Figure 4.3: *Curio*, 2023. Image courtesy of the author.

our cinematographer; Autumn Maria Reed, our composer; and my executive producers Hilary Giorgi and Andrew Kornhaber). After revisiting and simplifying the story of the original piece, I was able to lean more heavily into the elements of the story that I felt were most successful in the original stage version, specifically the handbell music and the dialogue excerpted directly from the archives. This chapter interweaves analysis of *Curio* alongside biographical and (auto)biographical archival remains of the McKoys to excavate the ways they created their uniquely fugitive sound.

Similar to the dreamscape that opens *Curio*, the opening of *Olio* positions the reader as a participant in the project of freedom when Jess notes immediately at the end of the section that he's titled "Introduction or Cast or Owners of This Olio,"

> Fix your eyes on the flex of these first-generation-freed voices:
> They coalesce in counterpoint, name nemeses, summon tongue
> to wit-ness.
> Weave your own chosen way between these voices. . . . [8]

Jess's invitation to "fix your eyes on the flex of these first-generation-freed voices" raises the question of what new freedom should and could sound like. How does such a person, living on the cusp of legal unfreedom and emancipation, sound to a modern audience? The newness and complexity of freedom for the performers, like the McKoys, who are discussed in Jess's collection ring out from the page in both his interrogations of form and his experimentation with language as a stand-in for music. In *Zong!*, Philip notes both on the cover of the text and in an author's note that the work within the collection was dictated or summoned to her through ancestral means, writing on the cover, "As told to the author by Setaey Adamu Boateng." Philip explains that "Setaey Adamu Boateng is the voice of the ancestors revealing the submerged voices of all who were on board the Zong."[9] Rather than voices ringing out on the arrival of freedom, Philip is grappling with voices silenced and lost to the murderous trajectories of violence inherent to the project of slavery. In these parallel beginnings, we see the traces of the voices of those forgotten or truncated by the archival records, made at once hypervisible through the mandates of slavery while also being rendered anonymous by those same logics. Each of these three openings demands that the audience (whether it is a live performance or a reading of the text) grapple with the question of voice under slavery. There is also significance in the fact that both Jess and Philip pay special attention to the voice as an instrument that both dictates and is to be listened to. What does it mean for Philip to say the world of *Zong!* was spoken to her by an ancestral voice or guide? What is the resonance of "first-generation-freed" voices? And in the case of *Curio*, how does a dreamscape sound? In each case the voice or interiority of the enslaved subject is the collective starting point of the sonic worlds and inquiries present in each text.

The centrality of the voice and the enslaved or free Black voice has been studied extensively by scholars such as Fred Moten, Roland Barthes, Masi Asare, Nina Sun Eidsheim, and Paige McGinley.[10] Voice and voicing have proved integral to Black performance traditions precisely because they allow performers who have been otherwise marginalized an avenue to express virtuosity, protest, pain, joy, and a host of other complex emotions. Yet I argue that the antithesis of voice (pointed silence) serves an equally pivotal role in the history of Black performance and protest. Silence, when chosen and not imposed, can send a message that is equally as powerful as the cry or scream of enslaved Blackness that was first noted by Frederick Douglass with his aunt Hester's scream and later theorized by scholars like Moten and Saidiya Hartman.[11] I argue that silence is one of the many sounds of slavery that make up the aural landscape of the plantation and also enslaved performance. In this chapter I will analyze the centrality of silence in both the performances and commemoration of enslaved life on- and offstage. In doing so I will illuminate the crucial role aural fugitivity plays in our understanding of enslaved autonomy and the critical questions facing contemporary artists who wish to animate these archival records.

Although this chapter deals with more modern source materials than the previous three, it is still intimately tied to the questions of enfreakment and slavery that are present throughout the book. In part, it is about reimagining the performance archives of the eighteenth and nineteenth centuries for modern audiences. In part it is an examination of the politics of refusal that these performers (and in turn the researchers and artists who engage with these stories) were participating in at the time of their peak popularity. But the largest factor that drives the temporal shift in this chapter is the previously mentioned theorizations of the future perfect. I argue that these poems, performances, and these three creative works are a realization of the future perfect present in the performance archives they explore. They are, in fact, the realization of the future-perfect impulse that drove the creation of these archives many years ago. When performers like Blind Tom and the McKoys (featured in *Olio* and *Curio*) were entered into the archival record both willingly and unwillingly, they left behind traces of resistance and performance ingenuity that are mirrored in the ways they are ultimately remembered in today's historical records. Even the *Zong* case had a sense of the future perfect in that it was deemed notable both in its own time and for generations of future scholars who would study it as an example of slavery's cruelest machinations. The opposite of the future perfect would be a sort of historical amnesia that leaves in its wake a void of understanding and obscurity. But if *Olio*, *Zong!*, and *Curio* stand as a testament to anything, it is that the records and archives of slavery were and still are deeply invested in the futurity of that project and memorialization was and remains a big part of that ambition. The future perfect is also a slippery tense, since one can assume but usually never accurately predict the future. For example, it may have been beyond the ability of white enslavers who entered these Black enslaved subjects into the historical record to imagine true freedom for these highly profitable enfreaked Black subjects. And yet, legal freedom did arrive, with all of its attendant failures and complications. So the leap forward here is less of a leap and more of a gesture back to the future perfect of historical production.

Part One: Aural Fugitivity Emerges

After the McKoy twins began to deny or severely limit doctors' publicized private access to their conjoined bodies (most notably their conjoined genitalia, which served as a point of continued examination and fascination for audiences and "medical men"), they began to engage in performance strategies that centered speech acts and sound over physicality. By withholding access to their bodies postemancipation, the twins set in motion a new way that they would be represented. The Smiths (their final owners) had the women taught multiple languages (in some cases it is reported as four, in others five or seven), singing, dancing, how to read, and how to play musical instruments.[12] Their act began to comprise a combination of these activities, with the medical reports and "verifications" limited to the texts of their promotional print programs. Instead, they focused on performing the skills they learned in their traditional ladies' education. Reports of Millie and Christine speaking to two different people on two different subjects, often in two different languages, proliferate the archive as their new main attraction postemancipation, replacing medical exams altogether. And suddenly in the archive, there is song where there once were only silent observations, a marked shift upward from the lower half of the twins' bodies to their faces that also moves us from visual material to aural material.

By identifying and amplifying the properties of music and sound in their archives, *Curio* first and foremost re-created a sense of their performance artistry and labor as it exists in the archive. It also spoke beyond the contradictory and challenging speech present in their (auto) biographies to get to the heart of the conditions under which they performed as formerly enslaved and later free women. Because the McKoys' lyric sheets were meant to be sung and not read, there was something deeply dissatisfying to me in simply reading the work as written text without hearing them. Thus, I embarked on a journey to find the properties of the work and animate them in ways that foregrounded theatrical research and praxis in equal measure. Nineteenth-century enslaved performers like the McKoys, in life and onstage, were at once highly valued as spectacles (someone to be gaped and gazed at) while still being deemed abjectly valueless through the systems of traditional enslaved labor that considered them unfit for "real work" because they couldn't bear children or enrich the estate through traditional manual or domestic labor. This is mirrored in the archive after death, where we still focus on the spectacle of these performers because we assume they are "unfit for bondage" (borrowing here from Dea Hadley Boster).[13] But it is precisely the impulses of curiosity and pleasure that continue to drive artists, scholars, and audiences to these works. The conditions of bondage under which they were created (regardless of whether the bodies were deemed fit or unfit) continue to ensnare and condemn us as a result. By sitting with and through the discomfort of my own complicity in creating this piece, I aimed to re-create conditions that mirrored the painful legacies of enslaved or unfree performance with methodologies that amplified the virtuosity of the McKoys' skills. This dual experience of discomfort and admiration existed both onstage for the actresses portraying the McKoys and throughout the audience who came to witness the staging.

With details of their (auto)biographies informing the action of the play, I turned my attention to the McKoys' lyric sheets sans music. I combined the conditions of unfreedom that permeated their archives before and immediately after emancipation with my own theorizations and research on how their world onstage should sound for twenty-first-century audiences. In order to do this, I made a few tentative assumptions as a writer but not composer and combined my assumptions and research with the efforts of student composer Elias Kotsis and the direction of Rosemary Malague for the 2018 production. The first assumption was that the McKoys' musical legacies largely centered on their speaking abilities, vocal stylings, and oral and linguistic dexterity. This assumption was confirmed by extensive archival research at Yale University's Beinecke Rare Book and Manuscript Library, as well as in the North Carolina Collection of the University of North Carolina at Chapel Hill and the North Carolina State Archives. My second assumption about the lyric sheets sans music was that parlor music usually delivered in this style has a few common characteristics that (as a nonmusician) I've anecdotally observed. They tend to be easy to sing, repetitive, and intended for singers and nonsingers alike to be able to join along extemporaneously. As a model for this, I thought of nineteenth-century parlor songs with rolling Southern pastoral themes and Black Christian gospel hymns. The imagery of the lyrics, with their idealized genteel antebellum South and traditional Christian themes, reinforced this feeling in me. I wanted to re-create the space of the freak show stage, where the McKoys' eager audiences (for an additional fee) could purchase souvenir programs like the ones I previously discussed that contain their (auto)biographies. But I still wanted to emphasize the conditions of unfree or fugitive performance in the archives of the McKoys. As a result, I was drawn to the handbell because bells were frequently used in torture devices meant to sound the alarm if repeatedly fugitive slaves attempted to escape. In incorporating the bells, I explored the potential of artistic fugitivity for performers such as the McKoys, whose family was involved in highly publicized legal disputes with their former owners to gain freedom for their children after emancipation.

It was these ongoing fights for freedom that caused me to explore the performance possibilities of the bell. Bell racks and devices like them were meant not only to protect slave owners from the loss of property but also to dehumanize and pathologize fugitivity. Writings centered on methods of torture and control often stressed hindering escape not only through physical impairment but also through psychological torture meant to destroy the emotional resilience of the enslaved, attaching pseudoscientific terms to them such as *rascality*, *drapetomania*, and *sullenness*. Similarly, freak shows often centered on displaying the medical disabilities of enslaved performers. *Curio* explores the connection between the bell as both a signal of capture and a method of music making. The piece attempts to unpack the use (or refusal) of medicalization onstage in the nineteenth century by investing in theory and sound over the purely visual spectacles favored in freak shows. In creating a performance piece out of the archival remains of the McKoy twins, I wanted to perform the methodological gesture of impartial observation that was so closely tied at its roots to the practice of displaying disabled and enslaved enfreaked bodies onstage. What occurred for these performers at the intersections of legality, disability, medicalization, and public performance? And what is our aim as scholars and artists when

Figure 4.4: A still from the stage performance of *Curio*. Courtesy of the University of Pennsylvania Theatre Arts Department.

Figure 4.5: A still from the short film *Curio*. Courtesy of the author.

we reanimate these contentious performance practices for contemporary audiences?

I became obsessed with the haunting resonance of the bell, both as it sounded to make music and as it was used to capture and further enslave fugitive bodies. The devices like the ones described by Domino in the epigraph show a particular cruelty in their design. Not only were they meant to constrict the movement of the enslaved through the use of heavy and cumbersome metal structures, but they also made invisibility (one of the key protective postures of the enslaved) impossible through auditory means. Escape is most often thought of as an act that is dependent on invisibility or the act of not being seen. What this fixation on the visual ignores is that the sounds of escape needed to be equally undetectable in order to ensure a fugitive body's safe passage. That these barbaric devices made the enslaved both more visible and more audible is their ultimate torture. The bells become transformed in Domino's mind as connected to the process of thwarted escape. In this vivid recollection, the bell becomes a method of capture, a way of ensuring the human property of plantations could not and would not make their repeated attempts at escape. The bell also unconsciously shows evidence of Black resilience and fugitivity, for why else would it be necessary to take these excessive measures if the enslaved were contented, as enslavers so often claimed?

This final question became particularly important in staging the lives of the McKoys postemancipation. The letters written on behalf of their parents to the Freedmen's Bureau show definitive evidence of attempted freedom and assertions of their rights to fair pay from their performance labor, which I detail in chapter 1. This stands in direct opposition to the contented, almost familial relationship between the McKoys and the Smiths that is portrayed in the (auto)biographies. Similarly, their refusal to be examined again after being granted legal freedom demonstrates not only an awareness of their legal rights as newly minted free women but also an acknowledgment of the boundaries they could now create onstage between themselves and white audiences. In choosing to enliven the McKoys' performances for contemporary audiences, I drew attention to this knowledge of unfreedom coupled with the growing pains of emancipation. Alongside this knowledge, I also had to reckon with the fact that in some ways the freak show stage offered limited possibilities to exercise new freedoms for formerly enslaved Black subjects precisely because it was dependent on an undergirding of medicalization and the objectification of disability. So even while I celebrated the McKoys' shift from physical display to more fully embracing the use of sound, I also recognized that this was a gesture with limited possibility for full freedom. Hence the bell became a symbol of their enslaved past, their newly won independence under legal freedom, and the limitations of that same freedom under the weight of ableism and white supremacy.

Transitioning the McKoys' theatrical work and worlds to film in 2023 proved to be a new challenge altogether. Outside of the difficulties of expressing myself in a new medium, there was also the question of how to build what I had learned through the collaborative process of the 2018 production. For example, in 2018 I was (like many new playwrights) significantly less restrained in my use of metaphor and also less concerned with narrative or plot. In this first production I wanted to capture the look, sensation, and feeling of the archival remains of the McKoys (including their hard-to-define sound acts) while still experimenting with surrealist elements in the work. As a result, I eschewed more realistic and literal approaches. However, I also (like other young writers) threw everything I had accumulated after six years of studying the McKoys into the script. For example, there were a variety of bells in addition to the live music (school bells, doorbells, alarm bells, etc.). I also heavily leaned into an autobiographical lens that mirrored the McKoys' own contested (auto)biography. Scenes involving a fictionalized version of myself were interspersed throughout the performance. I started with six characters in three pairs that I eventually (for the sake of time) whittled down to four characters in two pairs. There were other logistical constraints of the 2018 production that informed our artistic choices. The primary constraint was that we had to write, design, and perform a show that could easily travel overseas from Philadelphia to the Edinburgh Festival Fringe in Scotland. This meant that, for the most part, single-use props would be a burden in an already prop-heavy production and I had to craft a script that could be performed in our sixty-minute time slot during the festival.

The 2018 production provided an opportunity to workshop and develop my lens as a writer in a collaborative and encouraging environment created by the entire company. I sat in the back of the theater through every performance in both Philadelphia and Scotland to engage with and watch audience reactions to the piece. I consistently noted through these performances that the section where the audience was most engaged and alert tended to be during the bell music scenes and the autobiographical scenes involving the McKoys. Therefore, I leaned into this knowledge when considering rewrites of the script. Although

I had plans to continue workshopping and performing *Curio* onstage, the COVID-19 pandemic and the demands of the tenure track quickly halted and altered my plans. With theaters worldwide going dark in 2020, I effectively shelved the project with the hope that, when they reopened after the pandemic, I could revive the piece. An opportunity came in the form of COVID-19 research recovery grants at my university, administered through Northwestern University's Office of the Provost. The grants essentially offered faculty whose research had been significantly affected by the pandemic an opportunity to apply for funding to complete their research. I successfully applied for money to convert my performance piece into a short film version of *Curio* on the basis that (1) I had experience working in media and production with partners like PBS and the History Channel, and (2) film would provide a more stable medium during the ongoing pandemic since I would be able to show it without a live audience. But with this influx of funding came new challenges.

I took the full-length original ninety-minute script and the sixty-minute version that played in Philadelphia and Edinburgh as a starting point in my revision process for the twenty-minute short film script. My aim was not to accordion the longer scripts down into a shortened version but rather to excerpt the key parts that exemplified the McKoys aural fugitivity. I also wanted to lean into the visual elements of filmmaking (most especially saturated color and an architectural approach to lighting) to create a heightened sense of theatricality that would permeate the short film. If the aesthetic of the first stage production was maximalist and surreal, then the name of the game for this iteration of *Curio* was simplicity. I wanted to simplify the storyline, the visual language, and the aural material used in the world of the short film. What resulted was a color-saturated and visually unified piece that reflected the world I was attempting to create without additional metaphors muddying the waters. I feel that this latest iteration of *Curio* allows the soundscapes of the McKoys' world (composed and arranged by Autumn Maria Reed) to take center stage as the primary driving force of the work. I see it as an evolution rather than a rewriting of the original piece.

Although there were many inspirational touch points that went into the creation of *Curio*, the two poetry collections explored in this chapter served as crucial sites of research for my own creative work. Investigating the context of *Curio* led me to investigate other artistic works that attempt to intervene in conversations about the enslaved through archival research and archival silence. Animating my inquiries were the questions, What makes the figure of the enslaved and the enfreaked so urgent today? And why are contemporary poets and writers interested not only in exploring the archival space but also in laying bare the process through which an archive is created, manipulated, redacted, and truncated? These same questions animated my interest in analyzing contemporary poetic interventions in aural fugitivity. The two poetry collections that I analyze in this chapter, Tyehimba Jess's 2016 *Olio* and M. NourbeSe Philip's 2008 *Zong!*, both use archival source materials (Philip through direct citation from the *Zong* legal case in eighteenth-century Jamaica, and Jess from the nineteenth- and twentieth-century archives of US slavery, emancipation, and Black performance) to demonstrate a shifting landscape in what has been alternately named the break, the sites of slavery, the site of memory, and the scenes of subjection.[14] And although their forms and strategies mark each text as distinct, they both offer a lens for contemporary interpretations of these archives. Linking past archival incompleteness to present-day methods of virtuosic poetics and sound, both *Olio* and *Zong!* utilize complex forms of collaged text to highlight the limits of the archive's desire to present an all-encompassing account of enslaved life and performance. Transposing their interpretations of the sounds of slavery, which range from cries and groans to the impact of corporeal punishment against vulnerable bodies, to the melodies of staged songs, these poets expand the repertoire of slavery's sonic remnants.[15] By reimagining slavery's unknowable reverberations (in the case of *Zong!*, the thoughts and testimony of the enslaved who were thrown overboard and became the subject of the 1781 legal case materials Philip draws her text from, and in the case of *Olio*, the McKoys' audio prerecorded harmonies, Blind Tom's unrecorded piano improvisations, and the inner thoughts of each), both Jess and Philip are invested in articulating sonic discourse alongside embodiment. Although all of the subjects of these works were marked by either enfreakment (or staged and spectacularized disability), as is the case of Blind Tom and the McKoys, or abject disability (as was claimed by those who murdered the enslaved people on the slave ship *Zong*), these textual retellings manipulate sound and silence in order to expand our understanding of archival memory.

Both *Olio*, which is built out of late nineteenth- and early twentieth-century archives of Black performance, and *Zong!*, which is constructed entirely out of the texts found in the legal records of the *Zong* massacre case, are operating from a site of archival abundance that must be hyphenated and abridged to create a new work. This strategy differs from that of prose works like Toni Morrison's 1987 novel *Beloved*, in which she built an elaborate and richly detailed world out of reading a newspaper article on Margaret Gardner's life and trial for infanticide. Instead, *Olio* focuses its poetic interventions on highlighting the interwoven and often contradictory stories within the archives of late nineteenth- and early twentieth-century Black performers like Blind Tom, the McKoy twins, and the Fisk Jubilee Singers.

Jess's assertion in the opening that the cast of subjects who are the central actors in his poetry collection are also the current "owners" of his project as well as "first-generation-freed" casts a temporal uncertainty over the work that unfolds. He chooses not to center his own accounting and mastery over these narratives and voices but rather instructs his reader on how to receive them. We must "summon tongue to witness" while being simultaneously told to "weave your own chosen way between these voices." The images of our summoned tongues and these conjured voices harken to present-tense orality, while the concepts of summoning and choosing our way point to a directional geography of archival navigation. We are making our way through his olio, a word we are told on the opening page stands for a "hodgepodge," "a miscellaneous collection (as of literary or musical selections)," and "also the second part of a minstrel show which featured a variety of performance acts and later evolved into vaudeville."[16] This poetic work is a process of making visible the arc of this sonic, temporal, and physical traversal.

Similarly, M. NourbeSe Philip's collection *Zong!* is an exercise in spiritual summoning and geographical reckoning that is expressed as deeply personal and embodied, for both poet and reader. Philip makes this process known from the cover and opening pages of her text, where she lists Setaey Adamu Boateng as a coauthor of her poems. As previously mentioned, the front cover notes that the story of *Zong!* was "told to the author by Setaey Adamu Boateng," and the back cover couples Boateng's biography with Philip's, stating, "Setaey Adamu Boateng is the voice of the ancestors revealing the submerged stories of all who were on board the *Zong*."[17] Yet in contrast to Jess's *Olio*, which is full of textual facsimiles, re-creations, and revisions meant to mirror the forms taken in the archives of enfreaked nineteenth-century performance, *Zong!* is concerned with neither textual wholeness nor virtuosic facsimiles. It is also not explicitly connected to the archives of enfreaked performers. And yet I've connected these two works because of their shared strategies for wrestling with narrations of slavery. In discussing the methods of her work in the section "Notanda," Philip writes,

> *I enter a different land, a land of language—I allow the language to lead me somewhere—don't know where, but I trust.*
> *water of want*
> *Everything is here I tell myself—birth, death, life—murder, the law, a microcosm—a universe.*
>
> My intent is to use the text of the legal decision as a word store; to lock myself into this particular and peculiar discursive landscape in the belief that the story of these African men, women, and children thrown overboard in an attempt to collect insurance monies, the story that can only be told by not telling, is locked in this text. In the many silences within the Silence of the text. I would lock myself in this text in the same way men, women, and children were locked in the holds of the slave ship Zong.[18]

Philip's temporal summoning and invocation of a land that is inhabited by the inherited language of the archives of slavery speaks to the textual choices she makes in the body of her work. Part of the reckoning her work forces in conversations about how and when we begin to write about the archives of slavery is that there is no potential for creation without re-creation. Just as the McKoys could refashion and revise their (auto)biography toward their own performance ends while also reproducing narrative tropes that depended on the racist structures of antebellum slave fictions, Jess's and Philip's texts use the ambiguous terrain of ownership coupled with temporal and geographical displacement to drive their contemporary interventions.

These same temporal and geographic displacements are used to draw the reader into the fictions and history of the works, causing us to doubt our own fixed versions of history. Through form and experimentation, Jess and Philip each borrow and convert passages from historical texts with racist undergirding in order to subvert the reader's expectations of what a historical accounting can and should look like. Nothing is as indicative of this disorientation as my first encounter with *Zong!*

The first time I read the opening poem of *Zong!*, I am standing on the edge of a train platform in 2012, a platform aligned with the same train tracks that loop throughout the Northeastern states I have lived in my whole life. At first, my eyes trip back and forth over the words on the page, scanning sideways left to right and back again. I see shapes, fragments, words, and sentences. But nothing remains intact. I decide that despite my embarrassment and the stares I am attracting from other commuters, I need to read the words aloud. If I don't, I'll be on the first page all night, internally stuttering through phrases in my head. As I begin to articulate, the words and nonwords take form. I stammer, miss lines, go back and start again. I scan up and down, left to right. I read in order. I read out of order. But most shockingly of all, I hear voices. And now that I've started, I cannot stop. In spite of the stares I am getting. Despite the difficulty of articulating each phrase. In spite of the fact that these voices (like this work) are fictionalized from 142 dead nonfictional subjects.

The 142 subjects are enslaved Africans who were en route to Jamaica when the crew of the *Zong* ship decided that these captured bodies were so weakened by maltreatment, and supplies aboard the ship so scarce, that they should be thrown overboard in order to collect the insurance payments for "lost cargo" rather than completing the trip. Philip's haunting ruminations are drawn entirely from recovered legal texts. The voices are my attempt to reconcile the sounds I hear when I read the first page of the text: the terrifying gurgling of water filling lungs. Water creeping in through gaping mouths and open noses, the salt burning tongues, destroying evidence, and deadening cries. I am speaking Philip's words aloud mostly to do what Saidiya Hartman warns us to be cautious of in her essay "Venus in Two Acts": I am reconciling this painful encounter with a personally contrived romance.[19] I acknowledge Philip's intervention, and I layer on one of my own. I flinch when I see the fatalistic line, "such drab necessity/murder," because I realize the "necessity" of my own engagement.[20] Necessary, just like the financially motivated murder and disposal of bodies. And unlike Jess's text, Philip's opening poem doesn't offer a distinct or readily discernible road map. It has an amorphous and aquatic geography, both on the page and in my ear.

My eyes, now working in concert with my mouth, stop dead when they first encounter the Latin text in *Zong!* Neither organ is ready for the familiar unfamiliar words. I took Latin for a total of five years, and as I look down on it I remember those half-forgotten lessons. I had three different teachers over the course of my studies: one an ancient nun of indeterminate age who terrified the girls; the next one the principal of our school, another aged nun with a wry sense of humor who was well loved by the students; and the last one a hip recent grad in her late twenties. I remember these three women now because of the discordance in their pedagogical practices that relate directly to the function of language in *Zong!* The older nuns always taught us that we should pronounce hard *v*'s and soft *c*'s in certain words. So the infamous phrase phonetically sounded like "veni, vidi, ve-chee." I learned this "church Latin" pronunciation, somewhat indifferently, for many years. When our new teacher came along, she told us that what we had learned was wrong, a result of biased church practice that favored current Italian pronunciation. According to her, research showed that Romans pronounced *v*'s more like a soft *w* and *c*'s should sound like a hard *k*. Soon she had us all reciting "weni, widi, we-kee" in class. Although I see Philip doesn't use words with hard versus soft *c*'s, I stumble back and forth over her use of "video": I see. I think about Latin as a "dead language" and how much of the spoken word is lost to us. Yet why, then, is recitation always a crucial part of the learning process? Why hear what we are never expected to speak?

Why spend time speaking words that are supposedly dead? So now my reading stands at the crossroads of this dead language, these lost stories, and these dead bodies. To me this works most clearly not only with the text and project of *Zong!* but also with the larger impossibility of recovery that does not also have within its re-creation. Even in Latin, a language that has become almost synonymous with the monolithic workings of power and endurance in western European culture's desire to draw a neat and inaccurate direct lineage between Greco-Roman antiquity and modern realities, there is still the possibility of loss and vocal discord. Still the voices are gone and re-created. Even here we are in the process of speaking back to "an inaccessible blankness."[21] Like the enslaved people sinking to the bottom of the sea, Latin is supposed to be both "dead" and not dead, living on notably in Western practices for the production of legal records and medical texts—two foundational types of documents that bracket the lives of the enslaved, such as in the McKoys' parents' attempts to free them from false enslavement at P. T. Barnum's museum, and the doctors' exams that circulate in their archives.

Six of the ten sections of *Zong!* carry Latin names: "Os," "Sal," "Ventus," "Ratio," "Ferrum," and "Notanda," which mean "bone," "salt," "wind," "reason" (noted in the glossary as short for *ratio decidendi*, or the reason for a legal decision), "iron," and "a note" or "something that should be noted." Philip's decision to derive all of the words used in her poetry collection from the legal archives of the *Zong* case that are also being channeled to her through a system of erasure and spiritual summoning is echoed in the choice of section titles here. All of these Latin terms are attached to things that either are corrosive (like salt and wind) or have the ability themselves to be eroded or dissolved (legal reasoning, iron, written notes, and bones). Whereas Jess creates archival reproductions that highlight the impermanence and unreliability of the archive through virtuosic facsimiles, Philip chooses instead to insert these archival alterations at the textual level of her words on the page. They resist guided readings because they are broken and gapped. They are cacophonous and unruly in the ways that they sometimes run into each other or over each other. She notes in her glossary that the collection uses Arabic, Dutch, Fon, French, Greek, Hebrew, Italian, Latin, Portuguese, Spanish, Shona, Twi, West African Patois, and Yoruba alongside the English text. The proximity of these varied words and languages on the page alongside Philip's attempts to make a work out of the deafening silence of the voices of the murdered captives of the *Zong* upends a certain amount of linguistic hierarchy while also succumbing to the limitations of its source material. By limiting her own re-creation to what is already available in the archive, Philip creates a work that is a project of frustration, of an attempt to speak where so much institutional, legal, and archival might have always been invested in silence. And I argue that her use of Latin is essential to that confined disruption.

Although my earlier images of Latin lessons bring to mind rows of anonymous desks, slouched shoulders, and stern, sturdy teachers, much of my own introduction to Latin came through the filter of Catholicism.

Neither raised Catholic nor a convert, I was always rather annoyed that so much of our recitation revolved around the memorization of prayer—Ave Maria (Hail Mary), Our Father (Pater Noster). It wasn't until our third teacher that the supposedly linear connection between religious evocation and the institutional might of the Catholic Church, morality, and Western education was even questioned in the curriculum. In *Race: Antiquity and Its Legacy*, Denise McCoskey speaks to the emergence of modern classical studies in nineteenth-century Europe. She writes,

> Led by burgeoning theories of race, which increasingly cast race as the main engine of human development, many early classical scholars consciously aimed to uncover a racial genealogy closely linking the European past and present, claims that—absent the physical remains of ancient peoples or evidence of "real" bloodlines—were demonstrated primarily through language clusters or language "families." *Trying to explain who the Greeks and Romans had been from how they had spoken thus became closely linked to asserting claims about which modern European groups could lay claim to being their "legitimate" descendants, conclusions fraught with racial overtones.*[22]

Most interesting here (outside of the racial connections made between Greco-Roman antiquity, the teaching of Latin, and nineteenth-century European pedagogy) is the attempt to re-create in absence. Embedded in the foundation of contemporary Latin pedagogy was the keen knowledge of loss and absence. Voices had not been recorded. Bodies were not present. "Real" bloodlines were unproven. Yet the nineteenth-century Western presentation of Latin pedagogy espoused the belief that speaking the words of the dead could somehow stand in as a substitute for the physical remains, a historical abridgment of its own. These assumptions resonate with Philip's own project. The reader is keenly aware when reading *Zong!* that the specter of the sea is always present as a barrier against physical recovery. Concepts of "evidence" and "lineage" are disrupted by the very nature of the crimes committed—crimes of accounting, disposal, and disintegration.

In his 2011 TEDx Talk "Syncopated Sonnets," Jess similarly offers the audience a listening and reading practice.[23] Jess notes that his poems on the McKoy twins can be read in a multitude of ways. It can be read down either side to distinguish Millie's and Christine's individual voices or straight down the center to hear them metaphorically duet. Jess's rhetorical choice to distinguish the voice of each McKoy sister before blending their voices along the shared spine of the same conjoined verse is mirrored in print in his collection *Olio*. Although his delivery of the poem five years before the publication of the text instructs the audience on how to properly read its syncopation, the form of the words on paper also demands and guides such a reading. He even notes in his 2011 talk that the McKoys were well known for their singing and for their harmonies, a fact that drives the narrative form of his work. By naming this poem after syncopation, or a mixture of rhythms that unexpectedly places a stress on a usually unstressed beat, Jess tests the limits of poetic conjoined form in order to mirror the McKoys' signature acts of vocal performance, harmony, and quotidian conversational skills.

The shapes and sounds of Jess's poetics mirror both the appearance and form of the McKoys' conjoined bodies and the unanticipated nature of their improvisational sonic acts. The key to their staged performances of individualized personhood was capturing the unexpected notes that existed outside white audiences' expectations. By articulating words in two different languages to two people at the same time and also singing in harmony, the McKoys asserted individual identities outside their conjoined bodies and the shared sensations in their lower extremities, the latter of which was the subject of great discussion among white physicians, sideshow proprietors, audiences, and "medical men" in their antebellum act. Their new aural performance acts postemancipation in effect raised white viewers' eyes and attention from their shared sensations below their waistline to the points of their bodies that were linked but functioned independently. Jess looks to celebrate this performance shift, and the temporal moment when audiences' eyes were directed upward toward the McKoys' faces. And yet in consciously mirroring the shape of the McKoys' verbal and physical form, Jess's poem is also oddly reminiscent of the shape of a set of lungs.

The sonic, embodied, and textual residues of these performances and legal encounters have never settled, never been entirely placed, never offered a distinct geographical or temporal map, and never received a pause or an aural rest. It is fitting, then, that Jess's syncopated sonnet for the McKoys looks eerily like a set of lungs. The same lungs that helped produce the McKoys' songs and linguistic acts. The same lungs I heard filling in my first reading of *Zong!* And yet on second evaluation, the opening phrases in *Zong!* that I assumed were the noise of water filling lungs as they sank, unidentified, to the ocean floor could just as easily be the sound of air escaping as those forgotten bodies surface again.

Part Two: Staging Aural Fugitivity for Contemporary Audiences

When I began writing creative work out of the McKoy twins' archive, I drew inspiration from several artistic sources. The first (very surprisingly) was Audra McDonald's Broadway turn as Billie Holiday. During her critically acclaimed and transformative performance in *Lady Day*

Figure 4.6: Costume design for *Curio*. Courtesy of Sara Outing.

at Emerson's Bar and Grill,[24] McDonald as Holiday begins to recall her own musical predecessors Bessie Smith and Louis Armstrong. Taking these iconic performers as her musical antecedents, Holiday recalls how she always admired Smith's "big sound," which she was never truly able to emulate because "my voice isn't that way." However, when speaking of Armstrong's ability to convey emotion throughout his vocality, she laughs when she recounts that she never understood why he didn't "sing no words." In this moment, both McDonald (the performer) and Holiday (the performer, the character, the persona, the myth, the memory) are at their signature funniest. The audience is in stitches recalling Armstrong's scat, a loose connection of sounds, notes, and utterances that are as signature to his style as his most famous standards (e.g., "Hello Dolly" and "What a Wonderful World"). Here the performer takes an unexpected turn, lowering her voice to barely above a whisper, before uttering dreamily, "but I just wanted that *feeling*. You know?" McDonald's whispering raised for me fundamental questions of Black orality and musicality: What is mimicry and what is signification? What are the attendant values of ownership and possession inherent in delineating these two categories of artistic agency? Additionally, how do we measure style, that which is ephemeral and transient, intangible and essential? More specifically, how do these pieces encourage us to view modes of style as not only essential to performance but also essential to a Black performance tradition? What exactly is "that feeling," and is it familiar enough to all of us that Holiday's soft, questioning "you know" resonates with each of us in the same way? What does she ask us to know?

My own project, *Curio*, in the McKoy twins' archive focuses primarily on practices of consumption and performance labor as exercised by the McKoy family both before and after legal emancipation. In looking at the process through which a body can be categorized as "free" or "enslaved" and thinking about the ways the McKoys enacted a subtle but strategic freedom through their control of their own performance labor practices, I hope that *Curio* meets at the intersections of the "slave narrative" and emancipated labor. But looking again to Lady Day, a moment in the production that struck me as particularly poignant was Holiday's bemoaning to the audience that parole officers always showed up to stop her club performances because she had no work card, which she was no longer eligible for because she was a convicted felon. Although early on in the show she jokingly noted that a parole officer's role was to stop her from "having too much fun," here we hear a different refrain: "They won't let me work!" How is this knife's-edge balance between pleasure and labor a constant mire for the Black female performer? For those who turn their bodies, their narratives, their lives, their personhood, their freedoms, and too often their wellness and sanity into a consumable product? What are the attendant dangers of simultaneously spectacularizing and necessitating Black pleasure while also commoditizing it as a highly valuable product? What does an archive like those of the McKoy twins and Holiday say about the potential perils of these labor practices? What are the terms under which a Black performer's body enters the national and international consciousness (as Farah Jasmine Griffin so aptly notes in her essay "When Malindy Sings")?[25]

And lastly, what insights do we gain from seeing Audra McDonald, an actress whose meteoric and sustained success on the Broadway stage has become the central plot point of her public persona, making her employability significantly less tenuous than that of her antecedent Holiday, uttering the frustrated words of Lady Day, "They won't let me work"? What is the cry, the defiance, the frustration, or the failure of this moment? What bodily freedoms are left truncated or unrealized? And how does Holiday's insistence on performing until the end, in spite of its illegality, show a careful balance between an oppressive hypervisibility and a determined personal aural fugitivity so often expressed in Black performance?

The other side of my inspiration for the McKoy twins' performance didn't stem from music at all, but rather from the use of the bell in both torture devices and visual culture. At a point in the stage performance of my piece *Curio*, the two actresses (at this point moving through the motions of an academic lecture) stop to tell the audience about the origins of the word *drapetomania*:

RESEARCHER 1: A footnote: *Drapetomania*. A fictitious mental illness coined by Dr. Samuel A. Cartwright. Theorized as the reason that enslaved blacks fled captivity. Scientific racism, roundly disproven. Was popularized in 1851 the year the McKoy Twins were born.

RESEARCHER 2: You said that already.

RESEARCHER 1: I did?

RESEARCHER 2: Yes.

Then, about thirty minutes later, they return as different characters, one of whom notes,

> WOMAN 2: If Drapetomania is a mental disease, the insanity of the slave, then the Bell Rack is a medical device.

And finally another few minutes pass and they add,

> WOMAN 2: A footnote: *Drapetomania*. A fictitious mental illness coined by Dr. Samuel A. Cartwright. Theorized as the reason that enslaved blacks fled captivity. Scientific racism, roundly disproven. Was popularized in 1851 the year the McKoy Twins were born.
> WOMAN 1: Is it diagnosable drapetomania if you just *dream* of running away?
> WOMAN 2: What?
> WOMAN 1: If it's only dreaming?

When it came time to stage my versions of the McKoys' songs, it was this impulse at the back of my mind, along with my research, as well as images of Caribbean visual artist Joscelyn Gardner's 2012 work *Creole Portraits*, which was commissioned by and appeared in *Small Axe* 37. Gardner joins detailed and colorful etchings of the abortifacient flowers reportedly used by enslaved women to end unwanted pregnancies with images of torture devices and almost ventriloquized pseudo-medical and scientific language used throughout the eighteenth and nineteenth centuries to classify and define the Black female body. It was Gardner's coupling of Western medical pathology with the shared knowledge of Black enslaved women (through the abortifacients) and the tenderness evidenced by the intricate braiding designs that drew me to take some dramaturgical license when setting the McKoy twins' lyrics to music. Since I already knew that I wanted to keep the parts of the songs that were irrevocably existent in the archives (the lyric sheets) in their original form, the music was a place for me to explore instruments that were more in service of the show than historically accurate.

It was after puzzling over this for two or three years that I became interested in videos of all-girls handbell choirs online. At the time, I was looking for an instrument for my two actresses to play that would require

Figure 4.7: Joscelyn Gardner, *Creole Portraits*, 2012.

all four of their hands to move in coordination, but without obstructing our view of their bodies or faces. I needed the songs to be simple, repeatable, and easily taught and learned. And I wanted every prop that was written explicitly into the script to always serve at least two functions onstage. I already had the bells written in for the scenes of torture devices and the sounds of ringing bells, a noise that is (for me) haunted by their historical weight. But I found as I was watching more and more videos of handbell choirs (most of which were from the US South) that the bells also created a kind of haunting and resonant ringing tone that aligned with the themes of *Curio* more closely than the piano or guitar. So when the time came to have the pieces sung in *Curio* composed, our creative team looked to the handbells to provide insight into the complex conditions of freedom and fugitivity that the McKoys performed under, while also attempting to capture the otherworldly virtuosity of their live performances that reviewers and witnesses recount in their descriptions of their shows. The resulting performances of *Curio* demonstrated that the handbells were the most effective theatrical device in the show. While other segments felt strained or difficult for the actresses to embody (namely, ones that mirrored academic lectures or focused exclusively on autobiographical material), audiences tended to be drawn in and transfixed by the bells. The transition from musical instrument to torture device also proved to be one of the more instructive moments in the 2018 performance. It heightened audiences' awareness of the politics behind the McKoys' work while also providing another opportunity to hear the bell music in a different way when one actress (who was not wearing the device) reached over and rang the bell hanging high over her fellow cast member's head. The development of this moment came in collaboration with scenic designer Sara Outing and director Rosemary Malague as we discussed ways to make props more utilitarian onstage while also maintaining their dramaturgical functions.

Reflecting on the 2018 production and projecting ahead to future rewrites and restaging, I planned to amplify the use of the bell and decenter the use of more academic frameworks in the script of *Curio*. Although the work was and is intended as an excavation of an archival collection, I found the framing device of delivering a lecture somewhat restrictive in our attempts to illuminate the deeper theatrical properties of the McKoys' extraordinary lives. In future productions (such as the 2023 short film), I leaned into the impulses that originally drove *Curio*: namely, telling of the lives and performance strategies of these remarkable women while also working to limit or restrict the amount of historical harm inflicted in the process of retelling.

By focusing my research and theatrical staging on illuminating the properties of the archival materials rather than concerning myself with a strict historical reenactment, I offer in *Curio* a new critique of the McKoy twins' archival remains and performance legacies. The piece itself owes a great deal to the collaborative efforts of the entire company, without whom I would not have been able to stage the archival properties of the McKoys' songs for a general audience. There remains work to be done to bridge the gaps between the traditional scholarship of performance theory and theater history and praxis. I am deeply indebted to works of theatrical ethnography that paved the way for scholar-artists to find ways to enact and act on archives in innovative ways. The work I've done and continue to do with *Curio* lives in a world that intersects these ethnographic methods with artistic and scholarly praxis to create an ethnography of the archive through performance. By examining the sites that we as historians and scholars are indebted to in order to retrieve the narratives of performers like the McKoys, I hope that this project offers a lens into the economies of pleasure and pain that still haunt both the margins and the center of the McKoys' virtuosic legacies and aural fugitivity.

Reflecting artistic interests and points of inquiry that are similar to the ones I explore in *Curio*, both *Olio* and *Zong!* take up the question of performance alongside the realities of labor (particularly unfree enslaved labor) as a point of departure. For example, the entire premise of *Zong!* is based on the fact that the slave ship murders were treated as a case of insurance fraud rather than the grisly killing of dozens of African people. Therefore, the work of Philip, in conversation and dictation with the ancestral realm through Setaey Adamu Boateng, is an act of recovery. That act is in and of itself a labor. The art of transcription and dictation guides the sensibilities of the work. Philip asks us to listen closely and otherwise to the voices that have long been denied humanity in the archive. We are asked to read and listen against the grain of the legal record that remains in the archive.[26] The remains that *Zong!* is primarily concerned with have been eroded by salt and sea and forgotten. In the absence of physical records from the enslaved or a pinpointed resting place, we are left instead with an endless expanse of ocean and a finite white supremacist legal record from which to cull information about those who lost their lives aboard the ship. In lieu of physicality, *Zong!* uses sound as an alternative method of communicating enslaved labor through modern performance practices.

In "Syncopated Sonnets," Jess opens his lecture by introducing the subject of his poem: Millie Christine McKoy. He notes that they were "two women" born into slavery "who persevered to become some of the biggest stars of the nineteenth century." He continues to describe them using a list of terms. First he says that they were "differently abled." Then he expands his list to include a number of statements, all notably starting with the term "they." "They were smart." "They were talented." "They were ingenious." "They were disciplined." "They were," he says as he turns to click to a slide of the McKoy sisters standing posed for a visiting card, "Millie and Christine McKoy." After this short and energetic biography, Jess goes on to introduce how he will read from his own work on the McKoys, saying of his syncopated sonnet, "What they try and do is they try and bring two voices together to talk individually and also to share a conversation to share lines in the middle. . . . If we read down the left side we can read Millie's lines and if we read down the middle we can read the lines they share together and if we read down the [right] side we can . . . read the lines of Christine." Jess then rotates his body to the side, strolling confidently across the stage as he reads from the projected poem. He reads everything justified along the left as Millie's poem and everything justified along the right as Christine's, then triumphantly merges the two texts by reading straight across to combine the twins' voices.[27]

In the content and also the heading of his syncopated sonnet, Jess chooses to differentiate between the two sisters by creating two distinct voices and also by placing an "and" between their names. This gesture isn't all encompassing, since even in their individual verses they still refer to themselves as "we" rather than "I." Just as the McKoys' archival materials alternate between the pronouns "she," "I," "them," and too often "it," Jess's own intervention of creating two distinct McKoys is unstable and shifts throughout his poems. In some he notes that they are "Millie-Christine," particularly in poems about their performance acts. In others he refers to them as "Millie McKoy" and "Christine McKoy," making an effort to give them each distinct first and last names. But his syncopated

MILLIE AND CHRISTINE MCKOY

We've mended two songs into one dark skin   *We ride the wake of each other's rhythm*
bleeding soprano into contralto   *beating our hearts' syncopated tempo*
—we're fused in blood and body—from one thrummed stem
budding twin blooms of song. We're a doubled rose
descended from raw carnage of the South   *with a music all our own. With our mouths*
bursting open our freedom. We sing past rage   *seeped in the glow of hand-me-down courage*
grown from hard labor that made our mother shout,
spent with awe. We hymn to pay soft homage
to the worksong's aria. It leaves us   *drenched in spiritual a cappellas,*
soaked in history like our father's sweat   *flowing soul from bone through skin. We pay debts*
borne of and beyond the flesh: we are just
two women singing truths we can't forget
from plantation to grave. Lord, here we are,   *from broken chattel to circus stars,*
freed twin sisters who've hauled our voices far . . .   *we sing straight from this nation's barbwired heart . . .*

Figure 4.8: Tyehimba Jess, "Millie and Christine McKoy," in *Olio*.

sonnet attempts, through the manipulation of language and poetic form, to give voice to the McKoys through the structures of virtuosity. For as Jess notes in his opening remarks, he wishes to frame them as "ingenious" and "disciplined," the latter of which is a curious word choice in light of the twins' own connection to systems of prolonged enslavement. But even though the written work opens with a credit given to the McKoys and their contemporaries as owners of the text, the genre of the TEDx Talk and the widespread acclaim of *Olio* (which won the Pulitzer Prize in 2017 and garnered considerable attention and praise for Jess) seem to grant a good deal of ownership to the poet. He presented this work in a moment characterized by a keen desire to celebrate and elevate Black ingenuity. And part of the work of reclaiming the narratives of the McKoys from the archive, for Jess, is centering their performance virtuosity and "discipline." To that end, the description of the video notes that the McKoys were "multilingual," and this linguistic dexterity is mirrored in his textual approach to abridging their stories.

For even though he makes an effort to separate Christine as an individual apart from Millie, both halves of his poem "Millie and Christine McKoy" appear to be written in the same voice. There is no distinct discourse from one sister versus another. In some ways this is necessary to make the poem function as he intends it to, allowing it to be read in three different ways. Even if Jess used "I" instead of "we" and a hyphen between their names instead of "and," the syncopated sonnet requires a level of uniformity in the lines in order to work.

Jess's project varies from previous poetic interventions based on the McKoys' archive, such as Marilyn Nelson's, which seeks instead to present a complete individualized voice for only Christine. When Millie succumbed to tuberculosis, Christine went on to live for an additional seventeen hours,[28] long enough for the family to release the news of her sister's death to local newspapers before doctors euthanized her shortly thereafter. This final act is detailed in a booklet from the Columbus County Historical Society published in 1969: "Millie in her last illness was attended by Dr. W. H. Crowell, a Whiteville physician who was presented to Queen Victoria by the twins at one of their performances in London where Dr. Crowell was studying at the time. Toward the last Dr. Crowell contacted Johns Hopkins Hospital in Baltimore and asked about separation. *He was advised to give Chrissy massive doses of morphine at Millie's death, as separation was impossible.*"[29] Nelson imagines and narrates those final seventeen hours of Christine's life in her poem "Millie-Christine," in which she writes,

> My being owned. My being self-possessed. My girlhood of medical
> exams masking abuse. My years of childhood outrage, unexpressed. My violated privacy. My face.
> My powerless gender. My despised race. My sense of the beautiful.
> My ugliness. My faith that everyone's here to be of use.
> My mine-alone eyes. My eyes mine alone, at least.[30]

Cast entirely in the possessive terms of "my," the poem here portrays an imagined interiority that mirrors the vast unknown terrains of Millie's and Christine's voices. For while the archive provides a cacophony of resources surrounding their lives, from newspapers to their autobiographies to interviews, playbills, and legal documents, there still remains a relative silence surrounding the depth of their interiority as women, performers, and free agents in Jess's poetic performances. But Nelson's attempts to write Christine in the singular person, a rhetorical move that is mirrored by Jess when he inserts the "and" between their names in his poem's title, do not place sufficient tension on the McKoys' own desire to be articulated through the singular pronoun and a singular, hyphenated name. In fact, by positioning the twins as separate entities postmortem, Nelson ignores the mandates of their final will and testament, in which they continue to refer to themselves as a singular woman,[31] whereas Jess's curved and conjoined text more closely mirrors this strain in the McKoys' archival afterlives.

Form, for Jess, is a road map and guide for the reader. He instructs us how to read, digest, and hear his works through the manipulation of text. The full-length collection *Olio* is also an exercise in material dexterity. The text is wide and large for a single poetry collection, looking at first more like a book of sheet music than a volume of poetry. The forms inside the text often are made to look like archival letters or posters, with pages that fold out like inserts and require the reader to tip the book on its side to read them fully. One page in the center of the text has a neatly perforated edge, as if encouraging the reader to pull it out and share it. But such an act would render the collection incomplete, with pages that are quite literally missing. This invitation to truncate or abridge the text makes *Olio* an oddly satisfying physical puzzle because it mirrors the sensation of archival recovery. This "hodgepodge" is carefully and meticulously curated by Jess yet made to feel random and precarious. Pages can unfold unexpectedly or be torn out entirely. There were moments when, while reading the text, I stopped to wonder, "Is this a real excerpt/letter/figure/fact, or is it Jess's invention?" But through reading and careful rereading, Jess's audience is left to make up their mind about his incomplete facsimiles.

For while his text is made to look, feel, and function like the archival material that it is based on, it does not re-create it intact. The facsimile is most often apparent, causing readers of this poetic text to do the work of historical fact-finding in conjunction with Jess's conjoined verse. The future-perfect formulation here is focused on his textual movements, both those driven in the narrative form of the work and those he forces on his readers, who must turn and twist the pages and understandings of enfreakment to fully follow Jess's texts. I enjoy *Olio* as both a text and a literary intervention into the catalog of work on enfreakment. However, I found Jess's performances of the syncopated sonnets to be driven by a less critical celebration that chose to center imagined joy over the complexity of the McKoys' lived realities. As a result, audiences' pleasure was centered in ways that mirrored the McKoys' performances in life (something I consciously attempted to avoid in *Curio*).

At the opposite pole, Philip's poetics in her performances of *Zong!* seem to defy easy legibility. Combining music, dance, and durational readings from *Zong!*, her performances create a uniquely cacophonous world that offers little in the way of linear comprehension. The sensorium of Philip's world has no linguistic or poetic road map, no neat way of digestion and interpretation. At moments it is hushed and soft so as to be barely audible. At others, the combined music, movement, and verse create a world that is at once atmospheric and dense. The sounds and performances of *Zong!* (water in lungs, fragmented thoughts, oceanic discord) are all presented for the audience to decipher.

Dictation and erosion, as methods coupled together, create a landscape of aural fugitivity within the textual and performance worlds of *Zong!* Dictation naturally suggests a truncation of the text or a shorthand being employed in order to keep up with the rapid-fire progression of speech, whereas erosion lays waste to that very same assumed precision. The ancestral voice that Philip relies on as part of her core methodology has been eroded by the elements of time, salt, sea, and lived memory. It is fragmentary and incomplete in nature and by design. As she notes in the text, "There is no telling this story; it must be told."[32] By acknowledging the impossibility of the task alongside the imperative of breaking silence, Philip gives voice to the dichotomy of commemorating enslavement through performance. It will always be at once too much and simultaneously insufficient to capture the textures of the lived realities of the enslaved. Language and therefore sound will persistently fail us in this endeavor. Therefore the artistic possibilities of intentional silence or of sound that is difficult to dictate and record, possibilities revealed by acts of aural fugitivity, remain vital forms of archival resistance, obfuscation, and (perhaps) even countersurveillance.[33]

Frederick Douglass's Aural Fugitivity

> I now come to that part of my life during which I planned, and finally succeeded in making, my escape from slavery. But before narrating any of the peculiar circumstances, I deem it proper to make known my intention

> not to state all the facts connected with the transaction. My reasons for pursuing this course may be understood from the following: First, were I to give a minute statement of all the facts, it is not only possible, but quite probable, that others would thereby be involved in the most embarrassing difficulties. Secondly, such a statement would most undoubtedly induce greater vigilance on the part of slaveholders than has existed heretofore among them; which would, of course, be the means of guarding a door whereby some dear brother bondman might escape his galling chains.[34]

Sound and its antithesis, silence, have always been powerful freedom tactics for the enslaved and their descendants. The ability to "hold your tongue" or to "make a joyful noise" in the face of systemic violence should not be taken lightly, since often they could mean the difference between extended life and premature death. These same logics apply to the archival practices of recording enslavement. The aural fugitivity expressed by Douglass in the foregoing quotation is a canonical example of this deliberate obfuscation that allowed for the possibility of more life away from the glare of archival inspection. In the passage, Douglass notes that he will purposely not reveal the details of his escape north precisely because entering this sensitive information into the official record may limit the freedom of other fugitives attempting to self-liberate, while simultaneously empowering the enslavers with intracommunity secrets. In his act of sonic refusal (refusing to speak or write this secret truth), Douglass is also protecting other sacred Black sound. The whisper network of Black people attempting freedom. The shared stories of liberation passed from ear to eager ear like a torch. Douglass at once stands defiant of white curiosity (the curiosity of his primary readership) and takes a stand for Black opacity.

This act of refusal resonates on the page and in a story that takes great care to enumerate and explicate the other sounds of slavery. Douglass recounts in great detail his aunt Hester's screams, the cries of his fellow bondsmen, the lash of the whip, and the cacophony of lived violence. He meticulously and intentionally details the hymns and prayers of bondage. Douglass's world is uniquely noisy on the page. And yet here the noise ceases to exist, and Douglass slips beyond the edges of the page until he is out of view and earshot. The map north remains hidden from both the archive and our living memory, taken to the grave with all those who memorized it as the route to legal freedom. All of the utterances and whispers shared in secrecy are not immortalized here on the page but rather held close to the chest. Douglass holds his tongue, even as he states that there does indeed exist such a route north. He gives us evidence of its existence, even while he withholds the details. His intentional silence rings out.

But Douglass doesn't stop there. In the same passage, he goes on to chastise "our western friends" for their propensity to speak out of turn when he writes,

> I have never approved of the very public manner in which some of our western friends have conducted what they call the *underground railroad*, but which I think, by their open declarations, has been made most emphatically the *upperground railroad*. I honor those good men and women for their noble daring, and applaud them for willingly subjecting themselves to bloody persecution, by openly avowing their participation in the escape of slaves. I, however, can see very little good resulting from such a course, either to themselves or the slaves escaping; while, upon the other hand, I see and feel assured that those open declarations are a positive evil to the slaves remaining, who are seeking to escape. They do nothing towards enlightening the slave, whilst they do much towards enlightening the master.[35]

This searing historical shade directed toward "our western friends" does much to illuminate the social and political stakes of aural fugitivity for the enslaved. Through sound acts (such as improvisational speech, oratory, and whispers) that are impossible or hard to capture, the enslaved were able to make a world that defied the Western logics of archival wholeness. What we get instead is a record that has been in some cases deliberately and methodically wiped clean of any traces, resisting the Western historical record's demand for a complete story. Silence about the route north (and silence while on that same route, as evidenced by the epigraph of this chapter) was an essential tool of survival. So, in a crucial way, these historical sonic absences left by public figures and performers who were formerly enslaved (like Douglass and the McKoys) and their later descendants (such as Jess and Philip) offer us an avenue to consider silence alongside the long project of Black freedom.

Douglass then goes on to detail his desires regarding slaveholders and slave catchers when he writes,

> I would keep the merciless slaveholder profoundly ignorant of the means of flight adopted by the slave. I would leave him to imagine himself surrounded by myriads of invisible tormentors, ever ready to snatch from his infernal grasp his trembling prey. Let him be left to feel his way in the dark; let darkness commensurate with his crime hover over him, and let him feel that at every step he takes, in pursuit of the flying bondsman, he is running the frightful risk of having his hot brains dashed out by an invisible agency. Let us render the tyrant no aid; let us not hold the light by which he can trace the footprints of our flying brother.[36]

Focusing here on the sense of sight (rather than hearing), Douglass speaks of depriving the slave catcher of one of his most valuable tools. Summoning darkness and calling on his readers not to "hold the light" that would illuminate the position of the enslaved, Douglass paints a picture that reverses the roles of fugitive and pursuer. Now it is not the enslaved who are forced to move blindly through the underbrush, or to worry that the bells and torture devices welded to them will give away their location (as Amy Domino describes in the epigraph). Instead, by turning the language and logics of the slave catcher on their head, Douglass is able to summon a vivid picture: He wishes for the slave catcher to suffer the same fear and uncertainty felt by fugitive enslaved laborers. He wishes that they be left to search and hunt and worry in the same ways that fugitives would. He hopes that his silence from the archive leaves a mark of countersurveillance[37] on their psyches, causing them to doubt what they see and hear and perceive with their own senses. Douglass's route slips beyond the page, never to be recorded or saved for future generations of readers. He takes a decidedly antagonistic tone to both slave catchers and the loose-lipped "western friends" he describes. The silence and secret of his aural fugitivity stand even today as a safeguard of an intracommunity knowledge of Black freedom.

Douglass's declaration of silence as a freedom strategy in the face of white supremacist curiosities paints a map that generations of Black freedom workers have utilized in a variety of contexts. In the case of the McKoys and later performers of aural fugitivity, they were able to take these strategies of resistance to the stage. When coupled with theatricality, these strategies of silence take on new significance. Freak show audiences' expectations were often driven by a grotesque curiosity about the "monstruous" figures they had come to see perform. In fact, the act of appearance was almost as essential as the acts themselves. In many cases, the act of appearance *was* the act. Coupling that with the subjugation experienced by enslaved Black laborers and the act of holding one's tongue (so to speak) takes on a heightened significance. I contend that *Curio*, *Zong!*, and *Olio* all swim in the wake of Douglass's literary legacy through their uses of punctuated sounds and silence. Each text takes up questions of what should and should not be shared on the page in retelling the stories of enslavement. While *Olio* stands apart in some ways from the other two texts because of its more celebratory tone and performance, each piece nevertheless questions the politics and prudence of re-creating the conditions of enslavement on the page or in performance.

Conclusion

It is so nice to have faith in our Lord Jesus, Saviour of mankind. . . . Yes, there is nothing like being able to feel His Glorious presence when earthly friends are gone. . . . Yes, we will have trials and tribulation as long as we dwell here, but they are meant for a purpose and we will win crowns if we hold out to the end. . . . With much love to and from all, I am as ever, your very affectionate aunt, Chrissie-Mille.

—Millie Christine McKoy to their niece, care of their great-niece Addie Montgomery, April 1911[1]

Mille-Christine, born July 11, 1851. Columbus County, N.C., a child of Jacob and Monemia McCoy. She lived a life of much comfort owing to her love of God and joy in following His commands. A real friend to the needy of both races and loved by all who knew her. Christine-Mille, died October 8th and 9th, 1912, fully resigned at her home, the place of her birth and residence of her Christian parents. "They that be planted in the House of the Lord shall flourish in the courts of our God."

A soul with two thoughts. Two hearts that beat as one.

—Tombstone of Millie Christine McKoy[2]

I have lived alongside and searched for the McKoys since that fateful day in 2012 in the archives. In scraps of paper. In newspaper clippings. In state records. In tombstones and graves. I have wrestled with a performance world that exemplified the place where ableism and white supremacy touched in the nineteenth and early twentieth centuries. Yet despite the popularity in their heyday of performers like Blind Tom Wiggins, Millie Christine, Joice Heth, and Chang and Eng Bunker, there is a certain willful amnesia about these performers and their legacies today. Perhaps it is because freak shows largely went out of fashion by the mid-twentieth century. Perhaps it is because these performers' legacies remind us of painful histories of the past. And perhaps still it is because these popular performers oversaturated the market when they were at their peak, leaving behind a glut of evidence through souvenirs and memorabilia, but little evidence of lived memory once the generations of gaping audiences that went to see their shows ceased to exist. And once living memory evaporated, so too did the interest in these performers' lives, shows, archives, and strategies. In fact, according to the 1969 booklet from the Columbus County Historical Society that I cite in the epigraphs of this conclusion, "a guard was placed over the grave for nine months after the death to prevent grave robbery, as rumors had been circulated that the bodies would be exhumed for a sideshow attraction. The burial of Mille-Christine was the last in the little family graveyard, and soon brush and brambles overran the area. A large grave marker made from lead-like metal was placed over the grave, but some years later an extremely hot forest fire swept through the woods, destroying the marker. Few people visited the grave and soon the memory of Mille-Chrissy faded."[3] Although at the time of their death they worried that they would be forced to work again postmortem as a sideshow act, the hypervisibility they labored under during life was curiously absent in death. In part this is because of the legal and extralegal means they took to protect their remains, such as having a last will and testament and having a guard stand watch over their graves for many months. It wasn't until they were exhumed and relocated to a more prominent plot in the cemetery with a new tombstone that the McKoys reentered the public imagination in 1968 and 1969, at the urging of the newly formed Columbus County Historical Society.

But although the McKoys' efforts to achieve an anonymity in death that they were denied in life were ultimately unsuccessful in the long term, in the short term they reached their goal. For fifty-seven years between their deaths in 1912 and their exhumation in 1969, they were largely unknown and forgotten. Their return to the spotlight of history is perhaps counter to what they would have ultimately wanted, a fact that I have negotiated with every day while I wrote this book. I have asked myself countless questions over the years about the ethics of exhuming this story and, in turn, returning the McKoys to the glare of inspection that they suffered under on the freak show stage. These questions prove challenging to me because in large part they remain unanswerable. The McKoys are deceased, as are any family members who would have known them in their lifetime. All that remains are the archives, which are notorious for obscuring as much as they reveal.

In the epigraphs of this conclusion, I present two passages: one taken from a letter that was excerpted in the booklet produced by the Columbus County Historical Society in 1969, and the other from their remade tombstone that was restored by the same historical society. In each quotation, there is a preoccupation with death and Christian notions of eternal life after human life ends. It seems that the McKoys in their final days turned to their faith to guide them as they transitioned onward into the next phase of their journey. And regardless of my own complex feelings about and relationship to Christianity, I cannot help but notice the quiet dignity in both their letter to their niece and their tombstones. There is a steadfast dedication to their faith and their belief that what eluded them in this life (anonymity, peace, quiet) would surely be waiting for them in the next because of their dedication to God. And yet these simply expressed desires do not mean that the McKoys and their contemporaries (or fellow enfreaked performers) did not lead extraordinary and complex lives.

And nowhere was the complexity of those lives more evident than in the courtroom. When they were able to enter the courtroom, these performers were able to negotiate on their own behalf, setting boundaries and maneuvering through complex systems of newly found freedom and shifting legality. Outside the court, there were extralegal means that each performer used to maintain and protect their autonomy (the Bunkers' record books and their sons' letters to the doctors who performed their autopsy; Blind Tom's complicated custody battles; the McKoys' letters to the Freedmen's Bureau and the guard that stood watch over their graves; Joice Heth's "sonic of dissent"). However, the court and its fixation on documentation provide a unique window into the worlds of performers like the McKoys precisely because of the quantity of archival remains left behind. And one such example of this is the case of *Millie Christine alias Christine Millie v. Adam Forepaugh* in 1883. The McKoys, who would have been approximately thirty-two years old at the time of the case, sued Forepaugh for libel, claiming he was interfering with their ability to earn a living through his outrageous claims about their act.

The record states that at the time of the complaint, Millie Christine "was and is of good name and repute" and that because of their conjoined body, "she is rendered unable to perform manual labor but by reason of the same acts, the public have been desirous of seeing her and conversing with her" and that "she has by means of such desire been enabled by exhibiting herself, to obtain a livelihood, and to amass some means by which she hopes to become independent and beyond the danger of want."[4] The complaint goes on to note that Forepaugh, who operated a show competing with Batcheller and Doris's Great Inter-Ocean Railroad Show (where the McKoys were performing at the time), on May 20, 1882, "maliciously and with malicious intent to impune this plaintiff in her said business of exhibiting herself for gain," wrote and printed showbills defaming the McKoys and circulated them in Fort Wayne, Indiana, where both circuses were scheduled to appear. The complaint goes on to note the playbills' contents, saying they were

> containing among other things the false and defamatory matter following to wit, "The one great feature this concerns" (meaning thereby the said Batcheller & Doris' Inter Ocean Circus) "extensively advertises is a horribly repulsive Negro monstrosity. (meaning thereby that this plaintiff was and is a horribly repulsive Negro monstrosity.) "No lady would knowingly ever look upon it" (meaning plaintiff) "Little children cover their faces with their hands when encountering this frightful malformation," (meaning that plaintiff is so rightfully malformed as to inspire terror in children) "and the sooner this hideous human deformity is hid from public view the better it will be for the community." (meaning that this plaintiff is a hideous human deformity) "All good Christian people can but regret that this afflicted object should be hawked over the Country to satisfy the greed of a couple of side show exhibitors," all of which was composed and published of and concerning the said plaintiff by the said defendant with the malicious intent aforesaid.[5]

In response to his outrageous claims about the twins, the McKoys demanded $25,000 in compensation from Forepaugh. Unlike previous court cases and legal ventures involving the McKoys, which sought to prove their humanity and right to freedom, the case against Forepaugh was not that he denied them their right to liberty but rather that he prevented them from earning an independent living based on their enfreaked bodies. Their previous forays into the courtroom were initiated with liberty in mind. This case was largely financially motivated. Although they ended their lives concerned with the Christian rewards of everlasting life and eternal rest, during their lifetimes the McKoys were shrewd businesswomen, negotiators, and legal actors. Their suit against Forepaugh serves as evidence of this fact.

Yet if I've learned anything in my decade plus of studying enfreakment, sideshows, slavery, and disability, it is when to distrust the archive and when to dig deeper for unwritten potential meanings and intentions. The case with Forepaugh is a notable example of this. While it remains unclear to me if the McKoys were awarded anything (let alone $25,000) from Forepaugh, the audacity of two Black disabled formerly enslaved women suing a white man for libel in particular in 1883 is not lost on me. That they were able to assert a right not only to bodily autonomy (as they did when they refused further semipublic examination postemancipation) but also to an untarnished name and reputation is a radical Black feminist act in and of itself. The gall of Forepaugh to claim that "all good Christian people can but regret that this afflicted object should be hawked over the Country to satisfy the greed of a couple of side show exhibitors" I imagine may have especially rankled the McKoys, who were well known throughout their lives for their Christian faith and propriety.[6] To even insinuate that "good Christian people" should not attend their shows out of a sense of pity and decorum seems to work counter to every account of the McKoys that I have come across. For at the end of the day, outside of their remarkable acts of appearing onstage and aural fugitivity, the McKoys' most valuable asset was their name and reputation. By threatening that, Forepaugh threatened their livelihood and, in turn, their independence.

Much of the story of the McKoys and their contemporaries is a story of the fight for an independent life free from the constraints and perils of enfreakment. It is what drove the McKoys to purchase the land on which they were born and formerly enslaved before their home burned to the ground in a grisly fire. It drove Blind Tom's mother in her yearslong custody disputes for her son. It is present in Joice Heth's cry. Even the

Bunkers attempted to separate themselves from their freak show past by marrying white sisters and becoming enslavers themselves, two acts that granted them a tangential and impermanent connection to the planter class. Yet despite the (at times) overwhelming paper trails left behind by these artists, there remains very little I can clearly attribute to their own voices or hands. There are snippets of letters and a last will and testament (which may not be attributable to them) from the McKoys.[7] In fact the only copy of the will that I've encountered was a paper that had evidently been scanned and printed and rescanned several times before it reached my hands at the North Carolina State Archives in Raleigh. Years later when I contacted the archive for a better copy, even the scan was undiscoverable and the original proved challenging to track down, leaving me with only a blurry cell phone photo and my notes to go off of. There are the Bunkers' letters and ledgers, and Blind Tom's musical compositions stand as a certain kind of "voice" amid the archival noise. And Heth's debunking autopsy and her sonic disruptions are her sole voice (if they even can be considered that).

But what do these small moments in time captured on film or paper or microfiche actually amount to? And what are they evidence of? In more ways than one, these small acts of archival defiance are the counterweights to the currencies of cruelty I have excavated in this book. They are proof of an alternative ledger of enslaved labor that considers performance and performance labor equally alongside more traditional forms of manual enslaved labor. Because of the airs and graces of "refinement" that surrounded these acts of appearance, the presence of labor has long been discounted or underknown when studying the legacies of slavery. And yet this story should be told, as it sheds a valuable light on the histories of where disability and slavery meet.

There is and was much struggle at the interstices of enslavement and disability. There were the sideshow proprietors vying for the audience's attention and hard-earned dollars. There were the audiences, themselves a force that was equal parts objectifying and wondering at the performance acumen of these figures. There were contracts broken and undeniable harm done. And yet in spite of these drawbacks, there was also ingenuity, creativity, artistry, and survival. This case with Forepaugh stands today as just one example of this fact. The McKoys asserted that they had the desire to continue to perform their act after emancipation (although this desire was undoubtedly complicated by acts of coercion). They also asserted a right to perform free from harassment and the fear of losing their income.

In the prologue of this book, I recalled entering the Hayes Plantation Library at the University of North Carolina at Chapel Hill and how that encounter with the legacies and opulence of slavery shook me and brought me to tears. I still recall it as I pen the conclusion of this book—the deep feeling of an unsettled history that not only is transmitted through the mind but continues to resonate deeply in the body, what Christina Sharpe has named "the wake" of Blackness, Diana Taylor called the repertoire and the archives of performance, and Joseph Roach named surrogation.[8] It is the common transmission of the memory of performance through the body and through lived experience. It is the common corporeal language of the Black diaspora in the United States: the lived and embodied knowledge of loss and performance. But to name it entirely as loss or harm would be to apply a misnomer to the feeling. It is also the will to survive and do otherwise when the world seems determined to diminish you. I think that is what drove me the most in the completion of this book.

I have asked myself many times if this book needed to be written. I still have no definitive answer to that question. Instead, I think often of the length of time that Christine survived after Millie's unfortunate death. The estimates vary on the exact amount of time she continued on before she was euthanized. Some say it was a matter of a few hours; others estimate it closer to half a day or an entire day. Although I cannot fathom what was going through her mind as her lifelong companion lay motionless beside her, I imagine there was an insurmountable sense of grief. All of her life she had been in the company of her sister. They had common dreams and sensations, a united body and profession. They spent every conscious moment of their lives attached to each other and now, in death, Christine was finally alone. What thoughts must have crossed her mind as her sister lay motionless beside her? In the hours before doctors decided to euthanize her, did she feel Millie's presence still like a phantom limb? Did she remember their travels and their shared secrets? Their life on the road and in the spotlight?

I will never know the answers to these questions, and perhaps it is better that I don't. In her poem "Millie-Christine," Marilyn Nelson imagines just such a moment for the McKoys. Told from Christine's point of view after the death of Millie, it states,

Pray I will die before Millie grows stiff,
my heartbeat crushed by iron calipers.
Pray Millie-Christine will depart from life
as we came, side by side, through heaven's door.

I'm not afraid. Death's just another tour
to a place so impossibly far off
no one ever returns. And furthermore,
it has no mail service.
    She's growing stiff.

In bed we used to talk about the grief
of being the one left behind for hours.
Millie took comfort in her firm belief
that her heart would soon be crushed by calipers.

So this is independence. Lonelier
than we imagined. Heavier to lift
the weight of consciousness, not helped by her.
Pray Aunt Chrissie will soon be freed from life.

The cherubs will be asking for autographs.
Millie's making a place for her sister.
Peace, children. Always be the better half.
We're going side-by-side through heaven's door.

Maybe, someday, when I am nothing more
than playbills, three gold rings, and photographs,
we'll be remembered as an Ancestor
(or two). God bless you. Pray I won't be left
long, while Millie grows stiff.[9]

Told in seven parts, the poem details the McKoys' lives, rise to fame, kidnapping attempts, world travels, and ultimate demise. Imagining this final section from the perspective of Christine, Nelson dives into the interiority of their shared life and the agony Christine must have felt as she lay next to her dead sister, knowing it harkened not only her own death but also the potential intrusion of medical men, signaled by the repeated image of a heart or heartbeat soon to be "crushed by calipers." Nelson has Christine predict her future after avoiding autopsy, writing, "Maybe, someday, when I am nothing more / than playbills, three gold rings, and photographs." She consciously writes Christine (and therefore Millie) into the archive, naming the documents that remain pertaining to their lives. A photograph, like the one I first saw that drew me down the road to this book. The playbills I searched for any trace of the McKoys' unadulterated voices. The gold rings that remained when they were finally exhumed. These objects serve as touchstones for a future that Christine will not reach, when she becomes "an Ancestor / (or two)."

Nelson's telling of the McKoys' death details a careful engagement with the future perfect. She shows a Millie Christine who are deeply aware and concerned about how they will be remembered and what future generations will call them. This imaginary Christine projects into the future how she and her sister will be rediscovered and (quite literally) taken up again from the grave as historical subjects and objects in equal measure. This heightened self-awareness in death is punctuated by the repeating line that begins "Pray I . . ." and ends "Millie grows stiff." Christine offers up a prayer that her life will end shortly and she won't be left alive without her sister. And yet halfway through the section we learn "she's growing stiff." This flat line accentuates the realization of Christine's worst fear. So what began as a prayer that she would die before Millie grew stiff by the end of the poem is transformed into, "Pray I won't be left / long, while Millie grows stiff."

The subtle change here hints at a vulnerability that the McKoys, in life, did not often display for their paying publics. In Nelson's retelling there is a conversation, both between the sisters and between each sister and herself, that they were denied in life. For lives so well documented, the archive is curiously devoid of personal items related to the McKoys. I remember my shock at seeing such unusual items as the Bunkers' silverware displayed in the archives on my first trip to the University of North Carolina at Chapel Hill. Their archives (while still largely dominated by public-facing items such as playbills, newspaper articles, and photographs) have a comparative intimacy when looked at next to the McKoys'. I know the curvatures of Chang's and Eng's handwriting from their ledger books. I know when they spent money on postage and playbills and their household. I know from archival photos that their large brood of children produced many heirs, who would occasionally get together for family reunions at least until the 1980s and 1990s. (Although I didn't come across pictures from later dates, this does not necessarily indicate that these reunions didn't continue.) I know some of the names of the people they owned. I know the shapes of their bodies from the Mütter Museum's plaster display. I have seen their insides as a result of that same display.

The archive will never produce an entirely complete accounting of the lives and legacies of the McKoys and their contemporaries. It cannot be relied on for an accurate or impartial telling of the lives of those who were enfreaked, enslaved, and exploited throughout their lifetimes. To carry the expectation that it ever could would be unwise in the face of so much evidence to the contrary. But what the performance archive can provide is a way of examining the remains of the past with the question, "Why was this placed here?" at the forefront of our minds. We can continue to mine the archive for sites of contention and the future-perfect thinking that drove those who documented the past for future consumption to record these stories there alongside more well-known events like war or famine or political upheaval. In other words, we can attempt to articulate why these freak show and sideshow histories, although obscure, were deemed worthy of protection for future generations.

I have asked myself many times, "Why now? Why write this book on freak shows, a long-outdated and largely forgotten practice, today for a twenty-first-century audience?" The plainest answer is that I believe this work tells a story about the intersections of disability history and slavery that needs to be told. I am still the same person who was drawn to a simple photograph of two Black women in the nineteenth century standing proud and erect in front of the lens of the camera, their gazes unwavering and unflinching. I am still the woman who wondered at the fact that they grew old together, who felt she recognized, if not their identities, then something in their bearing that harkened to generations of Black women, defiant, holding the gaze of the onlookers who gaped at their forms. Corresponding (and even conflicting) truths can exist at the same time. For me, the import of this work has been to embrace the fact of my superstitious first encounter with the years I've subsequently spent researching and writing this book.

As their tombstone notes, Millie Christine were "a soul with two thoughts. Two hearts that beat as one." The distinction here of the mind as functioning in connection with but also separately from the body is striking to me. In asserting that they shared a singular soul but two independent minds and two hearts that worked in unison, the inscription highlights the complications of distinguishing the McKoys from each other. In life and even in death, they preferred the singular first-person pronoun *I* when referring to themselves. They signed their will as one person. They lived united, spending their time on the stage convincing paying audiences that they indeed had intelligent and separate minds. But in their death the question is raised again where to delineate Christine's and Millie's individual identities.

In the letter to their niece that is excerpted as the first epigraph in this chapter, the McKoys show a preoccupation with death and Christian notions of eternal life through God. This brief passage presents the closest I have come to locating the McKoys' unmediated voices, and yet even this excerpt proves unsatisfactory. Alternating between the first-person singular "I" and the first-person plural "we," the McKoys show a certain maudlin hopefulness at the prospect of dying. In some ways this offers us brief insight into their thinking as they approached the end of their lives, letting us know that they weren't fearful so much about the prospect of death as about the prospect of what would come after (namely, autopsy and further public display). In Nelson's imagining of their deaths, Christine traces the hours passing after Millie has died with a certain stoic fearfulness that contradicts this letter to their niece. I wonder now at the joint dreams that Millie Christine professed to have (noted in the introduction to this book). Where did dying factor into those dreams? Death for them represented not only an end to the physical ailments that plagued them at the end of their lives but also a reprieve from the humiliations and exploitations of the freak show stages they graced with their talents.

In their last will and testament (the authenticity of which was later contested by local historians), they bequeath the entirety of their remaining estate to their sister Clarrah Yeoman and four nieces, essentially guaranteeing that the women in their family would benefit most from their earnings. They write,

> Second,—I give *devise* and bequeath all the rest, residue and remainder of my estate both real and personal to my beloved sister Clarrah Yeoman to have and to hold to her my said sister during all of her natural life, after her death I give, desire, and bequeath the same all the right and title to all of my estate, both real and personal to my four nieces, namely: Millia Christine Chaney, daughter of *Coleman* McKoy, Flossey McKoy, a daughter of Josiah McKoy, Isabella McKoy, daughter of *Biston (Riston??)* McKoy, and Emma *Puree*, my younger sister's baby girl to have and to hold to them, equal share and share alike each one and unto them and their heirs and *assigns* forever.[10]

This expression of the desire to have the women in their family inherit their property serves as one final act of resistance on the part of the McKoys. All they fought for and earned, through their travels, performances, court cases, letters to the Freedmen's Bureau, and extrajudicial maneuvering, would enrich their direct female descendants. This serves as a powerful reminder of the business acumen and savvy they possessed, even during their dying days.

What is left to say about the lives of the McKoys and their freak show contemporaries? Today the remnants of their memories within popular culture are largely confined to shows and movies such as the 2014–15 season of Ryan Murphy's campy anthology series *American Horror Story* subtitled *Freak Show* and the film *The Greatest Showman*. The former presents a sideshow and freak show culture tinged by horror. The latter provided the direct opposite in the form of a saccharinely cloying retelling that centers largely on a sanitized life story of P. T. Barnum, played by a dashing Hugh Jackman. But the truth of the historical stories remains, located somewhere between these two poles.

The truth is that the highs and many lows of nineteenth- and early twentieth-century freak shows still remain in the margins of our collective cultural understanding of disability and performance. While teaching a course called Performing the "Freak" in Pop Culture in 2018, I opened the first lecture with a short screening from *American Horror Story: Freak Show*. The series unfolds as an anthology, each season starting a fresh storyline with no direct connection to the season before. The cast remains somewhat stable, most often anchored by veteran actress Jessica Lange. Each season is titled in the same way, beginning with *American Horror Story* and followed by a subtitle that identifies that season's theme. Sometimes the subtitle gestures toward a location (such as the seasons on "hotel" or "murder house"), and in others it's more of a reference to a cultural idea associated with psychological horror (such as "cult" or "coven"). In some instances these two are combined, so that the location is one that bears with it the implication of psychological horror. I would argue that the seasons *Roanoke*, *Asylum*, and *Freak Show* illustrate this particular function.

When asking my students about the opening scenes I showed of Murphy's campy, outlandish, garish, and intensely saturated world, I was surprised at the number of sideshow, circus, and freak show markers they flagged or recognized. They noted the warped and atmospheric organ music that reminded them of the circus. One student pointed to the use of helium balloons, another to the bodies of the conjoined twins (played by Sarah Paulson), and yet another to the turn-of-the-century style of the homes that peppered the background of those early scenes. They said that they knew what the music, the tents, the disabled bodies, and the horrified shrieks were supposed to signal. Yet when I asked if any of them had ever attended a live freak show with human performers, none of them raised their hands. In that first class I also showed a short excerpt from Tod Browning's 1932 film *Freaks*, which features actual circus and sideshow performers in the cast yet was widely criticized and later banned upon its first release. Again they understood a surprising number of puns and jokes. They mentioned familiarity with the love story farce of the conjoined twins who had two different husbands (played in the film by Daisy and Violet Hilton).[11] They mentioned the performer Josephine-Joseph, who was described as a "true hermaphrodite," with one side presenting as a man and the other as a woman, and was often the center of jokes. I questioned them on what made the show from 2014, with the theme of the "freak" at its center, so frightening. And I asked why they believed that Browning's *Freaks* remains, to this day, a controversial cult favorite with a relatively small circulation. Their answer to these questions, unexpectedly, came in the form of the milkman who stumbles upon a murder in the opening scene of *American*

Horror Story: Freak Show. They all claimed to know and recognize the Americana image of the "milkman" and they sensed something was awry as soon as they saw him approach the old porch that was filled with unopened milk bottles. They all recognized the milkman, from his white uniform down to his glass bottles and wire basket. None of them had ever seen a milkman in real life before or had their milk delivered. But his image was enough for them to recognize him, empathize with him, and fear for him as he entered the freak-inhabited home.

But if we set aside the presumptions of horror, disgust, or condescending empathy (in the case of *The Greatest Showman*), then what remains? I argue that the answer lies in something as layered and complex as Nelson's poem, or the McKoys' letter to their niece, or even the court cases against Adam Forepaugh. What remains is a complex portrait of lies so exceptional that they perhaps could never have escaped archival capture. And yet these same lies defy and resist the traditional bounds of archival capture at every turn. Instead what remains is the future-perfect anticipation that each performer engaged in to complicate their archival legacies and memories, even today. By being keenly aware of the ways that they were portrayed and ultimately remembered, each artist leaves behind a complex legacy of slavery, freedom, disability, and performance that this book only does a small part to unpack. The rest remains, perhaps for the best, lost in the margins of the archives, never to be told.

ACKNOWLEDGMENTS

As I near the end of a process more than a decade in the making, I am filled with no small measure of anxiety and awe. I feel anxiety because this book has grown alongside me through some of the most formative years of my life and I am now releasing it into an unpredictable world. It lived with me as a project that became the constant companion of my twenties. As a monograph, it has shadowed me through the early years of my thirties and the beginnings of my career as a professor. I, along with this book, have been an imperfect project in a constant state of progress and process. But I am in awe because both this book and this author would not exist without the loving generosity and support of my community. When the work (both great and small) felt insurmountable, the love of my community filled me to overflowing. I am forever in their collective debt. I will attempt here to name a few of the vast army of folks whose love is coded into the line breaks and margins of this work. I pray I do justice to the immensity of their kindness.

To begin, first and always, I would like to thank my parents, Ronald and Paulette. They gave me a capacious sense of identity and self-worth from an early age that made all things seem possible to me. Most importantly of all, they made me feel capable of great things even as a small child. Mama and Daddy, I love you so much. I hope that this book honors the investments of love and care you've made in me and makes you proud. To Brian and Kim: I'm honored to call you not only my siblings but also my friends. Thank you for growing with me all of these years. And to the newest addition to our family: Becky, you're a wonderful sister-in-law (and a damn good hype woman). I am so blessed to share deep kinship (and a last name) with all five of you. And to my irascible and wonderful grandfather Arthur McDonald: You make 102 years old look effortless. You and my three other grandparents started a project decades ago that instilled in your descendants the life-changing and world-making power of a good education. Thank you for always asking me if my schoolwork was done. Thank you for buying two ice creams for each of us at the ice cream truck (even though our mother hated it). And thank you for the gift of a strong sense of humor. Love you, Papa.

A friend once joked to me that I seem to have a mentor for every situation. And while it was meant in jest, it actually bears the ring of truth as all good jokes tend to do. I have been well mentored and guided on this academic journey from undergrad to now. I dedicate this book in part to the world-changing power and Black feminist praxis of good mentorship and care. To Thadious Davis, Tsitsi Jaji, and Salamishah Tillet: Thank you for your early commitment to me and my work. You took a (somewhat hardheaded) teenager and turned her into a scholar. To Rosemary Malague and Cary Mazer: Thank you for gifting me the magic and wonder of a life in theater as well as your early support and production of *Curio*. You gave me the education of a lifetime. To the students and collaborators from the University of Pennsylvania's 2018 Edinburgh Project, Duval Courteau, Aria Proctor, Breyasia Scott, and Hannah Spear; student composer Elias Kotsis; scenic designer Sara Outing; and production manager Eric Baratta: Thank you for bringing my early vision to life. And to the McKoys from my 2023 production of *Curio*, Charence Higgins and Felica Oduh; our director of photography Brian Inocencio; composer Autumn Maria Reed; my executive producers Hilary Giorgi and Andrew Kornhaber; graphic designer Mark Olsen; and the entire crew: You were immeasurably wonderful to work with. Thank you.

I would be totally remiss in my efforts at expressing gratitude if I did not take time to thank my mentors. To my dissertation chair Joe Roach: You stewarded this project with a support, wisdom, and grace that leaves me tender and teary-eyed when I recall it. Your work and our collective thinking are folded deep within the pages of this book. If this book touches even one student in the ways your work has touched me, it would be the honor of a lifetime. To the ever-brilliant and incandescently badass Daphne Brooks: Your arrival at Yale University, your mentorship, and your insistence that there was a multitude of ways for Black women to not only survive academia but thrive were world-altering. I cannot thank you enough. To the wonderful Elizabeth Alexander and Jafari Allen: Thank you for modeling a Black feminist praxis in real time. Your offices were always safe havens for me, and you've taught me that the most brilliant people are smart enough to know that kindness is the cure. I am honored by the kindness you both have shown me.

To my colleagues, friends, and comrades who have supported me on this journey since graduate school and beyond—Aldrin Abastillas, Raquel Adorno, Masi Asare, Lovell Bainbridge, Melissa Blanco Borelli, Joe Bowie, Stan Brown, Joshua Chambers-Letson, Esi and Monica Codjoe, Tracy Davis, Tommy DeFrantz, Patrice Delaney, Tom Delaney, Roger Ellis, Marcela Fuentes, Nadine George Graves, Hilary Giorgi, Henry Godinez, Shane Humphrey, Ryan Jobson, E. Patrick Johnson, Andrew Kornhaber, Susan Manning, Taylor O'Brien, Camille Owens, Kaneesha Parsard, Detra Payne, Miriam Petty, Dassia Posner, Ramon Rivera Severa, Christofer Rodelo, Tyler Rogers, Liz Son, Damian and Daniela Vergara, and everyone in Northwestern University's Departments of Theatre, Black Studies, and Performance Studies: Thank you for listening, carefully reading early drafts of this work, inviting me to give talks, writing letters of support for various fellowships and grants, cheering me on and shouting me out when I needed a boost, and extending general camaraderie and support. You are wonders and I am honored to work alongside you. You have sharpened my thinking through your care. A special thank-you to my tenure mentor Dassia Posner, whose unwavering support, optimism, encouragement, and grace under fire are truly a model for mentorship.

To the graduate students who served as my research assistants at key moments during the writing of this book, Deon Custard, Brandon Greenhouse, Sierra Rosetta, Emry Sottile, and Linnea Valdivia, and to my undergraduate research assistant Asha Navaratnasingam: Thank you for your time and attention to this work. To the undergraduate and graduate students in my Performing the "Freak" in Pop Culture seminar (which I've had the privilege to teach three times, once at Yale and twice at Northwestern): thank you for working and thinking alongside me to sharpen the questions I ask and the answers I seek. Additional thanks for the editorial work of Sara Brady, Mariellen Sandford, and Richard Schechner at *The Drama Review* and Patricia Herrera, Caitlin Marshall, Marci McMahon (as guest editors), and Peter Dickinson at *Performance Matters* for their guidance on key parts of the research that was published in these journals. I would also like to thank the anonymous reviewers for their careful and thorough notes and revision suggestions. This book is better because of your collective work.

To the librarians and archivists at the University of North Carolina at Chapel Hill, the North Carolina State Archives, and the Beinecke Rare Book and Manuscript Library (with particular note of Melissa Barton and Nancy Kuhl at Yale, whose early belief in this project was invaluable): Thank you. And to the librarians and staff of Northwestern's library system (with special thanks to Steven Adams, Dana Lamparello, and Jason Nargis): I am deeply appreciative of all the work you've done to support my classes and research in my time at Northwestern. To the faculty of Yale's Departments of African American Studies, American Studies, and Women's, Gender, and Sexuality Studies: Thank you. I'd estimate that by the time I finished grad school, I had probably gone to office hours with about 75 percent of you, and I always opened with some version of the same line: "Can you help me talk about freaks?" Your open doors and minds have buoyed me. And to all of the departments, summer institutes, working groups, and symposia that have given me the space and opportunity to workshop this project: You have my utmost gratitude. Key parts of this research were developed in conversation with scholars and colleagues at the American Society for Theatre Research, the Association for Theatre in Higher Education, the American Studies Association, the Northwestern Performance Studies Summer Institute, the Ford Fellows conference, the Society of Nineteenth-Century Americanists, the American Comparative Literature Association, Northwestern's Black Studies Department, Yale's Black Feminist Reading Group, and programs in women's, gender, and sexuality studies and LGBT studies. The completion of both this book and my companion project *Curio* would not have been possible without the generous support of Northwestern's Kaplan Center for the Humanities (which is run by rock stars), the Ford Foundation, the Beinecke, the Dean's Office of Northwestern's School of Communication, and Northwestern's Office of the Provost. I am thankful to the Mellon Foundation and the Northwestern Department of Black Studies for the postdoc year during which formulated much of my thinking for this book. To my editors Stephanie Batiste, Robin Bernstein, and Brian Herrera: I am immeasurably grateful for your continued championing of this book and of me throughout this process. Being a first-time author is daunting (to say the very least), and you have made this process unexpectedly joyful. A special thank-you to Robin for providing a careful eye on multiple early drafts and half-baked chapters, and to Stephanie for guiding me across the finish line. Your gentle and patient editorial work are appreciated and necessary. To Furqan Sayeed and Eric Zinner at NYU Press: Thanks for shepherding this book into the world.

And last in my mentions but first in my heart: to my partner, Amanda Suckow. You are everything a partner should be. Tender when I am tired, funny and irreverent when I'm down, so kind and good when I am stressed and drowning in work. The best parts of me are safe with you. I look forward to coming home to you (and our three naughty cats) every day. Without you this book would never have been finished. I love you so much, BBQ.

I often joke with the people I love that I'm so sarcastic that I misspell *sincerely* at the end of my emails. That is because while sincerity feels vulnerable, sarcasm can serve as a convenient shield. But I also have a habit of holding the people whom I cherish most with both of my eyes closed. And so I say with my most sincere heart: I hold all of you with both of my eyes closed.

NOTES

PROLOGUE

1 Examples of the intermingling of the autobiographical and the political in US autobiography and history are Glenda Elizabeth Gilmore, *Defying Dixie: The Radical Roots of Civil Rights, 1919–1950* (W. W. Norton, 2008); and Jonathan Scott Holloway, *Jim Crow Wisdom: Memory and Identity in Black America Since 1940* (University of North Carolina Press, 2013).

2 Notable examples of thinking about the role the imagination plays in archival recovery include Saidiya Hartman's work on "critical fabulation" in her monograph *Scenes of Subjection: Terror, Slavery, and Self-Making in Nineteenth-Century America* (Oxford University Press, 1997), as well as her work on silence in the archive in her article "Venus in Two Acts," *Small Axe: A Caribbean Journal of Criticism* 12, no. 2 (2008): 1–14.

3 Millie and Christine most often referred to themselves as a single person. This fact is noted in their "autobiography" as well as in interviews with surviving family members after they died. For the purposes of this book, I will refer to them mostly as Millie Christine to reflect this fact.

4 Hartman, *Scenes of Subjection*.

5 Toni Morrison, "The Site of Memory," in *Inventing the Truth: The Art and Craft of Memoir*, ed. William Zinsser (Houghton Mifflin, 1995); Salamishah Tillet, *Sites of Slavery: Citizenship and Racial Democracy in the Post–Civil Rights Imagination* (Duke University Press, 2012).

6 Hilton Als, "Remembering 'Gone with the Wind,'" *New Yorker*, July 1, 2011.

7 Saidiya V. Hartman, *Lose Your Mother: A Journey Along the Atlantic Slave Route* (Farrar, Straus and Giroux, 2007).

INTRODUCTION

1 Jenifer L. Barclay, "Mothering the 'Useless': Black Motherhood, Disability, and Slavery," *Women, Gender, and Families of Color* 2, no. 2 (2014): 115–40; Dea Hadley Boster, *African American Slavery and Disability: Bodies, Property and Power in the Antebellum South, 1800–1860* (Routledge, 2013); Therí A. Pickens, *Black Madness: Mad Blackness* (Duke University Press, 2019); Edna Edith Sayers, "From Freak Show to Jim Crow: A Siamese Twin and His Deaf Daughter in the Antebellum and Postbellum South," *Sign Language Studies* 22, no. 4 (2022): 553–89; Sami Schalk, *Black Disability Politics* (Duke University Press, 2022).

2 Saidiya V. Hartman, *Scenes of Subjection: Terror, Slavery, and Self-Making in Nineteenth-Century America* (Oxford University Press, 1997); Michel-Rolph Trouillot, *Silencing the Past: Power and the Production of History* (Beacon, 1995).

3 D. Soyini Madison, *Critical Ethnography: Methods, Ethics, and Performance* (SAGE Publications, 2005); Richard Schechner, *Performance Studies: An Introduction* (Routledge, 2013).

4 Tina Campt, *A Black Gaze: Artists Changing How We See* (MIT Press, 2021); Saidiya Hartman, "Venus in Two Acts," *Small Axe* 12, no. 2 (2008): 1–14; Lisa Lowe, *The Intimacies of Four Continents* (Duke University Press, 2015); Hortense Spillers, "Mama's Baby, Papa's Maybe: An American Grammar Book," *Diacritics* 17, no. 2 (1987): 65–81.

5 Daphne A. Brooks, *Bodies in Dissent: Spectacular Performances of Race and Freedom, 1850–1910* (Duke University Press, 2006); Uri McMillan, *Embodied Avatars: Genealogies of Black Feminist Art and Performance* (New York University Press, 2015); Cynthia Wu, *Chang and Eng Reconnected: The Original Siamese Twins in American Culture* (Temple University Press, 2012); Benjamin Reiss, *The Showman and the Slave: Race, Death, and Memory in Barnum's America* (Harvard University Press, 2001); Joseph Roach, *Cities of the Dead: Circum-Atlantic Performance* (Columbia University Press, 1996).

6 Rachel Adams, "Disability and the Circus," in *The American Circus*, ed. Susan Weber et al. (Yale University Press, 2012).

7 See Tyehimba Jess, *Olio* (Wave Books, 2016); as well as work by Marilyn Nelson, Glenda Gilmore, and Daphne Brooks.

8 Drawing on Saidiya Hartman's monograph *Scenes of Subjection*, the theoretical frameworks of the refinements of cruelty consider public performance spaces in which variously raced bodies intermingle in a complicated taxonomy of the consumption of manners. See C. L. R. James's *The Black Jacobins: Toussaint L'Ouverture and the San Domingo Revolution* (Vintage, 1963) and Jill Casid's monograph *Sowing Empire: Landscape and Colonization* (University of Minnesota Press, 2005) for further reading on the intersections of space, narrative, and historical reimagining, all of which are crucial to this work.

9 James, *Black Jacobins*, 8–13.

10 James, *Black Jacobins*, 13–14.

11 Ellen Samuels, "Examining Millie and Christine McKoy: Where Enslavement and Enfreakment Meet," *Signs* 37, no. 1 (2011): 53–81.

12 Judith Butler, *Giving an Account of Oneself* (Fordham University Press, 2005).

13 Stephanie Smallwood, *Saltwater Slavery: A Middle Passage from Africa to American Diaspora* (Harvard University Press, 2008); Miranda Joseph, "Making Debt," *Occasion: Debt* 7 (2014); Jennifer L. Morgan, *Reckoning with Slavery: Gender, Kinship, and Capitalism in the Early Black Atlantic* (Duke University Press, 2017); Daina Ramey Berry, *The Price for Their Pound of Flesh: The Value of the Enslaved from Womb to Grave in the Building of a Nation* (Beacon, 2017), Kindle.

14 "Some dead bodies were cultivated as cadavers, trafficked and sold to medical schools for human anatomy courses at major institutions throughout the North and South. Untangling what I call the domestic cadaver trade, I also address some aspects of enslaved people's ideas about the afterlife and their preferences for specific burial rituals, even when doctors wanted to harvest their bodies for dissection." Berry, *Price for Their Pound*, 3.

15 This improvisational umbrella of virtuosic enfreaked performance is also represented in Thomas "Blind Tom" Wiggins's piano playing and Joice Heth's "sonic of dissent" as theorized by Uri McMillan. The case of Chang and Eng Bunker, who rose to prominence as freak show performers and spent their later years as slave owners before returning to the sideshow stage after the Civil War, stands outside this formulation in some regards.

16 Moten uses the phrase "(anti-, ante-[slave]) narrative fashion" in *In the Break: The Aesthetics of the Black Radical Tradition* (University of Minnesota Press, 2003), 24. Tinsley states, "As we navigate the postmodern we must look for the fissures that show how the anti- and ante-modern continue to configure black queer broken-and-wholeness. At the same time, the meaningfully multi-blued Atlantic tells us that we must continue to navigate our field *metaphorically*." Omise'eke Natasha Tinsley, "Black Atlantic, Queer Atlantic: Queer Imaginings of the Middle Passage," *GLQ: A Journal of Gay and Lesbian Studies* 14, no. 2–3 (2008): 212.

17 Hartman, "Venus in Two Acts,"; Lowe, *The Intimacies of Four Continents*; Spillers, "Mama's Baby, Papa's Maybe," 65.

18 Daphne A. Brooks, *Bodies in Dissent: Spectacular Performances of Race and Freedom, 1850–1910* (Duke University Press, 2006); Uri McMillan, *Embodied Avatars: Genealogies of Black Feminist Art and Performance* (New York University Press, 2015).

19 W. E. B. Du Bois, *The Souls of Black Folk*, ed. Farah Jasmine Griffin (Barnes and Noble Classics, 2005).

CHAPTER 1. ALTERNATIVE LEDGERS OF ENSLAVED LABOR

1 Joanne Martell, *Millie-Christine: Fearfully and Wonderfully Made* (John F. Blair, 2000).

2 Martell, *Millie-Christine*, 205.

3 Judith Butler, *Giving an Account of Oneself* (Fordham University Press, 2005).

4 Millie Christine bio sketch, 1883, Beinecke Rare Book and Manuscript Library.

5 Linda Frost, *Conjoined Twins in Black and White: The Lives of Millie-Christine McKoy and Daisy and Violet Hilton* (University of Wisconsin Press, 2009).

6 This improvisational umbrella of virtuosic enfreaked performance is also represented in Thomas "Blind Tom" Wiggins's piano playing and Joice Heth's "sonic of dissent" as theorized by Uri McMillan. The case of Chang and Eng Bunker, who rose to prominence as freak show performers and spent their later years as slave owners before returning to the sideshow stage after the Civil War, stands outside this formulation in some regards.

7 Martell, *Millie-Christine*, 136.

8 See *New Berne (NC) Journal*, November 23, 1897; *Raleigh News and Observer*, October 10, 1912; *Raleigh News and Observer*, September 27, 1925; *Raleigh Register*, October 22, 1853; *News Reporter* (Whiteville, NC), December 10, 1925; *News Reporter* (Whiteville, NC), March 29, 1934.

9 See *New Berne (NC) Journal*, November 23, 1897; *Raleigh News and Observer*, October 10, 1912; *Raleigh News and Observer*, September 27, 1925; *Raleigh Register*, October 22, 1853; *News Reporter* (Whiteville, NC), December 10, 1925; *News Reporter* (Whiteville, NC), March 29, 1934.

10 See Millie Christine McKoy, last will and testament, North Carolina State Archives, Raleigh, NC.

11 Lieutenant Echelberry to General Allan Rutherford, August 17, 1866, Freedmen's Bureau Collection, National Archives, cited in Ellen Samuels, "Examining Millie and Christine McKoy: Where Enslavement and Enfreakment Meet," *Signs* 37, no. 1 (2011): 63–65.

12 Quoted in Samuels, "Examining Millie and Christine," 63–65.

13 After age fourteen the twins were never examined naked by a medical professional, with the exception of their 1871 visit to Dr. Pancoast when they were being treated for an abscess-like formation on their genitals. Samuels, "Examining Millie and Christine," 66–69.

14 Millie Christine bio sketch. Most versions of the (auto)biography list "receptions" that Millie Christine held for both public audiences and various European dignitaries as part of their touring routine. See also letter to the editor, *Wilmington (NC) Daily Herald*, June 9, 1859; Touchatout and La Fosse, *Trombinoscope*, November 1873; and reviews from the *Raleigh News and Observer*, October 10, 1912, and September 27, 1925; *Raleigh Register*, October 22, 1853; *New Berne (NC) Journal*, November 23, 1897; *News Reporter* (Whiteville, NC), December 10, 1925, and March 29, 1934; *Wilmington (NC) Daily Herald*, June 9, 1859; and *Wilmington (NC) Morning Star*, October 10, 1912. All sources cite the twins' multilingual performance skills as a central drawing force of their act as well as a primary mode of distinguishing the two sisters from each other.

15 Millie Christine bio sketch.

16 Millie-Christine [McKoy], *The History of the Carolina Twins: "Told in Their Own Peculiar Way" by "One of Them"* (Buffalo Courier Printing House, [18—?]), http://docsouth.unc.edu/neh/millie-christine/millie-christine.html.

17 National Museum of African American History and Culture, "Freedmen's Bureau and the McCoy Custody Battle," accessed January 21, 2025, www.searchablemuseum.com.

18 National Museum of African American History and Culture, "Freedmen's Bureau."

19 See Jennifer L. Morgan, *Laboring Women: Reproduction and Gender in New World Slavery* (University of Pennsylvania Press, 2004), and other works on financial motivations for slavery in the introduction chapter.

20 Bill of sale for two slaves sold to Chang and Eng Bunker, September 29, 1845, Chang and Eng Bunker Papers #3761, Southern Historical Collection, Wilson

Library, University of North Carolina at Chapel Hill. For the purposes of this book, I will refer to her as "Nicey."

21 Vincent Woodard, *The Delectable Negro: Human Consumption and Homoeroticism Within U.S. Slave Culture*, eds. Justin A. Joyce and Dwight A. McBride (New York University Press, 2014).

22 Receipt for a piece of land sold to David _____, December 9, 1840, North Carolina Collection, Wilson Library, University of North Carolina at Chapel Hill.

23 Bill of sale for slaves, November 20, 1855, Chang and Eng Bunker Papers #3761, Southern Historical Collection, Wilson Library, University of North Carolina at Chapel Hill.

24 An account of money received by Chang-Eng, 1833–1839, Chang and Eng Bunker Papers #3761, Southern Historical Collection, Wilson Library, University of North Carolina at Chapel Hill.

25 An account of monies expended by Chang-Eng, 1832–1841, North Carolina Collection Gallery, Wilson Library, University of North Carolina at Chapel Hill.

26 Harry Z. Tucker, "Siamese Twins Were Good Farmers," *Progressive Farmer*, November 1939 (this source reports seventy-five enslaved laborers); Joseph Andrew Orser, *The Lives of Chang and Eng: Siam's Twins in Nineteenth-Century America* (University of North Carolina Press, 2014), 151–52 (this source reports twenty-seven slaves on the estate as of 1860).

27 "Former slave of Eng Bunker," photograph, ca. 1880–90, Chang and Eng Bunker Papers #3761, Southern Historical Collection, Wilson Library, University of North Carolina at Chapel Hill.

28 "Former slave of Eng Bunker."

29 Benjamin Reiss, *The Showman and the Slave: Race, Death, and Memory in Barnum's America* (Harvard University Press, 2001).

30 Uri McMillan, "Mammy-Memory: Staging Joice Heth, or the Curious Phenomenon of the 'Ancient Negress,'" *Women and Performance* 22, no. 1 (2012): 36.

31 Bunker family, photograph, 1870, Ronald G. Becker Collection of Charles Eisenmann Photographs, Special Collections Research Center, Syracuse University Libraries.

32 Orser, *Lives of Chang and Eng*, 147.

33 Orser, *Lives of Chang and Eng*, 147.

34 See Uri McMillan, "Objecthood, Avatars, and the Limits of Human," in "Queer Inhumanisms," special issue, ed. Mel Y. Chen and Dana Luciano, *GLQ* 21, no. 2 (2015): 224–27; Uri McMillan, *Embodied Avatars: Genealogies of Black Feminist Art and Performance* (New York University Press, 2015); Millie Christine bio sketch; and Deirdre O'Connell, *The Ballad of Blind Tom* (Overlook Duckworth, 2009).

35 McMillan, "Mammy-Memory," 30–31.

36 Robin Bernstein, *Racial Innocence: Performing American Childhood from Slavery to Civil Rights* (New York University Press, 2011); Camille Owens, *Like Children: Black Prodigy and the Measure of the Human in America* (New York University Press, 2024).

37 Jenifer L. Barclay, "Mothering the 'Useless': Black Motherhood, Disability, and Slavery," *Women, Gender, and Families of Color* 2, no. 2 (2014): 117.

38 Orser, *Lives of Chang and Eng*, 151–52.

39 An account of monies expended by Chang-Eng, 1832–1841, North Carolina Collection Gallery, Wilson Library, University of North Carolina at Chapel Hill; an account of money received by Chang-Eng, 1833–1839, Chang and Eng Bunker Papers #3761, Southern Historical Collection, Wilson Library, University of North Carolina at Chapel Hill.

40 Edna Edith Sayers, "From Freak Show to Jim Crow: A Siamese Twin and His Deaf Daughter in the Antebellum and Postbellum South," *Sign Language Studies* 22, no. 4 (2022): 563.

41 Influential to my thinking here were Bernstein, *Racial Innocence*; Richard E. Howells and Michael M. Chemers, "Midget Cities: Utopia, Utopianism and the *Vor-schein* of the 'Freak' Show," *Disability Studies Quarterly* 25, no. 3 (2005); Michael M. Chemers, *Staging Stigma: A Critical Examination of the American Freak Show* (Palgrave Macmillan, 2008); Jayna Brown, "'Little Black Me': The Touring Picaninny Choruses," in *Babylon Girls: Black Women Performers and the Shaping of the Modern* (Duke University Press, 2008); and Tera W. Hunter, *To 'Joy My Freedom: Southern Black Women's Lives and Labors After the Civil War* (Harvard University Press, 1997).

42 For example, Blind Tom earned an average of $100,000 before the Civil War from sales of sheet music and performance proceeds. John Davis, "Blind Tom," in *African American Lives*, eds. Henry Louis Gates and Evelyn Brooks Higginbotham (Oxford University Press, 2004), 84–86.

43 Chemers, *Staging Stigma*; Howells and Chemers, "Midget Cities."

44 Davis, "Blind Tom," 84; Geneva H. Southall, *Blind Tom, the Black Pianist-Composer (1849–1908): Continually Enslaved* (Scarecrow, 1999); Geneva H. Southall, *Blind Tom: The Post-Civil War Enslavement of a Black Musical Genius* (Challenge Productions, 1979).

45 Davis, "Blind Tom," 85.

46 Davis, "Blind Tom," 85.

47 Davis, "Blind Tom," 85–86.

48 Millie Christine bio sketch. This biographical sketch of Christine and Millie features a fictionalized account of the twins' births, early lives, rise to fame, and travels. It follows a form commonly used in performance programs and publicity materials popular in American freak shows of the late nineteenth century. The program also includes several doctors' reports verifying the twins' conjoined status, lyrics from the songs they would perform (with instructions for the audience to sing along), and advertisements on each page for Merchant's Gargling Oil Linament, used for humans and animals alike.

49 Frost, *Conjoined Twins*, 40–49.

50 Samuels, "Examining Millie and Christine," 55.

51 Martell, *Millie-Christine*, 254.

52 Millie Christine bio sketch, 5.
53 Millie Christine bio sketch, 6.
54 Hortense J. Spillers, "Mama's Baby, Papa's Maybe: An American Grammar Book," *Diacritics* 17, no. 2 (1987): 74.
55 Jennifer L. Morgan, *Laboring Women: Reproduction and Gender in New World Slavery* (University of Pennsylvania Press, 2004).
56 Millie Christine bio sketch, 9.
57 Joan Dayan, "Legal Slaves and Civil Bodies," in *Materializing Democracy: Toward a Revitalized Cultural Politics*, eds. Russ Castronovo and Dana D. Nelson (Duke University Press, 2002).
58 McMillan, "Mammy-Memory," 39.
59 Davis, "Blind Tom," 85.
60 Audre Lorde, "The Transformation of Silence into Language and Action," in *Sister Outsider: Essays and Speeches* (Crossing, 1984), 40–44.

CHAPTER 2. SLAVE AUTOBIOGRAPHY AND THE PERFORMANCE ARCHIVE

1 Millie-Christine [McKoy], *The History of the Carolina Twins: "Told in Their Own Peculiar Way" by "One of Them"* (Buffalo Courier Printing House, [18—?]), http://docsouth.unc.edu/neh/millie-christine/millie-christine.html.
2 Linda Frost, *Conjoined Twins in Black and White: The Lives of Millie-Christine McKoy and Daisy and Violet Hilton* (University of Wisconsin Press, 2009), 16.
3 Joanne Martell, *Millie-Christine: Fearfully and Wonderfully Made* (John F. Blair, 2000), quoted in Frost, *Conjoined Twins*, 16.
4 Frost, *Conjoined Twins*, 16.
5 Rachel Adams, "Disability and the Circus," in *The American Circus*, ed. Susan Weber et al. (Yale University Press, 2012).
6 Frost, *Conjoined Twins*, 4 (emphasis mine).
7 [McKoy], *History of the Carolina Twins.*
8 "Clara Yeoman, their only surviving sister, has spent her life in Columbus County [North Carolina]. Her famous *sister were* older than her by about 6 years. Millie-Christine would have been almost 83 years of age, had they lived. When interviewed by newsmen on last Friday afternoon, one particular thing was noticed about Clara's conversation. *She always referred to Millie-Christine as one, and never in a plural sense.*" Article on Millie-Christine McKoy, *News Reporter* (Whiteville, NC), March 29, 1934 (emphasis mine).
9 Judith Butler, *Giving an Account of Oneself* (Fordham University Press, 2005), 21 (emphasis mine).
10 Ellen Samuels, "Examining Millie and Christine McKoy: Where Enslavement and Enfreakment Meet," *Signs* 37, no. 1 (2011): 69.
11 Dennis Tyler, *Disabilities of the Color Line: Redressing Antiblackness from Slavery to the Present* (New York University Press, 2022), Kindle.

12 Cynthia Wu, *Chang and Eng Reconnected: The Original Siamese Twins in American Culture* (Temple University Press, 2012), 3.
13 Samuels, "Examining Millie and Christine," 55.
14 Adams, "Disability and the Circus," 421.
15 Adams, "Disability and the Circus," 421–22.
16 See Robin Bernstein, *Racial Innocence: Performing American Childhood from Slavery to Civil Rights* (New York University Press, 2011).
17 Martell, *Millie-Christine*, 270.
18 Minnie McIver Brown, obituary for Millie Christine McKoy, *News Reporter* (Whiteville, NC), December 10, 1925, 6.
19 Millie Christine bio sketch, 5.
20 Millie Christine bio sketch, 6.
21 Harriet Jacobs, *Incidents in the Life of a Slave Girl* (Townsend, 2004), 149.
22 Brown, obituary.
23 This is shown in a 1925 obituary in the Whiteville *News Reporter* in which their sister notes that both she and they always referred to them in the singular tense, mirroring the advertising efforts that labeled them as a singular woman. See Sander Gilman, "Black Bodies, White Bodies: Toward an Iconography of Female Sexuality in Late Nineteenth-Century Art, Medicine, and Literature," in *"Race," Writing, and Difference*, ed. Henry Louis Gates Jr. (University of Chicago Press, 1986). Widely accepted within the medical community as an external demonstration of Black women's primitivism, propensity for sexual activity, and supposedly insatiable appetite for sex, the "Hottentot Apron" is well documented in eighteenth- and nineteenth-century medical texts. Named for Sarah Baartman, who was famously displayed as an ethnographic exhibit known as the "Venus Hottentot," this trait, which consisted of an "elongated" labia, was supposedly unique to Black women and viewed as a result of "inherent, biological variations rather than adaptions" (Gilman, 237). This soon evolved into a narrative that claimed there was an inherent difference in the genitalia of Black women and women of other races, particularly white women of European descent. Gilman describes how, by the latter half of the nineteenth century, this evolution led to the Black female body becoming synonymous with that of a prostitute (Gilman, 248).
24 Frost, *Conjoined Twins*, 40.
25 *Trombinoscope* can be translated literally to mean a group of photographs or an informational chart with pictures.
26 Unless otherwise noted, translations are my own. Touchatout and La Fosse, *Trombinoscope*, November 1873, 2.
27 Touchatout and La Fosse, *Trombinoscope*, 2–3.
28 Touchatout and La Fosse, *Trombinoscope*, 3.
29 Touchatout and La Fosse, *Trombinoscope*, 3.
30 Touchatout and La Fosse, *Trombinoscope*, 4.
31 Touchatout and La Fosse, *Trombinoscope*, 4.

32 Rachel Adams, *Sideshow U.S.A.: Freaks and the American Cultural Imagination* (University of Chicago Press, 2001), 164–66.
33 Adams, *Sideshow U.S.A.*, 165.
34 W. C. Coup, *Sawdust and Spangles: Stories and Secrets of the Circus* (Herbert S. Stone, 1901), xiv.
35 Weheliye, Alexander G. *Habeas Viscus: Racializing Assemblages, Biopolitics, and Black Feminist Theories of the Human* (Duke University Press, 2014).
36 Quoted in Joshua Bennett, *Being Property Once Myself: Blackness and the End of Man* (Harvard University Press, 2020), 1.
37 Bennett, *Being Property Once Myself*, 1–2.
38 Mel Y. Chen, *Animacies: Biopolitics, Racial Mattering, and Queer Affect* (Duke University Press, 2012), ProQuest Ebook Central.

CHAPTER 3. AUTOPSY AND ENFREAKMENT ON THE NINETEENTH-CENTURY STAGE

1 C. W. and J. D. Bunker to Harrison Allen, North Carolina Collection, University of North Carolina at Chapel Hill, April 1, 1874.
2 Joan Paulson Gage, "A Slave Named Gordon," *New York Times*, October 3, 2009, www.nytimes.com.
3 Carrie Mae Weems, "From Here I Saw What Happened and I Cried," photo exhibition, 1995–96, www.carriemaeweems.net.
4 See Ben Brantley, "Review: 'Venus' Recalls a Woman's Fortune, and Her Ruin," *New York Times*, May 15, 2017, www.nytimes.com. Brantley's review inaccurately opens by drawing a direct correlation between Baartman and reality star Kim Kardashian.
5 Daphne A. Brooks, *Bodies in Dissent: Spectacular Performances of Race and Freedom, 1850–1910* (Duke University Press, 2006); Daphne A. Brooks, "Fraudulent Bodies/Fraught Methodologies," *Legacy* 24, no. 2 (2007): 306–14; Farah Jasmine Griffin, "When Malindy Sings: A Meditation on Black Women's Vocality," in *Uptown Conversations: The New Jazz Studies*, ed. Robert G. O'Meally et al. (Columbia University Press, 2004); Saidiya V. Hartman, *Scenes of Subjection: Terror, Slavery, and Self-Making in Nineteenth-Century America* (Oxford University Press, 1997); Joseph Roach, *Cities of the Dead: Circum-Atlantic Performance* (Columbia University Press, 1996); Hortense J. Spillers, "Mama's Baby, Papa's Maybe: An American Grammar Book," *Diacritics* 17, no. 2 (1987): 64–81.
6 Hurston, Zora Neale, "The Characteristics of Negro Expression," *Negro: An Anthology*, ed. Nancy Cunard, (Frederick Ungar Publishing Co, Inc., 1970), 24–46.
7 Ellen Samuels, "Examining Millie and Christine McKoy: Where Enslavement and Enfreakment Meet," *Signs* 37, no. 1 (2011): 53–81.
8 *Oxford English Dictionary*, "future," accessed March 28, 2020, www.oed.com.
9 *News Reporter* (Whiteville, NC), December 10, 1925, 6.
10 Leslie A. Schwalm, *Medicine, Science, and Making Race in Civil War America* (University of North Carolina Press, 2023), 69.

11 "Millie in her last illness was attended by Dr. W.H. Crowell, a Whiteville physician who was presented to Queen Victoria by the twins at one of their performances in London where Dr. Crowell was studying at the time. Toward the last Dr. Crowell contacted Johns Hopkins Hospital in Baltimore and asked about separation. *He was advised to give Chrissy massive doses of morphine at Millie's death, as separation was impossible.*" Booklet on Millie Christine McKoy, Columbus County Historical Society, 1969 (emphasis mine).

12 Here I am referring to the biographies and other materials that were circulated surrounding Heth's performance as Washington's mammy and nursemaid: Lost Museum Archive, "The Joice Heth Exhibit," American Social History Project, Center for Media and Learning, Graduate Center, City University of New York, accessed March 17, 2025, http://lostmuseum.cuny.edu; *The Life of Joice Heth, the Nurse of Gen. George Washington, (the Father of Our Country,) Now Living at the Astonishing Age of 161 Years, and Weighs Only 46 Pounds*, 1835, http://docsouth.unc.edu/neh/heth/heth.html; Harry Thomas, summary of *Life of Joice Heth*, accessed March 17, 2025, http://docsouth.unc.edu/neh/heth/summary.html

13 Duncan F. Cameron, 1971. "Museum, a Temple or the Forum." *Curator* 14 (1971): 1:11–24.

14 Cynthia Wu, *Chang and Eng Reconnected: The Original Siamese Twins in American Culture* (Temple University Press, 2012).

15 Wu, *Chang and Eng Reconnected*, 67–68.

16 Christina Elizabeth Sharpe, *Monstrous Intimacies: Making Post-Slavery Subjects* (Duke University Press, 2010), 73–74.

17 Joseph Andrew Orser, *The Lives of Chang and Eng: Siam's Twins in Nineteenth-Century America* (University of North Carolina Press, 2014), 178–80.

18 The Bumpass family had several notable preachers. The quote is pulled from a letter Sidney Bumpass wrote to his wife, Frances, after a revival meeting the Bunkers attended. Sidney D. Bumpass, *Letter to Mrs. Frances M. Bumpass* (1838), Bumpass Family Papers (#1031), Southern Historical Collection, Wilson Library, University of North Carolina at Chapel Hill.

19 Orser, *Lives of Chang and Eng*, 147.

20 Orser, *Lives of Chang and Eng*, 147.

21 Millie Christine bio sketch, 1883[?], Beinecke Rare Book and Manuscript Library.

22 Photograph of Millie Christine McKoy titled "Temple of Art: Philadelphia, PA," n.d., Beinecke Rare Book and Manuscript Library.

23 After age fourteen a medical doctor never again examined the twins with their clothes removed, with the exception of Pancoast's exam. Ellen Samuels, "Examining Millie and Christine McKoy: Where Enslavement and Enfreakment Meet," *Signs* 37, no. 1 (2011): 69.

24 See Millie Christine bio sketch. Most versions of the (auto)biography list "receptions" that Millie Christine held for both public audiences and various European dignitaries as part of their touring routine.

25 Visiting card from Coup's Equescurriculum, 1879, Beinecke Rare Book and Manuscript Library.
26 For a discussion of the link made in eighteenth- and nineteenth-century medicine between Black women's genitalia and "abnormal" sexuality (starting with the "Hottentot Apron" named after Baartman), see Sander Gilman, "Black Bodies, White Bodies: Toward an Iconography of Female Sexuality in Late Nineteenth-Century Art, Medicine, and Literature," in *"Race," Writing, and Difference*, ed. Henry Louis Gates Jr. (University of Chicago Press, 1986).
27 Daphne Brooks describes this negotiation in *Bodies in Dissent.*
28 William H. Pancoast, "The Carolina Twins," in *Photographic Review of Medicine and Surgery*, vol 1, *1870–71* (J. B. Lippincott, 1871).
29 Michael Sappol, *A Traffic of Dead Bodies: Anatomy and Embodied Social Identity Nineteenth-Century America* (Princeton University Press, 2002).
30 Samuels, "Examining Millie and Christine," 69.
31 Mrs. Smith was the widow of the McKoys' late owner, Joeseph Smith, and remained their manager and pseudo-owner for years after his death.
32 Pancoast, "Carolina Twins," 44.
33 Pancoast, "Carolina Twins," 47–48.
34 Samuels, "Examining Millie and Christine," 66.
35 Minnie McIver Brown, obituary for Millie Christine McKoy, *News Reporter* (Whiteville, NC), December 10, 1925, 6.
36 Martell, *Millie-Christine*, 270.
37 Martell, *Millie-Christine*, 274.
38 Martell, *Millie-Christine*, 272–73.
39 Saidiya V. Hartman, "Venus in Two Acts," *Small Axe: A Caribbean Journal of Criticism* 12, no. 2 (2008): 1–14.
40 Uri McMillan, "Mammy-Memory: Staging Joice Heth, or the Curious Phenomenon of the 'Ancient Negress,'" *Women and Performance* 22, no. 1 (2012): 30.
41 Uri McMillan, "Objecthood, Avatars, and the Limits of the Human," in "Queer Inhumanisms," special issue, ed. Mel Y. Chen and Dana Luciano, *GLQ* 21, no. 2 (2015): 226.
42 McMillan, "Mammy-Memory," 30–31.
43 McMillan, "Mammy-Memory," 30.

CHAPTER 4. AURAL FUGITIVITY IN *ZONG!*, *OLIO*, AND *CURIO*

1 Ellen Samuels, "Examining Millie and Christine McKoy: Where Enslavement and Enfreakment Meet," *Signs* 37, no. 1 (2011): 53–81.
2 Article on Millie-Christine McKoy, *News Reporter* (Whiteville, NC), March 29, 1934.
3 Daphne A. Brooks, *Bodies in Dissent: Spectacular Performances of Race and Freedom, 1850–1910* (Duke University Press, 2006); Uri McMillan, "Mammy-Memory: Staging Joice Heth, or the Curious Phenomenon of the 'Ancient Negress,'" *Women and Performance* 22, no. 1 (2012): 36.

4 Janice Lowe, "Excerpt, Millie and Christine McKoy Sisters' Syncopated Sonnets, Text by Tyehimba Jess, Music by Janice A. Lowe," accessed January 22, 2025, www.janicelowe.com.
5 Marlene NourbeSe Philip, "Zong!," accessed January 22, 2025, www.nourbese.com.
6 See the epigraph to the introduction.
7 Hartman, "Venus in Two Acts," 11.
8 Tyehimba Jess, *Olio* (Wave Books, 2016), 3.
9 Marlene NourbeSe Philip, *Zong!* (Wesleyan University Press, 2008), front and back covers;
Marlene NourbeSe Philip, "Statement for Legal Opinion," *Set Speaks* (blog), April 2018, www.setspeaks.com/wp-content/uploads/2018/04/MNPs-statement-for-legal-opinion.pdf.
10 Fred Moten, *In the Break: The Aesthetics of the Black Radical Tradition* (University of Minnesota Press, 2003); Roland Barthes, *The Grain of the Voice* (Vintage Classic, 2010); Masi Asare, "Vocal Colour in Blue: Early Twentieth-Century Black Women Singers as Broadway's Voice Teachers," *Performance Matters* 6, no. 2 (2021): 52–66; Nina Sun Eidsheim, *The Race of Sound: Listening, Timbre, and Vocality in African American Music* (Duke University Press, 2019); Paige A. McGinley, *Staging the Blues: From Tent Shows to Tourism* (Duke University Press, 2014).
11 Moten, *In the Break*; Hartman, *Scenes of Subjection.*
12 Minnie McIver Brown, obituary for Millie Christine McKoy, *News Reporter* (Whiteville, NC), December 10, 1925.
13 Dea Hadley Boster, "Unfit for Bondage: Disability and African American Slavery in the United States" (PhD diss., University of Michigan, 2010).
14 See Moten, *In the Break*; Salamishah Tillet, *Sites of Slavery: Citizenship and Racial Democracy in the Post–Civil Rights Imagination* (Duke University Press, 2012); Toni Morrison, "The Site of Memory," in *Inventing the Truth: The Art and Craft of Memoir*, ed. William Zinsser (Houghton Mifflin, 1995); and Hartman, *Scenes of Subjection*, respectively.
15 Analysis of the scream can be found in the close readings of Aunt Hester's scream from Frederick Douglass's autobiography in the works of scholars such as Moten and Hartman.
16 Jess, *Olio*, front matter.
17 Philip, *Zong!*, front and back covers.
18 Philip, *Zong!*, 191.
19 Hartman, "Venus in Two Acts," 2.
20 Philip, *Zong!*, 69.
21 Gayatri Spivak writes, "If, however, we are driven by nostalgia for lost origins, we too run the risk of effacing the 'native' and stepping forth as 'the real Caliban,' of forgetting that he is a name in a play, an inaccessible blankness circumscribed by an interpretable text. The stagings of Caliban legitimizes the very individualism that we must persistently attempt to undermine from within." Spivak, "Three Women's Texts and a Critique of Imperialism." *Critical Inquiry* 12, no. 1 (1985): 245.

Spivak's critique here denies us the wholeness of stepping into the role of Caliban, whose own curse to Prospero is, "You taught me language; and my profit on't / Is I know how to curse" (*The Tempest* 1.2.517), condemning the idea that linguistic virtuosity and dexterity can serve as a stand-in for freedom.

22 Denise Eileen McCoskey, *Race: Antiquity and Its Legacy* (Oxford University Press, 2012), 5 (emphasis mine).

23 Tyehimba Jess, "TedxNashvlle [*sic*]—Tyehimba Jess—Syncopated Sonnets," TedxNashville talk, 18 min., 49 sec., April 2011, posted by TEDx Talks, May 18, 2011, www.youtube.com/watch?v=OmtHoA5mVnA.

24 *Lady Day at Emerson's Bar and Grill*, dir. Lonny Price, Broadway Theatre, New York, NY, March 25–October 5, 2014.

25 Farah Jasmine Griffin, "When Malindy Sings: A Meditation on Black Women's Vocality," in *Uptown Conversations: The New Jazz Studies*, ed. Robert G. O'Meally et al. (Columbia University Press, 2004).

26 Alex Vasquez, *Listening in Detail: Performances of Cuban Music* (Duke University Press, 2013).

27 Jess, "TedxNashvlle [*sic*]."

28 Eugene Warner, "The Carolina Twins Millie-Christine," *Sandlapper: The Magazine of South Carolina*, 1969.

29 Booklet on Millie Christine McKoy, Columbus County Historical Society, 1969 (emphasis mine).

30 Marilyn Nelson, "Millie-Christine," in *Faster Than Light: New and Selected Poems, 1996–2011* (Louisiana State University Press, 2012), 400.

31 Millie Christine, last will and testament, North Carolina State Archives, Raleigh, NC.

32 Philip, *Zong!*, 189.

33 Simone Browne, *Dark Matters: On the Surveillance of Blackness* (Duke University Press, 2015).

34 Frederick Douglass, *Narrative of the Life of Frederick Douglass, an American Slave* (Belknap, 1960), 86.

35 Douglass, *Narrative of the Life*, 87.

36 Douglass, *Narrative of the Life*, 87.

37 Browne, *Dark Matters*.

CONCLUSION

1 Booklet on Millie Christine McKoy, Columbus County Historical Society, 1969.

2 Quoted in booklet on Millie Christine McKoy.

3 Quoted in booklet on Millie Christine McKoy.

4 *Millie Christine alias Christine Millie v. Adam Forepaugh*, 1883, p. 1, Mixed Case Files, Record Group 21: Records of District Courts of the United States, National Archives, https://catalog.archives.gov/id/192044942.

5 *Millie Christine alias Christine Millie*, 3.

6 *Millie Christine alias Christine Millie*, 4.

7 According to the booklet on Millie Christine McKoy, "The last will and testament, dated September 1912, was apparently penned by someone other than Mille-Chrissy. The name is listed as 'I, Millia-Christine McKoy,' and the signature appears to have been written in a hand more feeble than the writing in the will itself. There are also some misspellings in the will, something never noticed in any of Mille-Chrissy's other ritings [*sic*]. The entire estate went to 'my beloved sister, Clarrah Yoeman.'"

8 Christina Elizabeth Sharpe, *In the Wake: On Blackness and Being* (Duke University Press, 2016); Diana Taylor, *The Archive and the Repertoire: Performing Cultural Memory in the Americas* (Duke University Press, 2007); Joseph Roach, *Cities of the Dead: Circum-Atlantic Performance* (Columbia University Press, 1996).

9 Marilyn Nelson, "Millie-Christine," in *Faster Than Light: New and Selected Poems, 1996–2011* (Louisiana State University Press, 2012), 400.

10 See Millie Christine McKoy, last will and testament, North Carolina State Archives, Raleigh, NC.

11 For more detail on the life stories of Daisy and Violet Hilton, see Linda Frost, *Conjoined Twins in Black and White: The Lives of Millie-Christine McKoy and Daisy and Violet Hilton* (University of Wisconsin Press, 2009).

BIBLIOGRAPHY

Adams, Rachel. "Disability and the Circus." In *The American Circus*, edited by Susan Weber, Kenneth L. Ames, and Matthew Wittmann. Yale University Press, 2012.

Adams, Rachel. *Sideshow U.S.A.: Freaks and the American Cultural Imagination*. University of Chicago Press, 2001.

Adams, Rachel, Benjamin Reiss, and David Serlin, eds. *Keywords for Disability Studies*. New York University Press, 2015.

Alexander, Elizabeth. *The Black Interior: Essays*. Graywolf, 2004.

Alexander, Elizabeth. *The Venus Hottentot*. University Press of Virginia, 1990.

Alexander, M. Jacqui. *Pedagogies of Crossing: Meditations on Feminism, Sexual Politics, Memory, and the Sacred*. Duke University Press, 2005.

Allen, Harrison. *Report of an Autopsy on the Bodies of Chang and Eng Bunker, Commonly Known as the Siamese Twins*. Collins, 1875. https://archive.org.

Allen, Jafari S. *¡Venceremos? The Erotics of Black Self-Making in Cuba*. Duke University Press, 2011.

Allen, James, ed. *Without Sanctuary: Lynching Photography in America*. Twin Palms, 2000.

Allen, Jeffery Renard. *Song of the Shank: A Novel*. Graywolf, 2014.

Allen, Robert Clyde. *Horrible Prettiness: Burlesque and American Culture*. University of North Carolina Press, 1991.

Als, Hilton. "'Remembering 'Gone with the Wind.'" *New Yorker*, July 1, 2011.

Andrews, William L. *To Tell a Free Story: The First Century of Afro-American Autobiography, 1760–1865*. University of Illinois Press, 1986.

Angelou, Maya. *The Collected Autobiographies of Maya Angelou*. Modern Library, 2004.

Asare, Masi. "Vocal Colour in Blue: Early Twentieth-Century Black Women Singers as Broadway's Voice Teachers." *Performance Matters* 6, no. 2 (2021): 52–66.

Bakhtin, M. M. *The Dialogic Imagination: Four Essays*. Edited by Michael Holquist. University of Texas Press, 1981.

Baraka, Amiri. *"Dutchman" and "The Slave": Two Plays*. Morrow, 1964.

Barclay, Jenifer L. "Mothering the 'Useless': Black Motherhood, Disability, and Slavery." *Women, Gender, and Families of Color* 2, no. 2 (2014): 115–40.

Barthes, Roland. *The Grain of the Voice*. Vintage Classic, 2010.

Barthes, Roland. *Mythologies*. Seuil, 1957.

Baucom, Ian. *Specters of the Atlantic: Finance Capital, Slavery, and the Philosophy of History*. Duke University Press, 2005.

Beckford, George L. *Persistent Poverty: Underdevelopment in Plantation Economies of the Third World*. Oxford University Press, 1972.

Beckles, Hilary. *Britain's Black Debt: Reparations for Caribbean Slavery and Native Genocide*. University of the West Indies Press, 2013.

Bennett, Joshua. *Being Property Once Myself: Blackness and the End of Man*. Harvard University Press, 2020.

Bernstein, Robin. *Racial Innocence: Performing American Childhood from Slavery to Civil Rights*. New York University Press, 2011.

Berry, Daina Ramey. *The Price for Their Pound of Flesh: The Value of the Enslaved from Womb to Grave in the Building of a Nation*. Beacon, 2017. Kindle.

Black, Stephanie, dir. *Life and Debt*. Blaq Out, 2007.

Boster, Dea Hadley. *African American Slavery and Disability: Bodies, Property and Power in the Antebellum South, 1800–1860*. Routledge, 2013.

Boster, Dea Hadley. "Unfit for Bondage: Disability and African American Slavery in the United States." PhD diss., University of Michigan, 2010.

Brand, Dionne. *A Map to the Door of No Return: Notes to Belonging*. Doubleday Canada, 2001.

Brantley, Ben. "Review: 'Venus' Recalls a Woman's Fortune, and Her Ruin." *New York Times*, May 15, 2017. www.nytimes.com.

Brooks, Daphne A. *Bodies in Dissent: Spectacular Performances of Race and Freedom, 1850–1910*. Duke University Press, 2006.

Brooks, Daphne A. "Fraudulent Bodies/Fraught Methodologies." *Legacy* 24, no. 2 (2007): 306–14.

Brooks, Gwendolyn. *Report from Part One: An Autobiography*. Broadside, 1972.

Brown, Jayna. *Babylon Girls: Black Women Performers and the Shaping of the Modern*. Duke University Press, 2008.

Browne, Simone. *Dark Matters: On the Surveillance of Blackness*. Duke University Press, 2015.

Browning, Tod, dir. *Freaks*. 1932.

Butler, Judith. *Giving an Account of Oneself*. Fordham University Press, 2005.

Butler, Octavia E. *Kindred*. Beacon, 2003.

Cameron, Duncan F. "Museum, a Temple or the Forum." *Curator* 14 (1971): 1:11–24.

Campt, Tina. *A Black Gaze: Artists Changing How We See*. MIT Press, 2021.

Carby, Hazel V. *Reconstructing Womanhood: The Emergence of the Afro-American Woman Novelist*. Oxford University Press, 1987.

Casid, Jill H. *Sowing Empire: Landscape and Colonization*. University of Minnesota Press, 2005.

Chemers, Michael M. *Staging Stigma: A Critical Examination of the American Freak Show*. Palgrave Macmillan, 2008.

Chen, Mel Y. *Animacies: Biopolitics, Racial Mattering, and Queer Affect*. Duke University Press, 2012. ProQuest Ebook Central.

Christian, Barbara. "The Race for Theory." *Cultural Critique* 6 (1987): 51–63.

Colbert, Soyica Diggs. *The African American Theatrical Body: Reception, Performance, and the Stage*. Cambridge University Press, 2011.

Copeland, Huey. *Bound to Appear: Art, Slavery, and the Site of Blackness in Multicultural America*. University of Chicago Press, 2013.

Coup, W. C. *Sawdust and Spangles: Stories and Secrets of the Circus*. Herbert S. Stone, 1901.

Davies, Carole Boyce. *Black Women, Writing, and Identity: Migrations of the Subject*. Routledge, 1994.

Davis, John. "Blind Tom." In *African American Lives*, edited by Henry Louis Gates and Evelyn Brooks Higginbotham. Oxford University Press, 2004.

Davis, Thadious M. *Games of Property: Law, Race, Gender, and Faulkner's "Go Down, Moses."* Duke University Press, 2003.

Davis, Thadious M. *Southscapes: Geographies of Race, Region, and Literature*. University of North Carolina Press, 2011.

Dayan, Colin. *The Law Is a White Dog: How Legal Rituals Make and Unmake Persons*. Princeton University Press, 2011.

Dayan, Joan. "Legal Slaves and Civil Bodies." In *Materializing Democracy: Toward a Revitalized Cultural Politics*, edited by Russ Castronovo and Dana D. Nelson. Duke University Press, 2002.

De Andrade, Oswald, and Leslie Bary. "Cannibalist Manifesto." *Latin American Literary Review* 19, no. 38 (1991): 38–47.

De Avila, Joseph. "Man Who Broke Window Depicting Slaves Gets New Job at Yale." *Wall Street Journal*, July 19, 2016.

Defoe, Daniel. *Robinson Crusoe*. Norton, 1975.

Deleuze, Gilles, and Félix Guattari. "Introduction: Rhizome." In *A Thousand Plateaus: Capitalism and Schizophrenia*. University of Minnesota Press, 1987.

Douglass, Frederick. *Narrative of the Life of Frederick Douglass, an American Slave*. Belknap, 1960.

Du Bois, W. E. B. *The Souls of Black Folk*. Edited by Farah Jasmine Griffin. Barnes and Noble Classics, 2005.

Dubreuil, Laurent. *Empire of Language: Toward a Critique of (Post)colonial Expression*. Cornell University Press, 2013.

Dussel, Enrique. "Europe, Modernity, Eurocentrism." Translated by Javier Krauel and Virginia C. Tuma. *Napantla* 20, no. 3 (2000): 465–78.

Edwards, Brent Hayes. *The Practice of Diaspora: Literature, Translation, and the Rise of Black Internationalism*. Harvard University Press, 2003.

Ehlers, Nadine. *Racial Imperatives: Discipline, Performativity, and Struggles Against Subjection*. Indiana University Press, 2012.

Eidsheim, Nina Sun. *The Race of Sound: Listening, Timbre, and Vocality in African American Music*. Duke University Press, 2019.

Elam, Harry, Jr., and Robert Alexander, eds. *The Fire This Time: African-American Plays for the 21st Century*. Theatre Communications Group, 2004.

Feimster, Crystal Nicole. *Southern Horrors: Women and the Politics of Rape and Lynching*. Harvard University Press, 2009.

Fitzgerald, Adam. "Tyehimba Jess on Excavating Popular Music Through Poetry: Exploring the Sustenance of Song and Historical Clapbacks." *LitHub*, May 5, 2016. http://lithub.com.

Fleetwood, Nicole R. *Troubling Vision: Performance, Visuality, and Blackness*. University of Chicago Press, 2011.

Frost, Linda. *Conjoined Twins in Black and White: The Lives of Millie-Christine McKoy and Daisy and Violet Hilton*. University of Wisconsin Press, 2009.

Gage, Joan Paulson. "A Slave Named Gordon." *New York Times*, October 3, 2009. www.nytimes.com.

Gardner, Joscelyn. *Bleeding and Breeding*. Station Gallery, 2012.

Gardner, Joscelyn. "A Collection of Creole Portrait Heads of the Female Sex." *Small Axe: A Caribbean Journal of Criticism* 16, no. 37 (2012): 71–118.

Gates, Henry Louis, Jr., ed. *"Race," Writing, and Difference*. University of Chicago Press, 1986.

George-Graves, Nadine. *The Royalty of Negro Vaudeville: The Whitman Sisters and the Negotiation of Race, Gender and Class in African American Theater, 1900–1940*. St. Martin's, 2000.

George-Graves, Nadine. *Urban Bush Women: Twenty Years of African American Dance Theater, Community Engagement, and Working It Out*. University of Wisconsin Press, 2010.

Gilman, Sander. "Black Bodies, White Bodies: Toward an Iconography of Female Sexuality in Late Nineteenth-Century Art, Medicine, and Literature." In *"Race," Writing, and Difference*, edited by Henry Louis Gates Jr. University of Chicago Press, 1986.

Gilmore, Glenda Elizabeth. *Defying Dixie: The Radical Roots of Civil Rights, 1919–1950*. W. W. Norton, 2008.

Gilmore, Glenda Elizabeth. *Gender and Jim Crow: Women and the Politics of White Supremacy in North Carolina, 1896–1920*. University of North Carolina Press, 1996.

Gilroy, Paul. *The Black Atlantic: Modernity and Double Consciousness*. Harvard University Press, 1993.

Glissant, Édouard. *Poetic Intention*. Nightboat Books, 2010.

Glissant, Édouard. *Poetics of Relation*. Translated by Betsy Wing. University of Michigan Press, 1997.

Gold, Sarah E. "Millie-Christine McKoy and the American Freak Show: Race, Gender, and Freedom in the Postbellum Era, 1851–1912." *Berkeley Undergraduate Journal* 23, no. 1 (2010): 1–43.

Goldsby, Jacqueline. *A Spectacular Secret: Lynching in American Life and Literature*. University of Chicago Press, 2006.

Greenwood, Emily, and Justine McConnell. "The Politics of Classicism in the Poetry of Phillis Wheatley." In *Ancient Slavery and Abolition: From Hobbes to Hollywood*, edited by Edith Hall, Richard Alton, and Justine McConnell. Oxford University Press, 2011.

Greeson, Jennifer Rae. *Our South: Geographic Fantasy and the Rise of National Literature*. Harvard University Press, 2010.

Griffin, Farah Jasmine. "When Malindy Sings: A Meditation on Black Women's Vocality." In *Uptown Conversations: The New Jazz Studies*, edited by Robert G. O'Meally, Brent Hayes Edwards, and Farah Jasmine Griffin. Columbia University Press, 2004.

Guy-Sheftall, Beverly. *Words of Fire: An Anthology of African-American Feminist Thought*. New Press, 1995.

Hall, Stuart. "Cultural Identity and Diaspora." In *Identity: Community, Culture, Difference*, edited by Jonathan Rutherford. Lawrence and Wishart, 1990.

Harris, Cheryl L. "Whiteness as Property." *Harvard Law Review* 106, no. 8 (1993): 1707–91.

Hartman, Saidiya V. *Lose Your Mother: A Journey Along the Atlantic Slave Route*. Farrar, Straus and Giroux, 2007.

Hartman, Saidiya V. *Scenes of Subjection: Terror, Slavery, and Self-Making in Nineteenth-Century America*. Oxford University Press, 1997.

Hartman, Saidiya V. "Venus in Two Acts." *Small Axe: A Caribbean Journal of Criticism* 12, no. 2 (2008): 1–14.

Hill Collins, Patricia. *Black Feminist Thought: Knowledge, Consciousness, and the Politics of Empowerment*. Routledge, 2000.

Holloway, Jonathan Scott. *Jim Crow Wisdom: Memory and Identity in Black America Since 1940*. University of North Carolina Press, 2013.

Holloway, Karla F. C. *Legal Fictions: Constituting Race, Composing Literature*. Duke University Press, 2013.

Horton-Stallings, LaMonda. *Funk the Erotic: Transaesthetics and Black Sexual Cultures*. University of Illinois Press, 2015.

Howells, Richard E., and Michael M. Chemers. "Midget Cities: Utopia, Utopianism and the *Vor-schein* of the 'Freak' Show." *Disability Studies Quarterly* 25, no. 3 (2005).

Hunter, Tera W. *To 'Joy My Freedom: Southern Black Women's Lives and Labors After the Civil War*. Harvard University Press, 1997.

Hurston, Zora Neale. "The Characteristics of Negro Expression." In *Negro: An Anthology*, edited by Nancy Cunard. Frederick Ungar Publishing Co, Inc., 1970.

Jacobs, Harriet. *Incidents in the Life of a Slave Girl*. Townsend, 2004.

Jaji, Tsitsi Ella. *Africa in Stereo: Modernism, Music, and Pan-African Solidarity*. Oxford University Press, 2014.

James, C. L. R. *The Black Jacobins: Toussaint L'Ouverture and the San Domingo Revolution*. Vintage, 1963.

James, Joy, and T. Denean Sharpley-Whiting, eds. *The Black Feminist Reader*. Blackwell, 2000.

Jess, Tyehimba. *Olio*. Wave Books, 2016.

Jess, Tyehimba. "TedxNashvlle [*sic*]—Tyehimba Jess—Syncopated Sonnets." TedxNashville talk, 18 min., 49 sec., April 2011, posted by TEDx Talks, May 18, 2011. www.youtube.com/watch?v=OmtHoA5mVnA&t=6s.

Jordan, June. *Directed by Desire: The Collected Poems of June Jordan*. Edited by Sara Miles and Jan Heller Levi. Copper Canyon, 2005.

Jordan, June. *Soldier: A Poet's Childhood*. Basic Civitas, 2000.

Joseph, Miranda. "Making Debt." *Occasion: Debt* 7 (2014).

Kafer, Alison. *Feminist, Queer, Crip*. Indiana University Press, 2013.

Kincaid, Jamaica. *My Brother*. Farrar, Straus and Giroux, 1997.

Kincaid, Jamaica. *A Small Place*. Farrar, Straus and Giroux, 1988.

Lee, Rachel C. *The Exquisite Corpse of Asian America: Biopolitics, Biosociality, and Posthuman Ecologies*. New York University Press, 2014.

The Life of Joice Heth, the Nurse of Gen. George Washington, (the Father of Our Country,) Now Living at the Astonishing Age of 161 Years, and Weighs Only 46 Pounds. 1835. http://docsouth.unc.edu/neh/heth/heth.html.

Lindfors, Bernth. *Ira Aldridge: Performing Shakespeare in Europe, 1852–1855*. University of Rochester Press, 2013.

Lorde, Audre. *The Audre Lorde Compendium: Essays, Speeches, and Journals*. Pandora, 1996.

Lorde, Audre. "The Transformation of Silence into Language and Action." In *Sister Outsider: Essays and Speeches*. Crossing, 1984.

Lost Museum Archive. "The Joice Heth Exhibit." American Social History Project, Center for Media and Learning, Graduate Center, City University of New York. Accessed March 17, 2025. http://lostmuseum.cuny.edu.

Lowe, Janice. "Excerpt, Millie and Christine McKoy Sisters' Syncopated Sonnets, Text by Tyehimba Jess, Music by Janice A. Lowe." Accessed January 22, 2025. www.janicelowe.com.

Lowe, Lisa. "The Intimacies of Four Continents." In *Haunted by Empire: Geographies of Intimacy in North American History*, edited by Ann Laura Stoler. Duke University Press, 2006.

Lowe, Lisa. *The Intimacies of Four Continents*. Duke University Press, 2015.

Martell, Joanne. *Millie-Christine: Fearfully and Wonderfully Made*. John F. Blair, 2000.

Mathes, Carter. "Circuits of Political Prophecy: Martin Luther King Jr., Peter Tosh, and the Black Radical Imaginary." *Small Axe: A Caribbean Journal of Criticism* 14, no. 2 (2010): 17–41.

McCoskey, Denise Eileen. *Race: Antiquity and Its Legacy*. Oxford University Press, 2012.

McCraney, Tarell Alvin. *The Brother/Sister Plays*. Theatre Communications Group, 2010.

McGinley, Paige A. *Staging the Blues: From Tent Shows to Tourism*. Duke University Press, 2014.

McKittrick, Katherine. *Demonic Grounds: Black Women and the Cartographies of Struggle*. University of Minnesota Press, 2006.

McKittrick, Katherine, ed. *Sylvia Wynter: On Being Human as Praxis*. Duke University Press, 2015.

McKittrick, Katherine, and Clyde Adrian Woods, eds. *Black Geographies and the Politics of Place*. South End Press, 2007.

[McKoy], Millie-Christine. *The History of the Carolina Twins: "Told in Their Own Peculiar Way" by "One of Them."* Buffalo Courier Printing House, [18—?]. http://docsouth.unc.edu/neh/millie-christine/millie-christine.html.

McMillan, Uri. *Embodied Avatars: Genealogies of Black Feminist Art and Performance*. New York University Press, 2015.

McMillan, Uri. "Mammy-Memory: Staging Joice Heth, or the Curious Phenomenon of the 'Ancient Negress.'" *Women and Performance* 22, no. 1 (2012): 29–46.

McMillan, Uri. "Objecthood, Avatars, and the Limits of the Human." In "Queer Inhumanisms," special issue, edited by Mel Y. Chen and Dana Luciano. *GLQ* 21, no. 2 (2015): 224–27.

Miller, Monica L. *Slaves to Fashion: Black Dandyism and the Styling of Black Diasporic Identity*. Duke University Press, 2010.

Morgan, Jennifer L. *Laboring Women: Reproduction and Gender in New World Slavery*. University of Pennsylvania Press, 2004.

Morgan, Jennifer L. *Reckoning with Slavery: Gender, Kinship, and Capitalism in the Early Black Atlantic*. Duke University Press, 2017.

Morrison, Toni. *Beloved*. Vintage, 1987.

Morrison, Toni. "The Site of Memory." In *Inventing the Truth: The Art and Craft of Memoir*, edited by William Zinsser. Houghton Mifflin, 1995.

Moten, Fred. *In the Break: The Aesthetics of the Black Radical Tradition*. University of Minnesota Press, 2003.

Murphy, Ryan, dir. *American Horror Story: Freak Show*. Aired 2014–15 on FX.

National Museum of African American History and Culture. "Freedmen's Bureau and the McCoy Custody Battle." Accessed January 21, 2025. www.searchablemuseum.com.

Nelson, Marilyn. *Faster Than Light: New and Selected Poems, 1996–2011*. Louisiana State University Press, 2012.

Nyongó, Tavia. *The Amalgamation Waltz: Race, Performance and the Ruses of Memory*. University of Minnesota Press, 2009.

O'Connell, Deirdre. *The Ballad of Blind Tom*. Overlook Duckworth, 2009.

Orser, Joseph Andrew. *The Lives of Chang and Eng: Siam's Twins in Nineteenth-Century America*. University of North Carolina Press, 2014.

Owens, Camille. *Like Children: Black Prodigy and the Measure of the Human in America*. New York University Press, 2024.

Pancoast, William H. "The Carolina Twins." In *Photographic Review of Medicine and Surgery*, vol 1, *1870–71*. J. B. Lippincott, 1871.

Parks, Suzan-Lori. *The America Play, and Other Works*. Theatre Communications Group, 1995.

Parks, Suzan-Lori. *The Red Letter Plays*. Theatre Communications Group, 2001.

Parks, Suzan-Lori. *Topdog/Underdog*. Theatre Communications Group, 2001.

Parks, Suzan-Lori. *Venus: A Play*. Theatre Communications Group, 1996.

Parsard, Kaneesha Cherelle. "Making Space: The Caribbean in Transnational American Studies." *American Quarterly* 68, no. 4 (2016): 1019–32.

Paton, Diana. *No Bond but the Law: Punishment, Race, and Gender in Jamaican State Formation, 1780–1870*. Duke University Press, 2004.

Perucci, Tony. *Paul Robeson and the Cold War Performance Complex: Race, Madness, Activism*. University of Michigan Press, 2012.

Philip, Marlene NourbeSe. "Discourse on the Logic of Language." In *She Tries Her Tongue, Her Silence Softly Breaks*. Ragweed, 1989.

Philip, Marlene NourbeSe. *A Genealogy of Resistance: And Other Essays*. Mercury, 1997.

Philip, Marlene NourbeSe. "Statement for Legal Opinion." *Set Speaks* (blog), April 2018. www.setspeaks.com/wp-content/uploads/2018/04/MNPs-statement-for-legal-opinion.pdf.

Philip, Marlene NourbeSe. *Zong!* Wesleyan University Press, 2008.

Philip, Marlene NourbeSe. "Zong!" Accessed January 22, 2025. www.nourbese.com.

Pickens, Therí A. *Black Madness: Mad Blackness*. Duke University Press, 2019.

Reiss, Benjamin. *The Showman and the Slave: Race, Death, and Memory in Barnum's America*. Harvard University Press, 2001.

Roach, Joseph. *Cities of the Dead: Circum-Atlantic Performance*. Columbia University Press, 1996.

Roach, Joseph. *It*. University of Michigan Press, 2007.

Rojo, Antonio Benítez. *The Repeating Island: The Caribbean and the Postmodern Perspective*. Duke University Press, 1992.

Rowell, Charles Henry. *Angles of Ascent: A Norton Anthology of Contemporary African American Poetry*. W. W. Norton, 2013.

Salih, Sara. *Representing Mixed Race in Jamaica and England from the Abolition Era to the Present*. Routledge, 2011.

Samuels, Ellen. "Examining Millie and Christine McKoy: Where Enslavement and Enfreakment Meet." *Signs* 37, no. 1 (2011): 53–81.

Sappol, Michael. *A Traffic of Dead Bodies: Anatomy and Embodied Social Identity Nineteenth-Century America*. Princeton University Press, 2002.

Sayers, Edna Edith. "From Freak Show to Jim Crow: A Siamese Twin and His Deaf Daughter in the Antebellum and Postbellum South." *Sign Language Studies* 22, no. 4 (2022): 553–89.

Schalk, Sami. *Black Disability Politics*. Duke University Press, 2022.

Schiebinger, Londa L. *Plants and Empire: Colonial Bioprospecting in the Atlantic World*. Harvard University Press, 2004.

Schwalm, Leslie A. *Medicine, Science, and Making Race in Civil War America*. University of North Carolina Press, 2023.

Scott, David. *Omens of Adversity: Tragedy, Time, Memory, Justice*. Duke University Press, 2014.

Sharpe, Christina Elizabeth. *In the Wake: On Blackness and Being*. Duke University Press, 2016.

Sharpe, Christina Elizabeth. *Monstrous Intimacies: Making Post-Slavery Subjects*. Duke University Press, 2010.

Siebers, Tobin. *The Body Aesthetic: From Fine Art to Body Modification*. University of Michigan Press, 2000.

Simpson, Lorna. *Lorna Simpson*. Edited by Okwui Enwezor, Helaine Posner, and Hilton Als. Abrams, in association with the American Federation of Arts, 2006.

Smallwood, Stephanie. *Saltwater Slavery: A Middle Passage from Africa to American Diaspora*. Harvard University Press, 2008.

Smith, Anna Deavere. *Fires in the Mirror: Crown Heights, Brooklyn, and Other Identities*. Anchor/Doubleday, 1993.

Smith, Mark M. *Listening to Nineteenth-Century America*. University of North Carolina Press, 2015.

Smith, Zadie. *White Teeth: A Novel*. Random House, 2000.

Southall, Geneva H. *Blind Tom, the Black Pianist-Composer (1849–1908): Continually Enslaved*. Scarecrow, 1999.

Southall, Geneva H. *Blind Tom: The Post-Civil War Enslavement of a Black Musical Genius*. Challenge Productions, 1979.

Spillers, Hortense J. *Black, White, and in Color: Essays on American Literature and Culture*. University of Chicago Press, 2003.

Spillers, Hortense J. "Mama's Baby, Papa's Maybe: An American Grammar Book." *Diacritics* 17, no. 2 (1987): 64–81.

Spivak, Gayatri Chakravorty. "Three Women's Texts and a Critique of Imperialism." *Critical Inquiry* 12, no. 1 (1985): 243–61.

Stowe, Harriet Beecher. *Uncle Tom's Cabin: Or, Life Among the Lowly*. Edited by Ann Douglas. Penguin, 1981.

Taylor, Diana. *The Archive and the Repertoire: Performing Cultural Memory in the Americas*. Duke University Press, 2007.

Thomas, Harry. Summary of *The Life of Joice Heth, the Nurse of Gen. George Washington, (the Father of Our Country,) Now Living at the Astonishing Age of 161 Years, and Weighs Only 46 Pounds* (1835). Accessed March 17, 2025. http://docsouth.unc.edu/neh/heth/summary.html.

Thompson, Barbara, ed. *Black Womanhood: Images, Icons, and Ideologies of the African Body*. Exhibition catalog. Hood Museum of Art, Dartmouth College, in association with University of Washington Press, 2008.

Tillet, Salamishah. *Sites of Slavery: Citizenship and Racial Democracy in the Post–Civil Rights Imagination*. Duke University Press, 2012.

Tinsley, Omise'eke Natasha. "Black Atlantic, Queer Atlantic: Queer Imaginings of the Middle Passage." *GLQ: A Journal of Gay and Lesbian Studies* 14, no. 2–3 (2008): 191–215.

Tinsley, Omise'eke Natasha. "Extract from *Water, Shoulders, into the Black Pacific*." *GLQ: A Journal of Gay and Lesbian Studies* 18, no. 2–3 (2012): 263–76.

Tompkins, Kyla Wazana. *Racial Indigestion: Eating Bodies in the Nineteenth Century*. New York University Press, 2012.

Trethewey, Natasha. *Bellocq's Ophelia: Poems*. Graywolf, 2002.

Trethewey, Natasha. *Native Guard*. Houghton Mifflin, 2006.

Trouillot, Michel-Rolph. *Silencing the Past: Power and the Production of History*. Beacon, 1995.

Tucker, Harry Z. "Siamese Twins Were Good Farmers." *Progressive Farmer*, November 1939.

Tyler, Dennis. *Disabilities of the Color Line: Redressing Antiblackness from Slavery to the Present*. New York University Press, 2022. Kindle.

Vasquez, Alex. *Listening in Detail: Performances of Cuban Music*. Duke University Press, 2013.

Von Eschen, Penny. *Satchmo Blows Up the World: Jazz Ambassadors Play the Cold War*. Harvard University Press, 2004.

Weems, Carrie Mae. *Carrie Mae Weems: Three Decades of Photography and Video*. Edited by Kathryn E. Delmez. Frist Center for the Visual Arts, 2012.

Weems, Carrie Mae. "From Here I Saw What Happened and I Cried." Photo exhibition, 1995–96. www.carriemaeweems.net.

Weheliye, Alexander G. *Habeas Viscus: Racializing Assemblages, Biopolitics, and Black Feminist Theories of the Human*. Duke University Press, 2014.

Warner, Eugene. "The Carolina Twins Millie-Christine." In *Sandlapper: The Magazine of South Carolina*, 1969.

White, Shane, and Graham J. White. *The Sounds of Slavery: Discovering African American History Through Songs, Sermons, and Speech*. Beacon, 2006.

Williams, Eric Eustace. *Capitalism and Slavery*. University of North Carolina Press, 1994.

Wood, Marcus. "John Gabriel Stedman, William Blake, Francesco Bartolozzi and Empathetic Pornography in *The Narrative of a Five Years Expedition Against the Revolted Negroes of Surinam*." In *An Economy of Colour: Visual Culture and the Atlantic World, 1660–1830*, edited by Geoff Quilley and Kay Dian Kriz. Manchester University Press, 2003.

Woodard, Vincent. *The Delectable Negro: Human Consumption and Homoeroticism Within U.S. Slave Culture*. Edited by Justin A. Joyce and Dwight A. McBride. New York University Press, 2014.

Wu, Cynthia. *Chang and Eng Reconnected: The Original Siamese Twins in American Culture*. Temple University Press, 2012.

Wynter, Sylvia. "Ethno or Socio Poetics." In *Alcheringa: Ethnopoetics: A First International Symposium*, edited by Michel Benamou and Jerome Rothenberg. Alcheringa/Boston University, 1976.

Wynter, Sylvia. "1492: A New World View." In *Race, Discourse, and the Origin of the Americas: A New World View*, edited by Vera Lawrence Hyatt and Rex Nettleford. Smithsonian Institution Press, 1995.

Young, Kevin. *The Art of Losing: Poems of Grief and Healing*. Bloomsbury, 2010.

Young, Kevin. *Book of Hours: Poems*. Knopf Doubleday, 2014.

INDEX

Page numbers in *italics* indicate photos.

ABOUT THE AUTHOR

Danielle Bainbridge is Assistant Professor in the Department of Theatre at Northwestern University and author of *Dandelion: A Memoir in Essays*. Shows she has worked on as a web series creator have received three Daytime Emmy nominations and one NAACP Image Award nomination.